HANDBOOK FOR MAGISTRATES

Third Edition

HANDBOOK FOR MAGISTRATES

Third Edition

Robert Allan, BA(Hons), Barrister

Pauline M. Callow, JP, LLM

Wildy, Simmonds & Hill Publishing

Copyright © 2013 Robert Allan and Pauline M Callow

Handbook for Magistrates, Third Edition

British Library Cataloguing in Publication Data
A catalogue record for this book is available from the British Library

ISBN 978-0854901-128

Printed and bound in the United Kingdom by Antony Rowe Ltd, Chippenham, Wiltshire

First published in 1997 by Blackstone Press
This edition published in 2013 by
Wildy, Simmonds & Hill Publishing
58 Carey Street
London WC2A 2JF
England

FSC
www.fsc.org
MIX
Paper from
responsible sources
FSC® C013604

Contents

Foreword

The medieval concept of the King's Peace created during the reigns of the earliest Plantagenets, applied and maintained by members of the local community and given legislative force by the Justice of the Peace Act 1361, although ancient, remains vibrant. The celebrations of the 650th anniversary of this statute in 2011 were amply justified. They reminded us both of the obvious and crucial importance attached by the community to the principle that they and their families should be allowed to live their lives in undisturbed peace and, simultaneously, that the enforcement of the laws to maintain it continued to rest very largely with the magistracy, in front of whom the overwhelming majority of criminal prosecutions are heard and decided. The various recent legislative changes to the structure of the judiciary mean that the twenty-seven thousand or so lay magistrates are now members of the judiciary, to be treated as such. They perform their responsibilities in the same professional, objective and independent way as the full-time judiciary, and their jurisdiction is no longer confined to criminal matters.

The second edition of the *Handbook for Magistrates* was published in 1997, which in contemporary terms is a very long time ago. The new edition takes account of landmark legislative changes, of which the Criminal Justice Act 2003 and the Courts Act 2003 provide two examples. Training requirements for magistrates have evolved, and the introduction of rules to govern the management of cases and the efficient use of resources has added to the responsibilities of magistrates.

This new third edition of the *Handbook for Magistrates* explains all these matters and their practical importance to the daily administration of justice with accuracy and clarity. It begins with the process of appointment and continues through to the logical conclusion of that rare event, disciplinary proceedings, which may arise when a magistrate has misconducted himself or herself in this important judicial office. The book is not, emphatically not, a textbook and does not seek to replicate the detail of legal technicality, which is found in, for example, *Stone's Justices' Manual*. It demonstrates that the energy of the ancient office of Justice of the Peace continues undiminished, by offering what I may reasonably describe as detailed information and thoughtful insight into the practical realities of the issues which magistrates are required to address, and the context in which these sometimes difficult issues may arise for consideration. It does so in comprehensive non-technical language, which will be appreciated both by serving and prospective magistrates and, indeed, anyone with an interest in this hugely important feature of the administration of justice in England and Wales.

Igor Judge
Lord Chief Justice of England and Wales

Preface

In writing this edition of *Handbook for Magistrates*, we have sought to provide a wide-ranging account of the work of magistrates in England and Wales. The book is intended primarily for those who might be thinking about becoming magistrates, those who have recently been appointed, and magistrates in their first few years on the bench. We hope it will also be valuable as a reference book for more experienced magistrates, especially those whose responsibilities include training their less experienced colleagues.

The work of the magistrates' courts affects many others besides the magistrates themselves, and we hope the book will be of some interest to them too. Individual defendants and witnesses, and the general public whom the magistrates' courts serve, may find something worth reading. Likewise the professionals – probation officers, social services personnel, court legal advisers, the police, the Crown Prosecution Service and other prosecutors, newly qualified lawyers, and teachers – perhaps may find some insights not easily available elsewhere.

Training courses for magistrates cover, in varying degrees of depth, a good proportion of what is said in this book, but we hope the book will prove a useful, permanent, and perhaps more comprehensive, source of reference. Other books for magistrates tend to concentrate on procedural and legal matters, but here we have tried to go beyond these, to give a flavour of what life as a magistrate is really like, touching on the pressures, responsibilities and rewards of the work. We have also sought to put the work of the magistrates into a wide context, for example, explaining the powers under which people are brought before the court in the first place, and linking what goes on in the magistrates' court to the court system as a whole and to certain broad principles on which the system of justice operates.

We examine how magistrates are appointed – a subject about which there are probably many misconceptions; what they are empowered to do; how their courts are organised and operated; the kinds of matters they deal with, such as criminal offences, traffic matters and civil work (notably in family matters); how they go about assessing evidence and deciding what to accept as true; how they decide whether defendants should be released on bail or kept in custody; the sentences they may impose and how they endeavour to make the punishment fit the crime. The popular press might have us believe that magistrates send people to prison with great frequency; in fact imprisonment is a sentence of last resort reserved for the most serious cases, and new magistrates soon come to realise that it is a rare outcome indeed. We also look at how legal aid works, a subject of continuing public and political concern. Last, but not least, we have tried to address some matters of concern to magistrates as individuals.

The book illustrates in detail the huge responsibility that magistrates take on their shoulders, and the fearsome consequences their decisions have on the people who come before them. It is no small matter for a person of hitherto unblemished character to face the possibility of being convicted of a criminal offence, or to have to await trial in prison rather than at liberty. It is a tribute to the diligence with which magistrates go about their tasks, and to the strenuous efforts of the Ministry of Justice and the Magistrates' Association to promote consistent principles, that public criticism is relatively rare.

In writing the book, we have tried to say what we have to say in a straightforward way, avoiding legal terminology when it was sensible to do so, but the nature of the subject limits the scope for this. We hope we have succeeded in explaining legal terms satisfactorily. This edition also includes, for the first time, a glossary listing and briefly explaining many of the terms used in the courts. It also gives the addresses of many websites where more information can be found.

The law is a dynamic subject and the criminal law in particular has been subject to many changes since the previous edition of this book was published. The landmark Criminal Justice Act 2003 gave rise to many changes in the workings of the courts, while the evolving Criminal Procedure Rules are revolutionising procedure. This third edition was prepared during the winter of 2011/2012 and, as far as the law is concerned, is up to date to 1 May 2012.

The authors will be glad to hear of any comments or suggestions for improvements in future editions of *Handbook for Magistrates*.

The authors take this opportunity to thank Neil McKittrick, co-author of the first and second editions of this book. Despite the extensive updating of the text, much of his original work remains.

Chapter 1

Becoming a Magistrate

BACKGROUND

The year 2011 was the 650th anniversary of the magistracy. It is well known that the office of justice of the peace or magistrate (the words are interchangeable for all practical purposes) can be traced back to before the fourteenth century. A statute of 1361 is still the source of certain powers of modern magistrates. Much has happened since those days of relatively primitive justice, but the disposal of the vast majority of criminal cases by people without special legal qualification, who are not paid for the work, remains unique in the world.

Magistrates deal with about two million criminal cases a year – something over ninety-five per cent of the total. These include assaults, theft, illegal possession of knives and other weapons, burglary, possession and supply of drugs, benefits fraud, harassment, obstructing police officers, public order offences and a host of motoring offences, to name but some. In all these cases, if the defendant pleads not guilty, the magistrates hear the evidence and decide whether or not the defendant is guilty or not guilty. Then they must select the most appropriate punishments for the guilty. In almost all the remaining five per cent of cases – the most serious – the magistrates have a role in the preliminary stages. This includes sending cases to be tried in the Crown Court, and deciding whether defendants are to be released on bail in the meantime. Magistrates also have an important role in cases which are not criminal in nature, principally family proceedings, discussed in Chapter 7.

There are about 27,000 magistrates, serving in some 280 courts in England and Wales. There are also about 140 district judges (magistrates' courts) and 150 deputy district judges (magistrates' courts). The district judges and deputy district judges are legally qualified and are paid (see also Chapter 4). They were first appointed in the eighteenth century, to deal with the increasing workload, and were then known as stipendiary magistrates.

In the early days, magistrates were selected from the 'great and the good', often the highest-ranking or wealthiest in society. The twentieth century saw the introduction of a far broader-based magistracy. The idea now is that magistrates should be drawn from all sectors of society. While that is fine in theory, in reality individual commitments and circumstances still restrict the sphere of people from whom magistrates can be drawn. Although employers are, strictly, obliged to allow people time off work to serve as magistrates, there is no requirement to pay them. Advertising in newspapers and even on the sides of buses has helped to attract a wider range of people, but the system probably still favours certain types and militates against others. Work and domestic responsibilities will always be inhibiting factors. The journal *Magistrate* reported in October 2009 on Judicial Office statistics which showed that 41 per cent of magistrates were in professional or technical occupations, 18 per cent in managerial or senior occupations, and 16 per cent in administrative or secretarial occupations. 10.5 per cent were not employed or unemployed, while small percentages were skilled tradespeople, sales people, self-employed or retired.

This is, however, an area in which women play a full part. The first woman magistrate was appointed in 1919, and 51 per cent of magistrates are now women. On the other hand, the make-up of some benches of magistrates is said not fully to reflect the social and cultural mix of the populations they serve. The website of the Judiciary of England and Wales describes 92 per cent of magistrates as white, 4 per cent as black and 2.7 per cent as Asian. Over half of magistrates are aged sixty or more, while just under 4 per cent are under forty.

Magistrates are not paid, although they can claim expenses. More about this is said in Chapter 12.

FINDING OUT

Many people may never give a thought to the possibility of becoming a magistrate. The justice system, in operation every day in the magistrates' courts, passes them by, and any knowledge they may have results from hearing about court cases in television news reports or the local press. But in recent years, the Magistrates' Association has been making unstinting efforts to provide information about who magistrates are and what they do. Much material about the work of magistrates is now available on the internet:

- the Magistrates' Association (www.magistrates-association.org.uk)
- Directgov (www.direct.gov.uk)
- the Ministry of Justice (www.justice.gov.uk)
- Judiciary of England and Wales (www.judiciary.gov.uk)

Other sources of information include the Magistrates in the Community project, which the Magistrates' Association launched in 1995 to increase public awareness of the role of magistrates. Almost every court area now has a panel of magistrates who go to workplaces, schools, colleges and community groups, explaining how magistrates are appointed and the work they do. Courts may hold 'open days', when those invited may tour the courts, and magistrates and staff are available to answer questions. A telephone call to the local magistrates' court will elicit further details.

The clerk to the justices, or deputy clerk to the justices, at the local magistrates' court will also assist with information, but the best way to get an insight into what magistrates do is to find out when the local court sits, and go along and watch. A list of courts is available at hmctscourtfinder.direct. gov.uk/HMCTS/. At least one such visit is required before a person applies to become a magistrate. All magistrates' courts are open to the public – justice in this country is administered openly – and all courtrooms have seats (sometimes called the 'public gallery') where ordinary members of the public can go. The public is not allowed into youth courts, that is, those dealing with children and young persons who have not attained their eighteenth birthdays. Nor is the public usually allowed into family proceedings courts, where sensitive matters involving families and the welfare of children are heard. The so-called 'secrecy' of the family courts has been a matter of controversy, and more will be said about this in Chapter 7.

Two or three visits to sit in the public gallery should give an excellent insight into what magistrates do, and the observer will also be able to identify the roles of those in court: the defendant, the prosecution and defence advocates, the court's legal adviser, witnesses, the probation officer, a press reporter perhaps, court security officers and the usher (or list caller). The role of the usher is critical to the smooth running of the courts, and ushers are usually unfailingly helpful. Try to have a few words with the usher and explain that you have come along to observe proceedings. The usher may well be able to tell you what is coming up in the court session, and may give you a copy of the court list which will enable you to follow cases easily. Ushers have many jobs to do: informing the legal adviser which cases are ready, calling parties into court, swearing in witnesses, rounding up advocates who may have cases in other courtrooms, and handing forms to the defendant and others involved in a case. Despite all these responsibilities, most will find time for those who are genuinely interested to know a little about how the court is run.

After a couple of visits, you will have an idea of whether the work is likely to be for you. You may have seen some interesting cases, and others which are fairly routine, where traffic offenders have been fined in fairly quick succession for exceeding the speed limit, or something similar. The important thing to remember is that, although routine, these cases may be of some significance to the defendants concerned, and the bench attaches the same care to dealing with them as to other more 'high profile' cases. You will probably also note that no two cases are ever the same, similar perhaps, but not the same. If you think that serving the community in this way might interest you, you will wish to consider taking it further.

THE COMMITMENT

There is no point, however, going further unless your personal circumstances allow you to do so. Magistrates are unpaid and they are expected to serve for a minimum of five years. They must perform a fair share of sittings on the bench. The precise number of sittings varies from bench to bench. A magistrate is expected to sit in court on at least twenty-six half days a year or the equivalent. A half day is, typically, three and a half to four hours. In some areas, magistrates sit for whole days rather than for a morning or afternoon, and whole-day sittings are becoming more common. The average is thirty-five half days, but in many areas, half a day a week, or a full day per fortnight, is normal. Magistrates must also be able to find time for meetings and training sessions.

If you are in work, you will need to know whether your employer will grant you time off for magisterial duties. Many are generous in this, but it is worth finding out, early on, whether time off is likely to be a problem.

If you know someone who is already a magistrate, make contact and find out more. If not, try to speak to the clerk to the justices or a legal adviser at your local court, who will do all he or she can to help.

THE LORD CHANCELLOR AND THE LOCAL ADVISORY COMMITTEES

Magistrates are appointed by the Secretary of State for Justice and Lord Chancellor (the Rt Hon Chris Grayling, at the time of writing), who does so on behalf of the Queen. The Lord Chancellor is a political appointee, a member of the cabinet, who is the Government's spokesman on legal affairs in the House of Lords. He also has numerous ceremonial functions. His department is the Ministry of Justice, formerly known as the Department for Constitutional Affairs. The Ministry is responsible for criminal law, sentencing, offenders, prisons and probation. Her Majesty's Courts and Tribunals Service (HMCTS), part of the Ministry of Justice, is responsible, in partnership with the judiciary, for the administration of justice in the courts. The Home Secretary is responsible for policing.

In practice, the Lord Chancellor appoints magistrates on the advice of local advisory committees. The Lord Chancellor appoints the members of the committee – most are magistrates – and liaises closely with them. The advisory committees may in turn appoint subcommittees. A list of advisory committees, contact names, addresses, telephone numbers and e-mail addresses is available at www.direct.gov.uk/magistrates. The listing also shows whether or not a particular advisory committee is seeking new magistrates.

QUALIFYING

Magistrates do not need legal qualifications, or indeed any kind of formal qualification. They are trained following appointment, and throughout their careers as magistrates. They are appraised regularly, and receive advice on the law from a legal adviser in court.

There are certain formal rules about who may be appointed. For example, a prospective magistrate must normally have lived in or near the area in which he or she will serve for at least a year, and should have a reasonable knowledge of the area. The candidate should be in satisfactory health, and in particular should be able to sit and concentrate for long periods of time. The minimum age for appointment is eighteen. It has been reported that someone as young as nineteen has been appointed. Since magistrates must retire when they reach the age of seventy, and are expected to serve for at least five years, those over sixty-five are not usually appointed.

British nationality is not a prerequisite, although all persons appointed must swear an oath of allegiance.

The candidate must also be able and willing to undertake a normal allocation of work, and to undertake training, as described above.

Certain people are ineligible to be considered for the magistracy:

- a serving police officer or a civilian employee of a police force. A former police officer or civilian employee of a police force must have left that employment at least two years before;
- a member of the Special Constabulary;
- a serving community support officer;

- a traffic warden (but parking attendants employed by a local authority are not disqualified);
- a Highways Agency traffic officer;
- anyone who has a spouse, partner or close relative who is employed as a police officer, special constable, a civilian employee in a police force or a traffic warden in the area to which the person might be appointed, and anyone whose spouse or partner has a close relative falling into one of these categories. A close relative means a father, mother, son, daughter, brother, sister-in-law or step-child;
- a full time member of HM Forces unless the person's commanding officer confirms that there is no realistic prospect of being posted abroad in the near future;
- anyone else whose work or community activities, or those of a spouse or partner, are clearly incompatible with the duties of a magistrate. This category includes employees of the Crown Prosecution Service, the Probation Service, a Youth Offending Team, Her Majesty's Courts and Tribunals Service, a bailiff or member of an enforcement agency, and store detectives;
- people employed in a penal establishment, by an organisation that is contracted to carry out work in such an establishment, or which is involved in the transport of prisoners;
- a security officer;
- a lay visitor to a police station or prison, unless willing to give up this activity if appointed;
- a person who undertakes field work for a victim support scheme (see Chapter 3), or as a 'McKenzie friend' (someone who is not a lawyer but who assists defendants in court – see Chapter 11) in the area in which he or she wishes to serve;
- anyone who is a member of the UK Parliament, the European Parliament or the Welsh Assembly, or has been adopted as a prospective candidate for election to either Parliament or Assembly;
- anyone who is paid as a full-time party political agent, if part of the constituency in question falls within the local justice area to which the person might be appointed.

Special restrictions apply to employees of the Royal Society for the Prevention of Cruelty to Animals (RSPCA). This is because officers of the Society prosecute certain offences (see Chapter 7).

While the above is a fairly long list, it is not exhaustive, and the selection process may bring to light some other reason for disqualification. Further, the Lord Chancellor does not appoint anyone:

- who (or whose spouse or partner) has been convicted of a serious offence, or a number of minor offences, if the advisory committee does not think that the public would have confidence in the person as a magistrate. An offence is regarded as serious for these purposes if it is anything other than a minor motoring conviction for which points were put on the offender's driving licence or a fine imposed;

- who has been convicted, in the preceding five years, of one motoring offence in respect of which six penalty points were imposed, or three such offences in respect of each of which three points were imposed;
- who has been disqualified from driving for twelve months or more within the preceding ten years;
- who has been disqualified for a shorter period within the preceding five years.

All those matters are fairly straightforward. The critical requirement for appointment to the magistracy is that a person must be of suitable character, integrity and understanding. The Ministry of Justice, in its notes for guidance on applying to become a magistrate, lists six key qualities of a good magistrate:

- *good character:* this comprises personal integrity, respect for and trust of others, respect for confidences, the absence of any matter which may bring the magistrate or the magistracy into disrepute, and a willingness to be circumspect in private, working and public life;
- *understanding and communication:* the ability to understand documents, identify and comprehend relevant facts and follow evidence and arguments, the ability to concentrate and the ability to communicate effectively;
- *social awareness:* an appreciation and acceptance of the rule of law, an understanding of local communities and society in general, respect for persons from different ethnic, cultural or social backgrounds and experience of life beyond family, friends and work;
- *maturity and sound temperament:* the ability to relate to and work with others, regard for the views of others, willingness to consider advice, maturity, humanity, courage, firmness, decisiveness, confidence, a sense of fairness and courtesy;
- *sound judgement:* the ability to think logically, weigh arguments and reach a balanced decision, open-mindedness, objectivity, the recognition and setting aside of prejudices;
- *commitment and reliability:* including willingness to undergo training with the support of family and employer.

This is a formidable list, illustrating the continuing dedication of the magistracy to justice and fairness, and the care taken in selecting new magistrates. It is for the advisory committee to decide, on the basis of a completed application form, references and interview, whether an applicant fulfils these many criteria.

THE APPLICATION

A person can apply to be a magistrate of his or her own initiative, or may be recommended by another person (perhaps someone who is already a magistrate), or by an organisation (for example, by an employer who has been approached by the Ministry of Justice with a view to finding new candidates). Useful guidance is given in the document 'Serving as a Magistrate – a detailed guide to the role of JP', to be found at www.direct. gov.uk/magistrates. For practical reasons, it is not a good idea to submit applications to more than one area at a time.

The application procedure is begun by completing a form, available at www. direct.gov.uk/magistrates. The form can be downloaded as a Word file and completed on the computer screen, or as a pdf file for completion by hand. For those who do not have access to the internet, or who have a disability, application packs are available from the clerk to the justices at the local court. The application form is accompanied by notes on the criteria for selection and on what is expected of those who are appointed.

As already noted, before making the application, applicants are expected to visit a magistrates' court (or courts) to observe what goes on. At least one visit is required, but two or three are preferable. Applicants are asked to state, in the application form, the court(s) visited and the date(s). When the time comes for interview, applicants may be asked about their experience observing in the courts. If you are employed, you should also find out, before beginning to complete an application form, if you will be able to have reasonable time off work.

The form opens by asking for the name of the court at which the applicant would prefer to sit. By this stage, you will probably have decided which court will best suit you – usually the one nearest to your home or place of work. The form then asks for the name of the appropriate advisory committee. This information should be available from the court itself, or from www.direct. gov.uk/magistrates. Applicants to courts in Wales are asked if they wish to be considered for any vacancies for bilingual magistrates.

Section 1 of the form calls for personal details, including the length of time the applicant has lived in the locality, and educational qualifications. Nationality is asked for, although, as noted above, applicants need not be of British nationality, but must be prepared to swear the oath of allegiance. There are also questions on ethnic origin, for statistical purposes. Ethnic origin is neither a qualification nor a disqualification.

Section 2 concerns current and past employment. Section 3 asks whether the applicant's spouse or partner is employed. Both these sections contain questions designed to identify candidates who may be ineligible on the formal grounds listed above.

Section 4 concerns criminal convictions and civil proceedings. Details of any conviction must be given, no matter how long ago, and no matter how minor. The guidance notes to the application form explain that this includes motoring offences dealt with by a fixed penalty or by attending a speed awareness course, penalty notices for disorder, warnings for possession of cannabis, anti-social behaviour orders and any police caution. The information to be given about any civil proceedings in which the applicant (or a company of which the applicant is a director) has been a party extends to bankruptcy, matrimonial and maintenance proceedings. Details about any pending or forthcoming criminal or civil proceedings are also to be declared.

Section 5 asks for reasons for applying, and what the applicant can bring to the magistracy. In deciding how to complete this part of the form, applicants may wish to reflect on their personal motivation for applying, in the light of the qualities required of magistrates and the commitment which would be required. It might be appropriate to highlight, for example, experience – whether at work or elsewhere – of social problems in the locality, or of dealing with disputes. Many magistrates volunteer out of a wish to contribute to their local communities.

In section 5, the applicant is also asked about past or present voluntary work, recreational interests and activities, and about the applicant's visits to observe a court in action.

Section 6 concerns health and disability. Applicants should give information about any relevant illness, and about any disability. An applicant's health should be good enough to allow for carrying out all the duties of a magistrate. An applicant's hearing (with or without a hearing aid) should obviously be good enough to follow proceedings in court, and it is important to be able to sit and concentrate for long periods of time. Applications from those with disabilities are encouraged.

Section 7 is headed 'Good character and declaration'. The applicant is asked if there is anything in his or her past, or private or working life, or (as far as the applicant knows) in the life of any family member or close friend, which, if generally known, might bring the applicant or the magistracy into disrepute, or call into question the applicant's integrity, authority or standing if appointed as a magistrate. An example might be where aspects of an applicant's private life have been exposed in the press, or where a family member has been convicted of a criminal offence. It is as well to be as open as possible and to declare anything which might be relevant, even if it seems trivial. If in doubt, it is worth contacting the clerk to the justices or the advisory committee for guidance. The approach of advisory committees is that it is better that any such matters be known at the outset, rather than risk embarrassment later. A person who makes a disclosure of this kind may still be appointed.

In signing the form, the applicant declares that he or she has read the guidance notes and agrees, if appointed, to carry out a fair share of duties and to undertake training.

Signing the form is not, however, quite the end. Candidates are asked to name three referees, from whom the advisory committee may later seek written references. Referees should have known the candidate for at least three years, but must not be relatives. At least one referee must be a person living in the same area as the applicant if the applicant has lived in that area for more than three years. One should be the applicant's employer if the applicant is employed and even if the employment has not yet lasted for three years. No more than one referee should be a magistrate, and a referee should not be someone – a police officer or solicitor, for example – likely to appear before the court to which the applicant may be appointed. Otherwise, referees may be a professional colleague, a local councillor or other person who can say something relevant to the candidate's suitability.

The completed application form should be sent to the appropriate advisory committee by post or e-mail, and will be acknowledged.

THE SELECTION PROCESS

On receiving an application, the advisory committee first checks it to ensure that the applicant is eligible in the terms outlined above. The committee also makes background checks to look into any apparent conflicts of interest or exceptional circumstances arising out of matters disclosed in the application. A check of the Criminal Records Bureau is also made.

If all is well in those respects, most applicants are invited to the first of two interviews. The purpose of the interview process is to assess candidates on merit against the six key qualities listed above. Interviews are usually conducted by a panel of three, at least one of whom is not a magistrate.

Interviewing panels are aware that candidates are putting themselves forward for a voluntary, unpaid role, come from different backgrounds, and have varying experience of being interviewed. While they must properly test candidates for the necessary qualities, they must do so with courtesy and professionalism.

A first interview usually lasts between thirty and forty-five minutes. Members of the interviewing panel should have carefully read the application form in advance, and the candidate is asked if there have been any material changes to the information given on the application form. The focus of the first interview is the key qualities of good character, commitment and reliability. The candidate can expect to be asked, 'is there anything in your private or working life, or in your past, or to your knowledge in that of your family or close friends, which, if it became generally known, might bring you or the magistracy into disrepute, or call into question your integrity, authority or standing as a magistrate?' This question appears also in the application form, and some advice about what an applicant should do if in any doubt about the answer has been given above.

The remainder of the first interview is on more general topics, but usually includes discussion of aspects of the criminal justice system, such as drink-driving, gang crime, knife crime or public disorder. Candidates can also expect to be asked to describe their visits to courts to observe proceedings – what they thought of how cases were handled, whether or not they agree with the sentences imposed. Candidates are also asked to confirm that they will be available to serve as magistrates for at least five years.

Applicants who successfully negotiate the first hurdle are invited to a second interview. It should take place between five and fifteen working days after the initial interview, and usually lasts for between forty-five minutes and an hour. Candidates are asked to bring with them a photograph of themselves, and a document of formal identification. They are invited to attend thirty minutes before the time for the interview. During this half-hour, they are asked to consider two exercises. One gives a list of offences and candidates are asked to rank the four most serious in order of seriousness as they see it. The second exercise usually focuses on a fictional offence.

The purpose of the second interview is to assess candidates for judicial aptitude – their qualities of understanding and communication, social awareness, maturity and sound temperament, and sound judgment.

The two exercises are discussed. A candidate might be asked what he or she might hope to achieve in sentencing in a given scenario, but clearly cannot be expected to suggest an actual sentence. The candidate may be asked questions aimed at assessing open-mindedness, and ability to listen to argument and reason on what has been said, and to proceed to a decision. Candidates can expect discussion about their views on crime and punishment, and what qualities they might bring to the magistracy. Would the candidate argue for a lower sentence because he or she believed the defendant was not guilty, when the majority view was that the defendant was guilty? (Sometimes a bench of three magistrates has to reach a decision by a two-to-one majority, and, as will be apparent from Chapter 9, dissent on the question of guilt is not a valid consideration in deciding the sentence.) Interviewees should probably expect questions of the 'name three adjectives your friends and family might use to describe you' variety; and fairly close questioning about motives for applying. The 'good character' question is also put once again. Questioning may well be rigorous, and while some may find this daunting, it is almost certainly essential and should be done sympathetically and professionally.

Since it is for the advisory committee to make recommendations for appointment to the Lord Chancellor, the question of suitability is entirely in the committee's discretion. All these matters apart, people are recommended for appointment only if they are needed. Thus, if there are only four vacancies, only the four who performed best at interview are appointed, even though others may be suitable. Candidates who come up to scratch but miss out because there are insufficient vacancies may, depending on local requirements, be offered the opportunity to be appointed as a magistrate in a neighbouring area, placed on a waiting list or invited to re-apply later.

In making appointments, advisory committees also have to seek to reflect the communities they serve, balancing the bench in terms of gender, ethnic origin, location, occupation, industry, age, disability and social background.

The committee should make its final decision within fifteen working days of the end of each series of interviews, and should notify each candidate within five working days of its decision on the application. At the end of this necessarily demanding and rigorous procedure, some are, inevitably, disappointed. Committees are not required to give detailed reasons for rejecting an application, but, when turning down an application, must explain that the applicant can ask for feedback. Any such feedback must be clear, concise and tactful, and unsuccessful candidates are entitled to ask for a review of the decision.

Many are, of course, successful in their applications and proceed to 'swearing in' and initial training.

DECLARATION AND UNDERTAKING

Before being formally appointed, new magistrates sign a form of declaration and undertaking, confirming their commitment to the role. This document sets out the responsibilities which each new magistrate takes on. It is a formidable list, covering not only practical matters such as the duty to undertake training, but the principles governing the administration of justice and conduct as a magistrate. New magistrates promise:

- to administer justice according to the law;
- to be circumspect in conduct and to maintain the dignity, standing and good reputation of the magistracy at all times in their private, working and public lives;
- to respect confidences;
- to complete all required training, and to offer to resign if the training is not completed without a good reason;
- to sit for at least thirteen days per year, or twenty-six half-days per year if they have commitments which prevent them from sitting full days, and to resign if that commitment is not met without a good reason;
- to resign if they become disqualified to sit or unable to perform their duties as a magistrate;
- to answer questions asked in surveys concerning balance of the bench;
- that their actions as magistrates will be free from any political, racial, sexual or other bias;
- to inform the chairman and the clerk to the justices of any court proceedings or professional disciplinary proceedings concerning them or a close relative, of their bankruptcy or other financial difficulties, or if they or a close relative joins the police service, the Crown Prosecution Service, the Probation Service or the Prison Service, or of any other matter which might disqualify the magistrate;
- to comply with any directions in relation to sitting as a magistrate, given by the Lord Chief Justice (or his delegate) with the agreement of the Lord Chancellor.

The document concludes with a declaration that the individual is not and has not been concerned in any relevant court proceedings, or, if that is not the case, a declaration setting out the matters in question.

This declaration and undertaking is by no means a formality, and all those who reach the point of being asked to sign it should consider carefully each and every paragraph, and the extent of the overall commitment. Being a magistrate is more than spending a few hours in court each week – it impinges on the individual's life as a whole. It is a way of life which carries with it serious long-term responsibilities, and should not be undertaken without full and due consideration.

'SWEARING-IN'

A new magistrate is officially appointed by being 'sworn in' before a judge, usually the magistrates' liaison judge for the area. All new magistrates appointed at the same time to the same bench are normally sworn in together, perhaps at the court where they will sit, or at the Crown Court for the area. Present at the ceremony, apart from the judge, are the chairmen of the relevant benches and the clerk(s) to the justices, as well as one or two of each of the new magistrates' family and friends.

Incidentally, the term 'bench' is used variously to refer to all the magistrates in a particular area, the magistrates sitting in a particular case, and the piece of furniture on which they used to sit.

The substance of the swearing-in is the oath of allegiance and the judicial oath. These may be made on the holy book relevant to the person's religious belief ('I swear by Almighty God ...' , for example) or by affirmation ('I do solemnly, sincerely and truly declare and affirm ...'). Both forms carry equal weight and no stigma attaches to those who do not espouse an organised religion.

The oath of allegiance is that the person making it 'will be faithful and bear true allegiance to Her Majesty Queen Elizabeth the Second, her heirs and successors, according to law'. And the judicial oath: 'I will well and truly serve our Sovereign Lady, Queen Elizabeth the Second, in the office of Justice of the Peace and I will do right to all manner of people after the laws and usages of this Realm without fear or favour, affection or ill-will'. The language is archaic, but the last sentence is at the heart of the work of the magistrate – that he or she will do justice in accordance with the law, regardless of any fear of the consequences or any improper influence. The oaths take only a few seconds to recite but are at the heart of everything the magistrate does in that capacity in the years to come.

After all the new magistrates have taken the oaths, the judge usually says a few appropriate words which emphasise the importance of the occasion, stressing the serious obligation of doing justice to one's fellow citizens.

While there is, of necessity, a degree of formality, the proceedings are often followed by a small social gathering between the new magistrates, the judge, and officers of the court.

BOOKS AND GUIDELINES

All new magistrates are provided with copies of the sentencing guidelines issued by the Sentencing Council, and the Adult Court Bench Book, issued by the Judicial College. These large (A4) loose-leaf volumes contain a wealth of vital information and are in constant use by all magistrates. They are updated from time to time, and revised pages are distributed. They are, however, rather large and cumbersome. A more convenient A5 version of the Sentencing Guidelines is available commercially from www.simonsden.co.uk (currently priced at £29 plus £4 postage and packing). Both books are also available on the internet and magistrates can simply download them and/or print their own versions (without charge), or even use their own portable devices in court to access the guidance.

INITIAL TRAINING

Each new magistrate is assigned a mentor – an experienced magistrate who has been trained and has demonstrated competence for the role. The mentor's job is to help, support and advise the new magistrate, and in particular, help him or her to achieve the knowledge, understanding and skills magistrates need. These qualities are described as 'competences' and all magistrates are expected to have the basic set of competences. These are:

- the ability to manage oneself, in the sense of being prepared for each hearing, conducting oneself effectively in the process and participating in continuing learning and development;
- the ability to work as a member of a team, making an effective contribution to the working and decision-making of the bench;
- the ability to make judicial decisions using appropriate processes and structures and maintaining impartiality.

Before they may sit in court with their mentors, newly sworn-in magistrates must complete induction training. This takes at least eighteen hours, usually spread over three days. It takes place at or near the courthouse and is often given by the justices' clerk or by one or more of the court's legal advisers. The training usually includes an introduction to the classification of offences, the procedure at a trial, the structured approach to making decisions, and the basics of sentencing and bail. All these topics are discussed in greater depth elsewhere in this book. The training also usually includes observing proceedings in court and visiting a number of penal institutions, such as prisons and young offender institutions. Chapter 3 contains more information about initial training.

FIRST SITTING

A magistrate's first sitting is a challenge for many, although some will be less fazed than others. You may be sitting with magistrates and a legal adviser whom you have not met before, but usually all magistrates sitting on the day will arrive at court fifteen or twenty minutes early, so there will be an opportunity for introductions. The legal adviser explains, before going into court, what kinds of case are to be dealt with, and whether any are likely to pose any particular problems. Initial training will have provided a background, but many magistrates feel that however good that initial training, it is not until they actually start to take part in hearing cases that things begin to fall into place. The views of all magistrates on a bench, whether they have thirty minutes' or thirty years' experience, are of equal importance. A new magistrate – indeed a magistrate of any number of years' experience – can always ask the chairman to explain anything which is not clear, or seek advice from the legal adviser.

The important point is to remember that you have been appointed because it is felt that you are a suitable person to do justice in this place, and the words of the judicial oath are your judicial birth certificate. The learning curve is steep in the early years, but if the magistrate tries to fulfil the obligation in the oath, it is difficult to go far wrong. The aim must always be justice, according to the law. That may sometimes be unpalatable, particularly where the law does not reflect what is seen to be the broader justice of the case, but such instances are rare. The law can be a surprisingly flexible companion, and the discretion vested in magistrates can be surprisingly wide.

Magistrates must remember, however, that they are not legislators, nor is it part of their function to assist others. They do not make law, they apply it. It follows that they must apply the law *as it is*, not as they might wish it to be. Some of the decisions they take do help defendants, as where the balance of the argument is that a rehabilitative sentence is called for, but while a just application of the law may help a defendant, that is not the purpose of the magistracy. Often a decision has to be aimed at balancing the interests of the offender before the bench against those of the wider and unseen public outside.

HELP

The chairman of the bench, the clerk to the justices and the legal team, and the mentor will do their best to make the new magistrate feel swiftly at ease. The new magistrate will have met those sworn in at the same time. They become 'the year of 2011' or 'the year of 2012' or whatever, and undertake their training together. Many magistrates appointed together become fast friends. The chairman of the bench is there to help if there is any difficulty. Chairmen cannot do enough to ensure their benches run smoothly, and the sooner new magistrates are made to feel at home, the better.

The clerk to the justices is also the legal adviser to the magistrates, jointly and individually. He or she, and members of the legal team, can always be consulted about a whole range of matters relating to the magistrate's duties. These days, clerks to the justices are responsible for fairly large areas, so you may meet the clerk only relatively rarely, but you will soon get to know many of the members of the team – the deputy justices' clerk(s) and legal advisers.

THE DUTIES OF A MAGISTRATE

Magistrates usually sit in court as a bench of three. They can sit in pairs, although this carries the risk that they may not be able to reach agreement, which could lead to a case having to be tried again later by different magistrates. A single magistrate can decide certain matters alone.

Magistrates always have the services of a legal adviser, or clerk as they are still sometimes known. All court legal advisers are qualified in law, and many are solicitors or barristers.

The magistrates make decisions about disputed facts – did this defendant hit this police officer in the back? They must then apply the law – did what happened amount to an assault? Perhaps the defendant was in a crowd of people, stumbled, and crashed into the back of the officer. If so, this was not an assault since the defendant did not have the necessary intention. In applying the law, the court's legal adviser will explain and interpret the requirements. Thus, to constitute assault, the defendant must have the unlawful intention of striking the other person. The way the magistrates come to their decisions is the subject of Chapter 10.

If a person pleads guilty or is found guilty, the court must then impose a sentence, ranging from an absolute discharge to imprisonment. Sentencing is dealt with in detail in Chapter 9.

Two types of case, 'summary' offences and certain 'either-way' offences, are dealt with entirely in the magistrates' courts. There is also a third category, 'indictable-only' offences. Summary offences are the least serious and must be dealt with by the magistrates. 'Indictable-only' offences are at the other end of the scale of seriousness and are heard at the Crown Court only, although, as we shall see, the magistrates have a role in the preliminary stages. 'Either-way' offences are in between in terms of seriousness. As the name suggests, they can be tried in either the magistrates' courts or the Crown Court. Where they are dealt with depends on whether or not the magistrates decide the case is suitable to be tried by them, and on the defendant's choice. This is dealt with in more detail in Chapter 5.

The kinds of case dealt with by a particular court vary enormously. Sometimes the reasons are obvious. Magistrates in areas without motorways will not come across motorway offences. Football hooliganism generally occurs in and around football grounds, and if there is no stadium in an area, there will be few, if any, such cases. Prosecutions for, say, car theft, may increase if the police decide to target this type of crime. Theft of livestock is confined largely to rural areas, while mugging, shoplifting and drug offences may be more prevalent in inner city areas characterised by social deprivation and unemployment. Motoring offences, however, make up a large part of all magistrates' work, even though many are dealt with by fixed penalty notices ('tickets') without coming before the courts.

Magistrates also deal with certain non-criminal matters, notably family cases. Family cases mostly concern orders to make maintenance payments, and matters under the Children Act, including emergency protection orders, care orders, and orders for contact between a parent and a child. Here the people appearing in court are representatives of the local authority, parents and other relatives of the child or children concerned, and sometimes even the child. As will be seen in Chapter 7, the approach to family court work differs in many respects from the approach to criminal court work.

Magistrates also have the unenviable tasks of dealing with council tax defaulters, non-payment of TV licences and road fund licences, and bus and train fare dodgers. They also have powers to authorise gas and electricity companies to enter buildings to install pre-payment meters or cut off supplies for non-payment. And again, they may have to deal with cases brought by the local authority under legislation designed to protect consumers – food safety and trade descriptions, for example. There are also cases on environmental matters, such as pollution of waterways or excessive smoke emissions, which may be brought by the local authority or by the Environment Agency. All in all, this is a wide remit and most magistrates would agree that there are rarely two days the same.

A great deal more will be said about all these matters in the chapters which follow.

THE MAGISTRATES' ASSOCIATION

The Magistrates' Association was founded in 1920 and provides a range of training programmes, some organised locally, others nationally. The advantage of training events organised by the Association is that they give those attending the opportunity to compare notes with members of other benches, who may have quite different perspectives. The Association has a number of local branches. It publishes the journal *Magistrate* and has a library which is open to members. All magistrates may join the Association on payment of an annual fee. It has an office in central London, employing a small, full-time staff. The Association is consulted frequently by government departments, particularly the Ministry of Justice, and is uniquely placed to represent the views of magistrates. The telephone number for general enquiries is (020) 7387 2353; the Association's website is at www. magistrates-association.org.uk.

Chapter 2

The Court System

INTRODUCTION

What place does the magistrates' court occupy in the hierarchy of courts in England and Wales? In this chapter it is sought to put the work of the magistrates' courts into the context of the legal system as a whole, by looking first at the structure of the courts, and then at the sources of English law.

CRIMINAL AND CIVIL CASES

Broadly speaking, the courts can be divided into two groups – civil and criminal – although there is some overlap, largely as a result of historical accident.

Criminal courts deal with people who are prosecuted, usually by the Crown Prosecution Service on behalf of the state, for behaviour which amounts to a crime. If the person pleads guilty or is found guilty, he or she is punished by the court on behalf of society as a whole.

Civil cases, on the other hand, usually arise out of disputes about rights and duties under the huge body of civil law. Often, the person bringing the case (the 'claimant') hopes, at the end of it, to receive money or some other form of compensation from the person against whom the claim is brought (the 'defendant'). For example, a printer might make a claim against a publisher for not paying bills for printing books. A patient whose surgery has failed might claim against the surgeon for professional negligence. A private householder might claim against a builder who made the leaking roof worse instead of better. Somebody who falls over a loose flag on a badly maintained pavement may claim compensation from the local authority for the injury caused. A petition for divorce and the proceedings concerning the children and maintenance are also civil matters. So too are matters of landlord and tenant – a landlord seeking to remove a tenant may have to go to court for an order. Disputes about wills likewise may find their way to the civil courts.

The parties in civil cases may be private individuals, companies and other types of corporation and government departments.

Sometimes, cases overlap. A person convicted of falsely claiming social security benefits (a crime) may also have to face a claim in a civil court for recovery of the money.

An important difference between criminal and civil cases is that in criminal cases, the prosecutor has to prove the case 'beyond reasonable doubt'. In civil cases, the person bringing the case must prove it on the less stringent 'balance of probabilities' test. More is said about these tests of proof in Chapter 10.

Almost all criminal cases start in the magistrates' courts, and over ninety-five per cent of them are dealt with entirely in those courts. The remainder are referred by the magistrates' courts up to the Crown Court as explained in Chapter 5. Magistrates' courts also deal with certain civil matters, notably under the Children Act 1989, although some of these cases can also begin in the civil courts.

Where a civil matter begins is not quite so straightforward, but most begin in the county court. Those which are more complex and feature claims for larger sums begin in the High Court.

Trial by jury

In the Crown Court, trial is by judge and jury, the jury making decisions on facts, the judge making decisions on points of law and on sentence. The judge also has the task of controlling the trial – deciding, for instance, whether the rules of evidence allow a particular matter to be put to the jury, summing up the evidence, and directing the jury on its duties. There are about 55 Crown Courts in England and Wales, compared with about 280 magistrates' courts.

Since the majority of criminal cases are dealt with entirely in the magistrates' courts, it is immediately apparent that, despite what popular culture may suggest to the contrary, and despite public debate about whether the tradition of trial by jury remains relevant and likely to deliver justice, juries deal with only a tiny proportion of cases, although they do include the most serious.

Appeals

Central to the concept of justice in English law is the freedom of a person in legal proceedings to appeal against a decision which the person believes to have been wrong. In criminal cases a defendant may appeal against the fact that he or she was convicted, or the defendant may accept that the conviction was correct but appeal against the sentence imposed. There are also a few, strictly limited, possibilities for the prosecutor to appeal against certain decisions. The reason the prosecutor's freedom to appeal is restricted is the rule against double jeopardy – the tradition that a person should not be tried twice for the same offence. This long-established rule was developed to avoid oppression and bad faith, although there are some important exceptions in relation to certain serious offences. The Crown Prosecution Service may now seek the re-trial of a person who has been acquitted of such an offence if there is new and compelling evidence, and if a retrial is in the public interest. These rules were invoked to facilitate the retrial, in 2011, of two defendants who were originally acquitted of the murder of teenager Stephen Lawrence in 1993.

In civil proceedings, any party may wish to appeal against an award of compensation or against a judge's decision not to award compensation, or against any of a host of other orders and decisions that may be made.

Rights of appeal are subject to a variety of rules, including time limits, and in some circumstances permission is necessary before an appeal can be brought.

Appeals against convictions for criminal offences and appeals against sentences imposed by magistrates' courts are dealt with by the Crown Court, where they are heard by a Crown Court judge sitting with two magistrates (see Chapter 4 for the role of the magistrate in the Crown Court). But appeals based on a point of law only go to the Queen's Bench Division of the High Court. Appeals from the Crown Court go up to the Criminal Division of the Court of Appeal, and, if there is a further appeal after that, to the Supreme Court. In most civil matters, permission to appeal is necessary and only one appeal is usually allowed. The appeal is heard at the lowest appropriate level in the system, although there is provision for cases which merit the attention of the Court of Appeal to go to that court.

Thus, at the bottom of the hierarchy are the magistrates' courts and the county courts; at the top is the Supreme Court, and in between, the Crown Court, the High Court and the Court of Appeal.

The adversarial system

The English trial process – and this applies to both criminal and civil trials – is of an 'adversarial' or 'accusatorial' nature. In a criminal case, the prosecution builds up a case against the defendant, presents that case in court, and it is then for the defendant to undermine the case. This compares with the 'inquisitorial' system, widely adopted elsewhere in Europe. In France, for example, extensive independent investigations are conducted by a professional examining magistrate (*juge d'instruction*) before a decision is made about whether or not to prosecute. The examining magistrate has wide powers to interview witnesses, and is in control of the police investigation. He or she gradually builds up a picture of the suspect, his or her background and the circumstances of the incident, and then decides whether or not charges should be brought, and if so what charges. When a suspect is charged with an offence, the examining magistrate withdraws from the case. The role of the examining magistrate – to pursue the truth – is far more neutral than that of anyone concerned in the pre-trial procedures under the English system.

By contrast, the police investigating a case here are motivated by, for example, the need to find the perpetrator of an offence and to make out a convincing case. The Crown Prosecution Service decides whether or not to pursue a case according to a number of published criteria, notably the likelihood of success and whether or not it is in the public interest to do so. There are many arguments about the advantages and disadvantages of the two approaches, which probably need not be aired here. But one consequence of an adversarial system is that the fate of a suspect depends very largely on what happens on the day of trial.

The county court

As has been seen, the county courts deal with a great many cases based on a broad range of civil matters. These cases are heard and decided by county court judges and the more junior district judges. Again, if a matter comes to trial, the adversarial approach applies, the claimant presenting all the evidence and arguments that can be mustered in favour of the case, the defendant seeking to discredit them. In civil cases, though, there is plenty of scope for extensive pre-trial negotiations between the parties. These often produce some kind of compromise so that the case can be settled without going before the court. Indeed, the rules governing the procedure are designed to encourage parties to co-operate and find a settlement.

The High Court

The High Court is divided into the Queen's Bench Division, the Family Division and the Chancery Division. It sits in London and in District Registries in other parts of the country.

The Queen's Bench Division is the busiest and deals with most disputes which are too large or complex for the county courts. It has two important subdivisions, the Divisional Court (in which decisions are made by at least two judges) and the Administrative Court (where decisions are made by a single judge). Appeals from the magistrates' courts on matters of law are heard either by a Divisional Court or by an Administrative Court.

The Commercial Court, as its name suggests, deals with commercial cases, and the Admiralty Court with shipping matters. Both fall within the Queen's Bench Division, as does the Technology and Construction Court.

The Family Division deals with divorce, maintenance and the division of money and other assets between divorcing and separating couples, and has all manner of tasks in relation to the welfare of children. It is also responsible for granting probate and letters of administration so that the affairs of a deceased person can be wound up.

Finally, the Chancery Division receives cases on financial matters, trusts, taxation and land.

The Court of Appeal and the Supreme Court

Moving up to the Court of Appeal, this is rather more logically divided into the Criminal and Civil Divisions, each dealing with cases of the appropriate category. The judges of the Court of Appeal, known as Lords Justices of Appeal, are selected from the ablest High Court judges.

Finally, appeals which get as far as the Supreme Court are heard by a panel of the country's most senior judges. The Supreme Court took over, in 2009, the judicial functions which used to be exercised by the House of Lords. The court whose decision is to be challenged, or the Supreme Court itself, must give consent to the bringing of an appeal to the Supreme Court. Consent is not forthcoming unless the case involves a point of law of general public importance, and the point is one which ought to be considered by the Supreme Court.

The Court of Justice of the European Union

Above all these courts there is now the Court of Justice of the European Union which sits in Luxembourg. It has the final word on all matters of European Union (EU) law, and although this rarely extends to criminal cases, it is important in civil matters, notably commercial interests in connection with trade and competition.

The European Court of Human Rights

Quite separate from the Court of Justice of the European Union is the European Court of Human Rights which sits in Strasbourg and which was established under the European Convention on Human Rights. The Convention was negotiated and agreed at the instigation of the Council of Europe. This is nothing to do with the European Union, but is an international, intergovernmental organisation which seeks to protect human rights and democracy. Among notable recent decisions was the court's judgment that police powers of stop and search under UK anti-terrorism legislation were too wide, and breached the right to private and family life. Even more controversial have been its decisions bearing on the proposed deportation from the United Kingdom of the radical cleric, Abu Qatada.

Other ways of settling disputes

Finally, it may be worth noting that in civil matters a number of other mechanisms exist to settle, or to seek to settle, disputes. These may be preferred because they are cheaper or less confrontational than the courts, or because they bring special skills to resolving conflict. For example:

- arbitration. People entering into a contract may agree in advance that if any dispute arises it will be settled by arbitration. The contract may go on to specify how the arbitrator – usually a person with special knowledge of the subject matter of the contract – would be appointed. This is commonly done in building contracts and the travel trade, and is increasingly favoured in many other areas;
- employment tribunals deal with claims under employment protection legislation – for unfair dismissal, for example;
- a great many other tribunals exist to deal with particular matters such as social security benefits, immigration and mental health cases;
- certain professional bodies, such as The Law Society, the General Medical Council and the General Dental Council, have their own tribunals to deal with disciplinary matters;
- many bodies provide mediation in cases of marriage breakdown, in an endeavour to help spouses find agreement rather than take a dispute to court;
- other methods of 'alternative dispute resolution'.

THE SOURCES OF LAW

One of the great fascinations of the law is that it reflects history, politics, economics and changing social values. Politicians come and go, public concerns fluctuate, sometimes with remarkable speed, theories of behaviour developed by sociologists and criminologists find favour then fade, moral values differ from individual to individual, but the law is the code by which society formally regulates its behaviour. That code comes from two sources: legislation and the common law.

Legislation

Much of our law derives from specific legislation – Acts of Parliament proposed, debated, and amended in the Houses of Commons and Lords and finally accorded Royal Assent by the Sovereign. Recent years have seen an increasing volume of new legislation – some say too much. Among the measures relevant to the criminal law have been legislation to counter terrorism, to amend the provisions on detaining suspects who have not been charged and to amend road traffic law, to mention but a few.

Acts of Parliament are increasingly supplemented by rules made by Statutory Instrument. Thus, an Act may lay down legal principles, but give authority to a particular government minister to make rules, having the force of law, on secondary matters such as procedure or dates of implementation. Perhaps the most relevant example is the Criminal Procedure Rules, made pursuant to the Courts Act 2003. The rules govern how cases are to be dealt with in the criminal courts, and set out the overriding objective that criminal cases are to be dealt with justly. The rules are discussed in greater detail in Chapter 4. Rules and regulations such as these are drafted by government departments, or (as in the case of the Criminal Procedure Rules) by a dedicated rules committee. They become law by being laid before Parliament for the requisite period. They may be subject to 'positive' or 'negative' resolution – either Parliament must specifically approve them before they become law, or they become law in the absence of any objection. The latter is the more common method, although it has attracted some criticism as more and more matters are controlled by Statutory Instrument and are not subject to full Parliamentary scrutiny.

Local authorities may also be given powers to make by-laws applying in their own areas only. For example, they can introduce requirements that dog-walkers in their area 'poop scoop'.

The common law

Unlike many other countries, English law has not been fully codified into statute, and many important provisions do not appear in any written law, but remain based, wholly or partly, in the common law – established custom as adopted and developed by judges over the years. For the details of this kind of law, it is necessary to refer to reported judgments. The most important example of a common law offence is murder: the constituents of 'malice aforethought' and an intention unlawfully to kill or cause grievous bodily harm, derive from what judges have said in the past, not from any Act of Parliament which says that murder is a crime.

Precedent

In the interests of fostering certainty, the principle of legal precedent promotes consistency in decision-making. Thus, largely, higher courts should follow their own earlier decisions, and decisions made in higher courts are binding on lower courts: what the Supreme Court says is binding on the Court of Appeal; what the Court of Appeal says applies in all lower courts. The principle of precedent applies to both civil and criminal cases, and to the interpretation of both common law and statute-based law.

Magistrates' courts and the Crown Court are not bound by their own earlier decisions, although, as we shall see, strenuous efforts are made to try to ensure consistency in sentencing. But they are bound by the decisions of the higher courts. Sometimes, earlier cases are referred to in court, perhaps to illustrate what has in the past been taken to amount to a 'special reason' for not disqualifying a driver who would otherwise be disqualified automatically.

The tradition is to name criminal cases in the style *'R v Smith'*, where *R* stands for *Regina*, all cases still strictly being brought by the prosecutor on behalf of the Sovereign, and *Smith* being the name of the defendant; or *DPP (Director of Public Prosecutions) v Smith*, the Crown Prosecution Service prosecuting on behalf of the Director of Public Prosecutions. Yet again, the case may be referred to simply as *'Smith'*. Reports published in the official law reports, the All England Law Reports and the Weekly Law Reports may well be mentioned.

Judicial interpretation

Although English legislation tends to be drafted in a fairly detailed way by comparison with that of other European countries, and certainly compared with EU legislation, the draftsmen cannot always contemplate every conceivable situation, and are not always as precise in their wording as might be desirable. Gaps, inconsistencies and ambiguities are dealt with by 'judicial interpretation' in individual cases. Sometimes such interpretations reveal gaps in the law. Tax lawyers and accountants are adept at seeking out gaps (often called loopholes) which can be used to the advantage of their clients. Sometimes a court will refer to *Hansard* to clarify the intention of Parliament in passing a particular piece of legislation, in an endeavour to interpret it in the right spirit. Interpretations of this kind are, like everything else, subject to the rule of precedent.

Some judges have been said to be rather too imaginative in interpreting the law to the extent, some say, that they make law in usurpation of the prerogative of Parliament.

The European Convention on Human Rights

The Human Rights Act 1998 made the European Convention on Human Rights of 1950 enforceable in the United Kingdom. Before the Act came into force, it was necessary to go to the European Court of Human Rights in Strasbourg to enforce those rights. The rights enshrined in the Convention include the rights to:

- liberty;
- a fair trial;
- respect for private and family life; and
- freedom of thought, conscience and religion.

The Act requires that when any court is deciding a question concerning any of these rights, it must take into account, among other matters, the judgments and decisions of the European Court of Human Rights (see above). It also requires that legislation be interpreted in a way which is compatible with these rights, and makes it unlawful for a court or other public authority to act in a way which is not compatible with a Convention right. In recent years a debate has arisen about the extent to which the domestic courts must actually follow the decisions of the European Court of Human Rights, some now arguing that those decisions need not be unquestioningly applied.

European Union law

Finally, the courts of England and Wales are subject to EU law, which takes priority over all domestic law. The Union makes laws by means of Directives (which must then be implemented in each member state by domestic legislation), Regulations (which are directly binding on the member states) and Decisions, which concern particular matters and are addressed only to the individual member state concerned. The system of law-making – in which the European Commission, which is not directly elected, has the greatest say – has long been controversial. Most of the EU's legislative activities do not, however, affect the criminal courts, although environmental protection is an increasingly important exception.

Text books

Text books have no formal place in making and interpreting the law, but advocates in court often refer to certain established works when seeking to persuade the court of a particular point of view. Arguments on doubtful points of law are fairly rare in the magistrates' courts, but leading books are often referred to in order to explain the relevant law, even though it may not be in doubt. Among authoritative books sometimes referred to are Archbold (*Criminal Pleading*), Blackstone's (*Blackstone's Criminal Practice*), Stones (*Stone's Justices' Manual*) and Wilkinson (*Wilkinson's Road Traffic Offences*). Generally, the more editions of a book that have been published, and where it is referred to by its author's (or original author's) name alone, the more authoritative it is!

The Law Commission

Again, although it is not a direct source of law, it is worth mentioning the work of the Law Commission. This is a body of authoritative lawyers drawn from all walks of legal life who undertake extensive reviews of particular areas of law and make recommendations for improvement, clarification, simplification, amendment, restatement or even abolition. The Commission is highly respected in legal circles and, for example, in the 1980s it produced detailed proposals for codifying the criminal law, although, as has been the case with many other well researched and carefully presented proposals of the Commission, parliamentary time was not devoted to it and it has not been acted on.

Royal Commissions and other reports

Royal Commissions may also influence how law is made. Royal Commissions are appointed on an *ad hoc* basis by Government to investigate specific matters and make recommendations, but again, their advice is not always taken. For example, although a Royal Commission recommended no change to an accused person's right to silence, the law was nevertheless changed by the Criminal Justice and Public Order Act 1994 to allow a court, in certain circumstances, to draw an adverse inference from a defendant's failure to explain himself or herself.

Other special reports may be commissioned to inform government policy. Sir Peter North was requested by the Secretary of State for Transport to conduct a study of the drink- and drug-driving laws, and reported in 2010. Although he made a number of recommendations – notably to lower the drink-drive limit – it seems unlikely that any of them will be acted upon in the short term.

Chapter 3

The Organisation of the Magistrates' Courts

In this chapter we take a look at the magistrates' courts themselves – how they are organised and administered, and the personalities to be encountered there.

FACILITIES

Like most other publicly-provided buildings, courthouses vary enormously, from the architecturally elegant to the downright scruffy. They may house a single court or two dozen (although the trend is towards fewer buildings, each housing more courts), as well as offices for the administrative staff, cells, a reception area, interview rooms, a public gallery and magistrates' retiring room(s).

Courtrooms also come in a wide variety of shapes, sizes and standards of comfort. But common to them all is that the magistrates sit at one end, usually on a raised platform, often beneath the Royal Arms. In front of them and usually a little below, normally facing in the same direction as the magistrates, sits the legal adviser. Facing the magistrates and the legal adviser are seats and desks for the lawyers. The prosecutor and the defence lawyer usually take the front row, those waiting their turn sitting behind.

Behind them, or perhaps to the side, is accommodation for the public, generally known as the 'public gallery' although in some cases that may be a rather grandiose term for the accommodation actually provided. Almost all proceedings in magistrates' courts (with the exceptions of family cases and youth court cases) are open to the public; for justice must not only be done, it must be seen to be done. We have already noted that prospective new magistrates can make use of the public gallery for their preliminary observations of proceedings. There may be a separate place for representatives of the press, or they may have to take their chances in the public gallery.

To the right and left are the witness box, the dock, and a place for a probation officer to sit. In 'secure' courts, the dock leads directly to the cells, and cases concerning defendants in custody are usually allocated to these courts. Other courts may not have direct access to the cells, and are generally used for cases involving defendants on bail and for cases where imprisonment is unlikely to be the final outcome.

There is an excellent illustration of a typical magistrates' court on the website of the Judiciary of England and Wales: www.judiciary.gov.uk/interactive-learning/interactive-courtroom/mags+ct+scene.

In the family proceedings court and the youth court the physical arrangements are less formal. In the family court, the emphasis is on the welfare of the child, and arrangements which less reflect the 'adversarial' approach are preferable. Likewise in the youth court, where engaging with the defendant is a primary consideration, a less formidable appearance is conducive to that purpose. Some courthouses have courtrooms specifically designed and furnished as youth courts and family courts; elsewhere, it may be a question of moving the furniture around before the session begins.

SECURITY

Private firms are contracted to transport defendants in custody between prison and the courts, and to be responsible for them while at court. This service is known as the Prisoner Escort and Custody Service (PECS), and, at the time of writing, is contracted out to two companies – Geo Amey PECS and Serco Ltd. Prisoners are brought into the dock by a PECS officer (sometimes two) who remains with the prisoner throughout the hearing.

If the defendant is not in custody, the court usually sits without a security officer present in the room, although one of the court's own security officers can be summoned from elsewhere in the building if necessary. Most courtrooms have a 'panic button' or similar system to call someone quickly in the – fortunately rare – event that someone has to be forcibly removed for disruption or other misbehaviour.

Security officers employed by the court are empowered to search people entering, or trying to enter, a court building, and also search anything in such a person's possession. They may forbid entry to anyone who does not co-operate. They may restrain and/or remove a person if necessary to enable court business to be carried on without interference or delay, to maintain order, or for the safety of anyone in the building. They may also remove a person from a courtroom at the request of a magistrate. They can use reasonable force. It is an offence to assault a court security officer in the execution of his or her duty.

Magistrates who wish to view the cells, reception area and other 'front of house' facilities can usually arrange to do so by asking a member of the court staff.

RETIRING ROOMS

Again, retiring rooms, and the standards of comfort they offer, vary. Some courthouses have a separate retiring room behind each court; others have a single retiring room which is used by all the magistrates. Whether the retiring room has five stars or none, this is the place where the magistrates deliberate, discuss and reach decisions. Here also, the legal adviser briefs the magistrates before the court session, pointing out any cases which might present particular difficulty or prove particularly interesting, and on matters concerning case management (discussed in more detail in Chapter 5).

It is an inexplicable fact of life that magistrates tend to be voluble, and this may be distracting in a shared retiring room, but in the absence of anything better, it simply has to be tolerated. The consolation is that it is becoming more and more common to provide a quiet place, however small, for reading pre-sentence reports, papers in family cases and so on.

The retiring room may also have a more general function as a meeting place. All sorts of social activities may be organised. Notice boards announce training courses, rota vacancies, reports of appeals, dates of meetings, sports fixtures and so on. Friendships may be made and lost here. Getting to know other magistrates on the same bench may take some time, given that the rota system may mean seeing a particular person only once or twice a year, but it is valuable in that it eases discussing cases, especially expressing differences of opinion.

THE LEGAL ADVISERS

As noted in Chapter 1, magistrates always sit in court with a legal adviser. Each local justice area has a clerk to the justices, who has overall responsibility for advising the magistrates on the law. At the time of writing, there are forty-nine clerks to the justices. They are assisted by a number of legal advisers (technically, assistant justices' clerks, and still sometimes called 'clerks'). Justices' clerks and legal advisers are qualified in the law and most are solicitors or barristers. The trend is towards requiring all those who advise magistrates on the law to be qualified solicitors or barristers.

Most justices' clerks and many legal advisers belong to the Justices' Clerks' Society, a long-established and respected body which represents their professional interests and provides a forum for consultation among themselves and with the Government and other agencies. Legal advisers and staff may, alternatively, be members of the Public and Commercial Services Union or Prospect.

The principal function of the legal adviser as far as the magistrates are concerned is to advise on the law. Advice may relate to the law itself, questions of mixed law and fact, practice and procedure, the penalties for a particular offence, decisions of higher courts, any relevant guidelines and decision-making structures. The justices' clerks and the legal advisers have complete independence when advising magistrates, and their task is to give full and accurate advice as to the law without regard to convenience, expedience, expense or other extraneous matters. For more about the role of the legal adviser at a trial, see Chapter 5.

The magistrates may themselves seek advice. Since the system of justice should be as transparent as possible, it is as well to ask questions openly in court unless there is a particular reason for confidentiality. Thus, the chairman of the magistrates may ask the legal adviser 'What are our powers of sentencing for this offence?' or 'Please recap the elements of this offence'. But if the bench is considering disposing of a case in a particular and perhaps unusual way, and wishes to check it has power to do so, it may not wish to prejudice its final decision by saying publicly what it has in mind. Thus, although it is preferable to avoid whispered conversations, this may have to be resorted to for a question like: 'We are thinking of deferring sentence for six months; do we need the defendant's consent?'

The legal adviser may also give advice of his or her own initiative. For example, if there is a decided case which the legal adviser considers relevant to the case in hand, and it has not been mentioned by either the prosecutor or the defendant's lawyer, the legal adviser may bring it to the attention of the magistrates, and does so in open court in case either side wishes, say, to argue that that decision is in fact not relevant. Likewise, the legal adviser may intervene if the magistrates are going wrong, as where, for instance, they have misunderstood something which has been said. It is no disgrace, but rather a confirmation of the strength of the system, for a chairman to have to say something like: 'The bench is corrected. The defendant is indeed entitled to make a new application for bail'.

Interaction between the bench and the legal adviser reflects that the role of the legal adviser is confined to matters of law, and decisions on the facts are the sole province of the bench. For this reason, the legal adviser does not usually retire with the magistrates. If the chairman of the magistrates thinks the bench will need the help of the legal adviser in the retiring room, it is good practice openly to invite the legal adviser to join the magistrates. There is no prohibition on giving advice in private. Indeed, privacy may be necessary so that questioning by the magistrates can be free and uninhibited. But any legal advice given to the magistrates in private should be considered provisional until repeated in open court.

Unfortunately for them, legal advisers also have to be available outside court hours, to advise on, say, an application for an emergency protection order made directly to a magistrate at home in the evening.

Because the workings of the court should be as self-evident as possible, it is sometimes said that the magistrates, and others in court, should address the legal adviser as 'Mister/Madam legal adviser'. Some may find this too cumbersome and artificial, and may prefer plain 'Mr Smith' or 'Mrs Jones', specifically explaining who the legal adviser is to anyone directly involved to whom it may not be obvious.

The legal advisers also play an important role in advising defendants who do not have lawyers, explaining the procedure and, perhaps, that what they have said amounts in law to a defence and that they should consider changing their plea from guilty to not guilty. The legal adviser may also assist in formulating questions for witnesses. With the reduction in the availability of legal aid (see Chapter 11), this role is increasingly important, and one which legal advisers often carry out with great skill and impartiality.

The legal advisers also make notes of evidence, record who is present and what is decided, write up bail notices and perform a range of administrative duties, for example arranging for the Driver and Vehicle Licensing Agency in Swansea to provide a 'printout' of a driver's record. Courtrooms are now equipped with computer terminals to assist in these functions.

The clerk to the justices shares certain functions with the magistrates. These have increased in recent years and now broadly equate with what a single justice is empowered to do. Thus, the justices' clerk can issue a summons, extend bail, adjourn cases, and request a pre-sentence report, and may delegate this work to his or her staff. The powers of justices' clerks are listed in more detail in Chapter 4.

THE USHERS

It has been noted in Chapter 1 that the court ushers (or list callers) occupy a unique place 'at the sharp end'. It is they who record the arrival of defendants, witnesses and lawyers, tell defendants where they can find the duty solicitor, and supplement the posted court lists by telling people in which courts their cases are to be heard. They, together with the lawyers, often have to take the brunt of the anger, frustration, disappointment and distress of defendants and witnesses.

The ushers usually decide the order in which to bring on the cases (although they can be overruled by the bench), checking which are ready to go ahead, and which defendants are still talking to their lawyers. Often they so manage things that all the cases in which a particular solicitor is involved are heard in sequence so that the solicitor can finish his or her court work for the day. They may also arrange for work to be switched between the courts. Perhaps Court 1's list has turned out to be shorter than expected but Court 2 is overloaded, so the usher, in consultation with the legal advisers, brings some of Court 2's work into Court 1. Transferring cases in this way may also be necessary if a magistrate has to disqualify himself or herself from a case (see Chapter 12), perhaps because he or she knows the defendant in some personal or professional capacity.

The ushers also have a host of other tasks in ensuring the courts work as smoothly as possible. In their 'spare time' when the courts are not sitting or have finished early, they are often deployed helping with general administrative work in the offices.

ADMINISTRATION

The administrative staff of the court are responsible for a range of 'backroom' duties, including:

- organising the magistrates' timetable;
- preparing the lists for each court day, making sure the files are complete and ready;
- following up after a case has been in court – sending out adjournment notices, for example;
- recording payments of fines and dealing with defaulters;
- collecting maintenance payments under orders made in family proceedings, and passing the money to those entitled to it;
- collecting money due under fixed penalty notices issued in road traffic matters (see Chapter 6).

THE LAWYERS

Lawyers in England and Wales come in two different kinds – solicitors, and barristers or counsel. This is a curious division which contrasts with the situation in many other countries which have only a single variety of lawyer: the *avocat* in France; the *rechtsanwalt* in Germany; the *advocaat* in the Netherlands; the *abogado* in Spain.

The reason we have two branches of the legal profession here is largely historical, and although proposals to fuse the two professions have been abandoned, the differences are being eroded little by little. For example, until 1990, only barristers had the right to conduct cases in the higher courts, including the Crown Court, but solicitors may now qualify to do so. It used to be said that the principal difference between the two professions is that barristers are specialists and solicitors are generalists. That remains true to some extent, and many barristers act as senior consultants on highly specialised areas of law, spending much of their time researching cases referred by solicitors and providing 'opinions'. But they do not train specifically for a particular specialisation. They are generalists when first 'called to the bar' on qualification, and specialisation tends to emerge over the years. That said, however, many solicitors now specialise more and more, for example offering (perhaps via the internet) specialised services to motorists charged with road traffic offences. In the civil law, proceedings to secure compensation for personal injuries have burgeoned, and that body of law has developed considerably over recent years, leading some solicitors to become specialists in this area.

A barrister of a certain number of years' experience may 'take silk' (having the privilege of wearing a silk rather than a stuff gown), becoming a Queen's Counsel (QC). Selection is by the Lord Chancellor in consultation with advisors in his department and at the bar. Taking silk usually leads to increased status and the possibility of later being appointed a High Court judge; it may also produce an increase in earnings. All barristers who are not silks are juniors, no matter how old they are, although experienced juniors are sometimes referred to, rather contrarily, as 'senior juniors'. Usually, a silk does not appear in court unless assisted by a junior.

The only common element in the training for each profession is that both study the same body of law. Thereafter, the barrister's life is characterised by a number of antique customs that need not concern us here, other than to note that in the magistrates' courts they do not wear their wigs and gowns. Although there has been some liberalisation of barristers' practices, an ordinary person still cannot consult a barrister directly, but must do so through a solicitor. The document in which a solicitor refers a case to a barrister, or 'instructs' the barrister, is called a brief, hence the expression, 'I want to see my brief'.

Most solicitors deal with a great variety of work. Thus High Street firms comprising perhaps two or three qualified solicitors are usually general practitioners, undertaking domestic and commercial conveyancing, writing wills and winding up estates, advising and conducting proceedings in divorce and other family matters, advising on disputes in civil cases, drawing up contracts and many other matters. In larger firms, notably big city firms, some having more than 100 partners, individual solicitors tend to specialise in particular areas, for example, shipping, trusts, company mergers, commercial contracts and so on. Many spend most of their time in their offices and rarely venture within the precincts of a court of any kind. But a large proportion of ordinary solicitors undertake criminal work and deal with a case from start to finish.

Solicitors may work on their own, in which case they are 'sole practitioners' and self-employed, or in partnership with others in which case they share office accommodation, facilities and fees. Or they may be employed by a firm of solicitors or in the legal department of a commercial organisation, receiving a salary rather than a share in the fee income. The long-standing rule that only lawyers may own solicitors' firms was relaxed in 2011. This reform, commonly referred to as the introduction of 'Tesco law', means that non-lawyers may now own and invest in law firms. It is controversial in that, on the one hand, it is said that consumers will benefit from greater competition, while on the other hand, there are fears that commercial considerations will undermine the quality and independence of legal services. Either way, it does seem that change is afoot.

Barristers, on the other hand, may not operate in partnerships and instead work independently, although by tradition they usually group together in a 'set', sharing offices, or 'chambers'. For historical reasons, barristers each belong to one of the four Inns of Court – Gray's Inn, Lincoln's Inn, Middle Temple and Inner Temple. Barristers are represented collectively by the Bar Council.

Barristers operate on what is known as the 'cab rank principle' which means exactly what it suggests – they take the case which is at the head of the queue, provided the barrister is available and the subject is one with which the barrister is familiar. They may not first examine the prospects of success, because the idea is to ensure that every person accused of an offence, particularly the distasteful offences such as rape or child abuse, can have the services of a lawyer.

One of the criticisms of the system is that a barrister often does not receive a brief until the last minute, perhaps only a couple of hours before a trial comes on in court. This may be because the barrister originally briefed has been detained by another case going on longer than expected, with the result that the brief is returned to chambers to be reallocated to another barrister. This is doubly frustrating for the client who may feel he or she is having to accept second best (although that may well not be so), and who may not meet the barrister until just before the case is called on in court.

In truth, whether the lawyer in court happens to be a barrister or solicitor is not terribly important in the day-to-day business of the magistrates' courts. Magistrates listening to lawyers may not even know whether they are solicitor or counsel, and it matters little. Many lawyers are good, some are indifferent and a few are plain bad. What does matter to magistrates is that they should not let their decisions be influenced by the fact that a lawyer may be irritating, condescending, unduly provocative, pompous, or, on the other hand, ingratiating, eloquent, courteous or especially fluent – none of these in itself has anything to do with the defendant's culpability or the heinousness of the crime.

Many solicitors deal with their clients' cases throughout, from first meeting the client through to sentence. But they may instruct counsel to deal with court appearances, either because they think counsel is better equipped to do so, or because they do not have the manpower to do it themselves. QCs rarely appear in the magistrates' courts, their expensive services generally being reserved for serious cases in the Crown Court and appeals to the Court of Appeal.

The steady reductions in the legal aid budget over the past decade, and the consequent erosion of the real income of many lawyers, are a cause of considerable concern, not only in relation to the loss of income to many experienced specialist lawyers, but also because of the fear that the quality of the process in the criminal courts is at risk. This is discussed further in Chapter 11.

In cases brought by local authorities, for example, prosecutions under food safety or trade descriptions legislation, a lawyer employed by the local authority may appear to present the case, or an outside solicitor or counsel may be instructed. Likewise, in cases brought by other non-CPS prosecutors, such as the RSPCA, or bus and railway companies, the prosecutor may be a lawyer employed by the prosecutor, or an independent lawyer instructed for the purpose.

And finally on the subject of lawyers, they do tend to use language which sometimes seems rather quaint. They often refer to other lawyers as 'my friend' even though they are on opposite sides of the case. They may say to a witness, 'are you quite sure you are remembering that correctly?', implying, 'that doesn't make sense', or 'that contradicts what Officer So-and-So said'. Or they may say, 'I put it you that you were at the Dog and Duck on Thursday evening' rather than, 'you can't possibly be right in saying you were at home at the time'. These ways of putting things, which may at first seem rather strained and indirect, derive from tradition and conventions of courtesy, avoiding direct confrontation. It rapidly becomes clear to new magistrates that they do not in any way detract from the force of what the lawyer is saying.

THE CROWN PROSECUTION SERVICE

Until 1986, prosecutions were conducted by the police. The main objection to this was that it was not in the interests of fairness that the police, who are responsible for investigating alleged crimes, should also have the conduct of the prosecution. As long ago as 1929 a Royal Commission said that it was important to separate 'on the one hand, the duty that lies on the police of preventing and detecting crime, and, on the other, the duty of bringing to justice people who have broken the law'. There was also considerable variation in practice between the different police forces in England and Wales, and an excess of weak cases coming before the courts. In the interests of independence, and of consistency and certainty in practice, an independent prosecuting body was desirable. This finally led to the establishment, in 1986, of the Crown Prosecution Service (CPS).

The CPS is divided into thirteen areas across England and Wales. Each area is headed by a Chief Crown Prosecutor. The service employs almost 8,000 people, about one third of whom are barristers or solicitors. The Director of Public Prosecutions (DPP) is the head of the service. Although politically neutral, the DPP is accountable to the Attorney General. The offices of DPP and Attorney General are of much more ancient origin than the CPS, the first DPP having been appointed in 1880. The present DPP is Keir Starmer QC. He may himself prosecute a case if it is particularly difficult or of exceptional importance.

The CPS is responsible for prosecuting all criminal offences, except traffic offences in respect of which it is possible to plead guilty by post. In 2010/11, the CPS brought over 840,000 cases in the magistrates' courts, 86.5 per cent of which resulted in convictions. Also within the CPS's remit are cases of serious or complex fraud, which are handled by its Central Fraud Group, and Serious Crime Group. These sections of the CPS prosecute cases investigated by the Serious and Organised Crime Agency, the UK Border Agency, and Her Majesty's Revenue and Customs, as well as terrorism, fraud and other cases requiring special experience. There is a special procedure for many of these cases to commence in the Crown Court without first coming before the magistrates' court. The magistrates therefore take no part in these intriguing and challenging cases.

Even if the CPS decides not to prosecute a case, there is no reason why an individual cannot bring a private prosecution, and this does sometimes happen, although doing so may well require exceptional application and perseverance. The prior consent of the DPP is required before bringing a prosecution for certain unusual offences, including incest, aiding and abetting suicide, and riot, none of which is the common stuff of the magistrates' courts. The CPS may take over a prosecution begun privately. It is noted elsewhere that certain cases are brought by prosecutors other than the CPS, for example, local authorities, the Environment Agency, and the Federation Against Copyright Theft, but the CPS prosecutes the vast majority.

In most cases, it is for the police, having investigated, collected evidence and identified a suspect, to decide whether or not to charge the suspect. They may consult the CPS before doing so. The CPS may advise on matters such as lines of inquiry and the evidence needed, but may not direct the police. In more serious or complex cases, the CPS decides whether a person should be charged with an offence. After charge, the CPS reviews the case to decide whether or not to proceed to prosecute the offence charged, or a different offence, or additional offences. The CPS is not obliged to bring a prosecution simply because a person has been charged. The charging process is discussed further in Chapter 5.

The decision whether or not to prosecute is guided by a Code for Crown Prosecutors. Crown prosecutors must first be satisfied that there is enough evidence to give rise to 'a realistic prospect of conviction'. They must take into account any likely defences. A realistic prospect of conviction means that a jury or bench of magistrates, properly directed and acting in accordance with the law, is more likely than not to convict the defendant.

The crown prosecutor must also consider that the evidence is both admissible and reliable.

If the evidence passes the test, the crown prosecutor must next apply the 'public interest' test. In 1951, the then Attorney General said in the House of Commons that, 'It has never been the rule in this country – and I hope it never will be – that suspected criminal offences must automatically be the subject of prosecution'. This remains the view to this day, and prosecutions are not brought unless it is in the public interest to do so. The Code for Crown Prosecutors lists a number of factors which would favour proceeding with a prosecution, for example:

- conviction is likely to result in a significant sentence;
- a weapon was used or violence threatened when the offence was committed;
- the victim was a person serving the public, such as a police officer, nurse or bus driver;
- the defendant was in a position of trust;
- the victim was vulnerable and was put in considerable fear, or suffered some kind of personal attack;
- the offence was motivated by some form of discrimination.

On the other hand, certain other features may be persuasive that it is not in the public interest to prosecute; for instance, where:

- the offence was committed as a result of a genuine mistake or misunderstanding;
- prosecution is likely adversely to affect the victim's physical or mental health;
- the defendant is elderly or suffers from significant mental or physical ill health (although this factor alone is unlikely to be conclusive);
- if a prosecution went ahead, details which could harm sources of information, international relations or national security, might be made public.

While the CPS should take into account the views of direct victims of crime, or of their families, this is only one factor in assessing the overall public interest.

If the CPS decides to proceed with a prosecution, the case is presented in the magistrates' court by a lawyer employed or instructed by the CPS, or, in certain cases, by a member of the CPS staff who is not qualified as a lawyer. The CPS usually instructs counsel to deal with cases that go to the Crown Court.

The CPS has obligations to observe confidentiality to protect witnesses, victims, suspects and defendants.

THE PROBATION SERVICE

The Probation Service can trace its history back over a hundred years, but it has undergone significant change in recent years, with more still to come. Along with the prison service, it is part of the National Offender Management Service (NOMS), which in turn is part of the Ministry of Justice. It is administered by thirty-five probation trusts, which are responsible for overseeing both those serving community sentences and offenders released on licence from prison. Probation staff are also responsible for preparing pre-sentence reports for the courts to enable them to choose the most appropriate sentence. They also facilitate and supervise community orders. It is these aspects of their work which are most familiar to magistrates, and more is said about them in Chapter 9. A probation officer may be present in court in anticipation of being asked to provide a pre-sentence report, or to deliver an oral report, or to elaborate on a written report. The court may wish to hear from a probation officer about progress under an order already in place, or about an offender's response to an earlier order.

Regular liaison meetings between the magistrates' courts and the Probation Service take place. These help keep magistrates abreast of developments in matters such as sentencing and resources, as well as assisting the Probation Service in understanding and meeting the needs of sentencing benches.

HER MAJESTY'S COURTS AND TRIBUNALS SERVICE

While the chairman of the bench and the clerk to the justices have overall responsibilities for the quality of justice dispensed in their courts, the task of organising and managing the courts falls to Her Majesty's Courts and Tribunals Service (HMCTS). HMCTS is an agency of the Ministry of Justice, and is responsible for the administration of all courts and tribunals in England and Wales. It is headed jointly by the Lord Chancellor (a political appointee), the Lord Chief Justice, and the Senior President of Tribunals. The Lord Chancellor has a statutory duty to uphold the independence of the judiciary. This is in keeping with the principle of the separation of powers, i.e. that judicial and administrative functions should be kept apart from each other to avoid the possibility that justice might be compromised by factors which are not directly relevant, such as budgetary or political constraints. The Lord Chief Justice is the president of the courts in England and Wales and his statutory duties include providing training and guidance to the judiciary, and representing the views of the judiciary to government. The Lord Chancellor and the Lord Chief Justice play no part in the day-to-day running of HMCTS, which has its own board and chief executive.

The aim of HMCTS, according to its framework document of April 2011, is to run an efficient and effective court system, which enables the rule of law to be upheld and provides access to justice for all. Members of the judiciary are expected to work with HMCTS in pursuit of the effective, efficient and speedy operation of the courts. HMCTS staff are, however subject to the directions of the judiciary in relation to the conduct of the business of the courts in matters such as listing, case allocation and case management. This is discussed further in Chapter 5.

BENCH COMMITTEES

Many benches elect a number of statutory and non-statutory committees and panels with specific tasks. These usually include:

- the Bench Training and Development Committee – see below;
- the youth court panel. Magistrates sitting in the youth court need special aptitudes and training to deal with the different approach taken when dealing with the young – see Chapter 7;
- the family court panel: again membership of this panel requires special training – see Chapter 7;
- a probation committee, to liaise with the local probation service – see above.

There may also be all manner of less formal groups – a 'magistrates in the community' group, for example (see Chapter 1), and social or sporting groups.

THE POLICE

At one time, the magistrates' courts were commonly referred to as 'police courts', but this expression disappeared following a change in the law in 1948. The privatisation of court security and the prison escort service has further reduced the number of police officers regularly present in the courts.

It is widely accepted that one of the strengths of the police service is that it operates independently of central or local government. This again accords with the general principle of the separation of powers – that the police, the judiciary and government bodies should each approach their work free of influence from each other. There are forty-three police areas in England and Wales, the areas being roughly equivalent to administrative counties.

The principal functions of the police are to keep law and order, protect people and property, prevent crime, detect criminals, liaise with the CPS and control traffic. Volumes could be, and have been, written about what these duties entail. Only a few general principles are noted here. Thus, the police are subject to the law in the same way as everybody else. They may not bend it or break it, but they do have special powers, notably powers to detain, arrest, search and question people. Their powers are regulated by the provisions of the Police and Criminal Evidence Act 1984 (PACE), and by the Codes of Practice made under the Act, which are discussed in more detail in Chapter 5. It has been said that: 'The Codes of Practice are to protect the individual from the might of the state. An individual is at a great disadvantage when arrested by the police even when there is no impropriety'.

Police officers regularly appear as witnesses in the criminal courts. They have no special status as witnesses and there is no presumption that what they say is more likely to be true than what anybody else says. Lady Ralphs and Geoffrey Norman, in their book, *The Magistrate as Chairman* (Butterworths, 1992), refer to a 1974 case, where a conviction was overturned on appeal, because the chairman of the magistrates had made the wholly unacceptable statement that:

> Quite the most unpleasant cases that we have to decide are those where the evidence is a direct conflict between a police officer and a member of the public. My principle in such cases has always been to believe the evidence of the police officer, and therefore we find the case proved.

On the other hand, the police are trained to observe people, events and surroundings accurately, and to make reliable notes, and magistrates have this in mind when deciding what credibility and weight to assign to their evidence. But police officers are not immune from making genuine errors or misconstruing events. Worse still, wrongful convictions based on bad faith or malpractice by police have occasionally come to light, and magistrates should be conscious of that possibility, however remote.

SUPPORT FOR VICTIMS AND WITNESSES

Victims of crimes often have to give evidence about what happened to them, and others may be called as witnesses. This can be a difficult, and sometimes frightening, prospect, especially bearing in mind that many may never have been inside a courtroom before. The independent charity Victim Support provides free and confidential help to victims and other witnesses. It runs the Witness Service in every criminal court, providing help and support, and information about what to expect. The service can even provide someone to go into the courtroom with a witness, to help the witness feel a little more at ease. This is an invaluable service not only for the witness, but for the court, in the sense that a witness who is relaxed is likely to testify more coherently and comprehensively than one who is not.

TRAINING

Bench Training and Development Committees

The training of magistrates has changed considerably over the years. Training for both new and experienced magistrates is now a far greater commitment than ever before. The present regime is governed by the Justices of the Peace (Training and Development Committee) Rules 2007, made under the Courts Act 2003. Each local justice area has a Bench Training and Development Committee (BTDC), comprising six or nine justices, elected by the magistrates. Two or more local justice areas may have a combined BTDC. There may be a separate committee for the family panel and the youth panel.

The tasks of the BTDCs are to:

- arrange for justices to attend appropriate training;
- identify training needs and report those needs to the relevant Magistrates' Area Training Committee (see below);
- set up and run a scheme for appraising justices (see below); and
- maintain a list of approved court chairmen (see below).

Before sitting in the adult court, the youth court or the family proceedings court, or as a chairman in any of those courts, a magistrate must first complete the appropriate training.

Training may take place at the magistrate's 'home' court, a neighbouring court, an office of HMCTS or other organisation, or perhaps at a hotel or conference centre. Plenty of notice is given and expenses (see Chapter 12) can be claimed.

Magistrates' Area Training Committees

Each courts board area has a magistrates' area training committee (MATC). It comprises magistrates and a justices' clerk from the area. Also on the MATC there may be a district judge (magistrates' courts), a family court judge and a Crown Court liaison judge. The roles of these judicial personalities are explained elsewhere.

The purpose of the MATC is to consider the training needs identified by the BTDC. A training plan is drawn up each year, setting out the proposed types of training, where and when it will take place, and the number of justices who are to receive training. The MATC also reports on its activities each year to the Lord Chief Justice.

The Judicial College

The Judicial College oversees and guides the training of all the magistrates at the national level. It promulgates training materials, and trains the trainers. It is also responsible for the training of other judicial office-holders in all courts and tribunals in England and Wales.

Initial training

Once they have been sworn in, new magistrates are invited to an introductory meeting at their 'home' courts, usually lasting about three hours. It allows them to become familiar with the layout of the courthouse, and to learn about the roles of the justices' clerk, the BTDC and others. Details of the mentor scheme, the training programme and first appraisal are also introduced.

Induction and core training follow, usually comprising about eighteen hours, before first sitting in the court. This training may take place over a long weekend, or in shorter sessions over several weeks, or anything between. Observing courts in session is also required. There may be one or more visits to prisons or young offender institutions, and perhaps a visit to observe an unpaid work project or other activity under a community sentence.

The aim is to achieve the three core competences needed in the ordinary adult court:

- managing oneself, in the sense of preparing for each sitting, conducting oneself effectively in the judicial process and engaging in continuing training and development;

- the ability to work as an effective member of a team; and
- the ability to think and act judicially, using appropriate processes and structures and acting impartially.

The focus is basic law and procedure, including:

- the different classes of offence;
- procedure at trials, fairness and the judicial approach;
- the structured approach to decision-making and sentencing;
- the most common sentences;
- bail;
- case management.

The training may take the form of reading, presentations by tutors, videos, role play and group discussions.

Mentors

As mentioned in Chapter 1, each new magistrate is assisted by an experienced magistrate who has been selected and trained to act as a mentor and provide support and guidance. During the first year, a new magistrate sits with the mentor six times. Each sitting is followed by discussions about the proceedings, reflecting on how the new magistrate has applied the knowledge and skills derived from the induction and core training.

Appraisals

After about the first year of sittings, it is time for consolidation training in preparation for the magistrate's first (or threshold) appraisal. Consolidation training comprises about twelve hours' work, and provides an opportunity for new magistrates to review progress, reflect on their growing experience and understanding, revisit their initial training, and generally prepare for appraisal. All serving magistrates are appraised every three years either as wingers or chairs in the adult courts, while members and chairmen of the family and youth panels are periodically appraised for competence in those special roles.

Appraisals are conducted by experienced magistrates who have been trained and approved by the BTDC for the purpose. The focus at a first appraisal is on the core competences listed above, and the purpose of the appraisal is to confirm that the magistrate has demonstrated those competences. The magistrate being appraised is provided with a document listing the types of behaviour, knowledge and understanding the appraiser is looking for, such as the ability to contribute to discussions assertively, but without being dominating or submissive. The justice being appraised and the appraiser usually meet beforehand to go through the process. While the procedure may sound intimidating, appraisers understand that those being appraised are often apprehensive, and usually do all they can to put them at ease so that they can perform to their best. Appraisers are specially trained for the task, and, like all magistrates, are themselves subject to appraisals from time to time. They are expected to conduct appraisals sympathetically and supportively, but sufficiently robustly to maintain standards.

The tasks of the appraiser include:

- making a record of the magistrate's performance against the competence framework;
- encouraging and assisting the magistrate to assess his or her own performance against the competence framework;
- giving the magistrate feedback on his or her performance;
- together with the magistrate, identifying any training needs and ways of meeting them;
- completing the necessary documentation and reporting to the BTDC.

The appraiser does not make the assessment of competence; this is the task of the BTDC once it has received the information recorded by the appraiser. This may mean a wait of some weeks before the magistrate receives a letter saying whether or not he or she came up to scratch. In practice, most magistrates do satisfactorily complete their first appraisals, as is to be expected given the extent of training and support afforded by the mentor and others concerned.

Chairmanship

After a few years' experience on the bench, and providing they have successfully undergone threshold appraisal and one three-yearly appraisal, many magistrates are asked if they wish to undertake training for chairmanship. The BTDC decides who will be invited. Training for chairmanship focuses on managing judicial decision-making, and covers matters such as the ability to lead (but not dominate) discussions in the retiring room, to make effective and appropriate use of the legal adviser's services and to announce the decisions of the bench clearly and dispassionately.

Training for new chairmen is a considerable undertaking, taking the form of at least twelve hours' work, spread over two days. Having completed the initial 'out of court' stages, the trainee chairman takes the chair, sitting with an appraiser for the first few (three to six) sittings, and may also be supported by an experienced chairman sitting as a winger. Providing these sittings establish that the necessary chairmanship competences are in place, the fledgling chairman is 'qualified'. Chairmen must take refresher training in chairmanship skills at specified intervals, and be reappraised to ensure that standards are maintained.

New developments

Apart from competences and skills training, the constant flow of new legislation often calls for training on specific subjects. Training sessions for the entire bench may deal not only with new laws but with, for example, new sentencing guidelines or matters of particular concern, such as the enforcement of fines or recent developments in case law.

THE CHAIRMAN AND DEPUTY CHAIRMEN OF THE BENCH

Apart from chairmen of the courts, each local justice area has its bench chairman and deputy chairmen. Statutory rules establish the procedure for electing the chairman and deputies each year, by secret ballot, at the bench annual election meeting held in October. A procedure to identify a shortlist of candidates in advance of the election is often adopted. A chairman may hold office for not more than five consecutive years, although in many areas this is in practice reduced to three or four.

The task of the chairman is to act as the bench's leader, representative and spokesperson. The chairman also has a pastoral responsibility for members of the bench, and is there to advise and support them when needed. The chairman is often the first person involved if there is a complaint concerning a magistrate, and it may fall to the chairman to decide whether the subject of the complaint is a question of competence, which would be a matter for the BTDC, or of conduct, which would be a matter for the area advisory committee.

The chairman needs to maintain and promote good working relationships with the justices' clerk and the court staff, and with a variety of outside agencies; promote and participate in training; represent the bench at a variety of outside fora; and generally keep up to date with developments. In this work the chairman is aided by a number of elected deputy chairmen. The outlook of the chairman and deputies tends to rub off on the bench as a whole, so that, generally, a positive, constructive and supportive approach is conducive to a harmonious, well-trained and efficient bench of magistrates.

All this calls for a wide range of skills and personal qualities – sensitivity, tact, balance, impartiality, objectivity, approachability, familiarity with the views of members of the bench, firmness – a formidable list. The view that persons may be particularly eligible for election as chairman by reason of length of service alone has largely fallen into disfavour. Experience matters, of course, but the trend is towards emphasising the search for the qualities of leadership which go to make an effective chairman.

Newer members of a bench may have difficulty in deciding who is to have their vote for chairman, since they may not know the candidates well, or even at all. The extent of canvassing or distribution of information about the candidates varies from place to place, some magistrates apparently taking the view that such activities are unseemly, others seeing no reason to outlaw these elements of a democratic process.

THE TIMETABLE

Each court has a system for timetabling, registering and recording the number of times magistrates attend. How often a magistrate sits in court clearly depends on how many magistrates there are on the bench, how many cases are being brought, and the number of courtrooms and other facilities available. It has already been mentioned in Chapter 1 that the minimum is thirteen full day sittings or 26 half-day sittings a year, but in busy areas magistrates may sit twice as often as this.

How sittings are planned varies from place to place. In some areas, individual justices are allocated to a particular day of the week, and so may be 'Monday justices', 'Tuesday justices' and so on. This type of arrangement is sometimes said to have the weakness that the practices of the justices of a particular day may become entrenched, with the result that, say, the 'Tuesday justices' may be considered more lenient, or more severe, than the 'Wednesday justices'. In an extreme case, this may lead parties to seek to have matters listed on a particular day because they perceive that as conducive to the result they desire. This system also restricts the opportunities justices have to meet each other and exchange views and ideas.

Another system features advance allocation at random (although, as is noted below, there are many considerations which restrict how random the process can in fact be), so that justices constantly sit with different colleagues. This meets the two criticisms of the 'day' system mentioned above. Rotas devised in this way may be compiled quarterly, half-yearly or annually, and justices may be given the opportunity to notify in advance the dates or days on which they are not able to sit.

Whichever system is adopted, those drawing up the lists have an unenviable task, for this is a clear example of 'you can't please all the people all the time'. These are just some of the factors that have to be taken into account when drawing up the rota:

- a balance between men and women;
- an appropriate mix of experience;
- sufficient qualified chairmen to take the courts of the day;
- if a family or youth court is to be in session, the appropriate number of members of the youth panel or family panel are needed;
- the courts have to be arranged so that new magistrates sit with their mentors on the required number of occasions;
- if an individual magistrate is coming back for the sentencing of an offender on whose trial that magistrate sat, that magistrate must be assigned to the appropriate court.

There are also varying arrangements for dealing with the situation where a magistrate is unable to sit on a date allocated, perhaps because of work commitments or because some emergency arises. In some courts, magistrates can simply arrange between themselves to exchange sessions. It is good practice to exchange with a colleague of the same sex and of roughly equal experience, and for qualified chairmen to exchange with other qualified chairmen, to maintain balance. In other courts, exchanges are channelled through a member of the court staff. 'Advertisements' seeking exchanges may appear on the retiring room notice board.

The custom of the court may be that all magistrates attending on a particular day are allocated in advance, by the rota clerk, to individual courts. Or they may be assigned to particular courts just before the session begins, by a senior magistrate who is 'chairman of the day'.

The rota can be a vexatious matter since it is often impossible to meet every magistrate's preferences – and people often do not know what their commitments will be at the time a rota is prepared. Again, different people have different views about priorities. If a particular date is difficult, some seek to change the court date; others seek to change the other, conflicting engagement. Flexibility on the part of magistrates is always appreciated, but sometimes work or family must be the primary consideration. If a magistrate cannot attend at the last minute because of illness or some sudden emergency, the simple courtesy of a telephone call is of course essential.

It is possible that two magistrates assigned to the same court do not get along with each other particularly well. By and large, this is probably just too bad and they have to get on with it – broad-mindedness is an attribute of a good magistrate, and life would be tedious indeed if we were all the same; but there may come a point when it is wise for the individual concerned to question where the difficulty lies. If a magistrate has a real and continuing problem working alongside another individual, particularly perhaps if he or she perceives that the other person exercises certain preconceptions, then it may well be a matter on which the chairman of the bench should be consulted.

Chapter 4

Jurisdiction

INTRODUCTION

This chapter concerns the jurisdiction of the magistrates and of the magistrates' courts – their authority, their powers, and the limits on those powers. The magistrates' courts are responsible for dealing with a wide range of cases, and have correspondingly broad powers. But there are limits on the offences which they may try, and on the sentences which they may impose. There are also certain time limits.

THE STATUTORY BASE AND THE COMMON LAW

Magistrates' courts are often said to be 'creatures of statute', meaning that their powers derive from, and are constrained by, legislation. The distinction between statute law (or legislation) and common law was explained in Chapter 2. The general trend is for common law powers to become less important as statute law becomes more comprehensive. The common law remains important, however. The higher courts have power to interpret legislation to fill gaps not provided for in the particular statute, or to deal with ambiguities or other uncertainties of meaning, and their interpretations bind lower courts under the doctrine of precedent. For example, in road traffic law, the High Court has developed a substantial body of case law on the meaning of the expression 'special reasons' for not disqualifying an offender from driving (discussed further in Chapter 6). These cases are often referred to in the magistrates' courts to guide decision-making, and indeed challenges to the interpretation of 'special reasons' continue to be brought before the High Court.

A number of offences still derive from the common law and have not been incorporated into statute. The most important are murder and manslaughter, which are tried at the Crown Court, although the magistrates may have a role in the early stages.

The most important common law power still retained by the magistrates is the centuries-old power to deal with a breach of the peace by binding over the person(s) responsible to keep the peace and/or to be of good behaviour. This power has survived challenges under the European Convention on Human Rights, when it was argued that the expression 'breach of the peace' was too imprecise for people to be able to foresee the circumstances in which they might be arrested for it.

THE STATUTORY FRAMEWORK OF MAGISTRATES' COURTS

The Courts Act 2003

From its common law beginnings in the fourteenth century, the constitution of the magistrates' courts is today largely governed by the Courts Act 2003. The Act also contains provisions relating to the county courts and to the higher courts. It gives the Lord Chancellor (see Chapter 1) responsibility for ensuring that there is an efficient and effective system to support the work of the courts. It empowers the Lord Chancellor to employ staff or to contract out services, to discharge that overall duty, but he may not employ staff or outside contractors to carry out any judicial function. It also authorises the provision, equipment, maintenance and management of courthouses and offices. These functions are carried out for the Lord Chancellor by HMCTS (see Chapter 3).

The Lord Chancellor may direct where, on what days and at what times magistrates' courts are to sit, and how work is to be allocated to them. This allows for great flexibility in when and where courts may sit – through the night in exceptional circumstances, or perhaps in unusual places. The arrangements must be such that a person charged with an offence appears in a court in the area in which the offence is said to have been committed, or where the person lives, or where the witnesses (or most of them) live, or where other cases raising similar issues are being dealt with. It was under this latter provision that the cases arising out of the riots in 2011 were allocated to a limited number of courts, to achieve consistency of approach, to make best use of the small number of prosecutors assigned to bringing the cases, and to deal with the large number of cases as expeditiously as possible.

The 2003 Act also contains provisions establishing a Criminal Procedure Rule Committee, a Family Procedure Rule Committee and a Civil Procedure Rule Committee. Each of these committees promulgates rules relating, respectively, to the three areas of law. The Criminal Procedure Rules are considered further below, and the Family Proceedings Rules in Chapter 7.

The Act also contains the principal provisions allowing for the training and appraisal of magistrates, discussed in Chapter 3.

The Magistrates' Courts Act 1980

The main statute governing the day-to-day work of the courts is the Magistrates' Courts Act 1980, which brought together a number of former provisions into one Act. The 1980 Act is certainly not a comprehensive measure, because much material governing the work of the courts is to be found elsewhere – the Criminal Justice Acts 1967–1991, the Police and Criminal Evidence Act 1984 and the Crime and Disorder Act 1998, for example. A host of other legislation deals with specific areas of law, defining offences and setting maximum penalties – the Theft Act 1968, the Road Traffic Act 1988, the Bail Act 1976, the Protection from Harassment Act 1977, to name but a few. The procedure in the courts is also subject to the Criminal Procedure Rules, mentioned below and discussed further in Chapter 5.

The 1980 Act is, however, the first base for anyone considering the powers of the magistrates' courts. It deals with a number of important aspects of the law. Part I deals with the criminal jurisdiction and procedure of the court and contains fifty sections which cope with everyday procedures followed by all magistrates' courts in England and Wales. Part II deals with civil jurisdiction and procedure. As noted earlier, the magistrates' courts retain a substantial range of powers to deal with non-criminal matters, notably, though not exclusively, in the field of family law. These sections in the Act start from the commencement of civil proceedings by the issue of a complaint (or application) through to the enforcement of a civil debt, and the imposition of penalties for non-compliance with non-monetary orders of the court. Part III deals with satisfaction and enforcement generally, Part IV with witnesses and evidence, Part V with appeals from the magistrates' courts whether to the Crown Court or by case stated to the High Court, Part VI with recognizances (solemn obligations or promises backed by a sum of money) and Part VII with miscellaneous and supplementary matters. There is in addition a number of schedules dealing in more detail with particular aspects of the jurisdiction.

For legal advisers, the 1980 Act is a familiar, accessible source of the law used day in, day out. It is the first Act that a trainee lawyer in the courts has to master. Many of the provisions will gradually become familiar to the new magistrate. Other Acts and case law decisions often need to be interpreted against its provisions. Various legislation may be of particular importance at different times depending on the issues arising during a sitting, but the Magistrates' Courts Act 1980 is *always* important.

Subordinate legislation

As mentioned in Chapter 2, an Act of Parliament, even an important one, may provide a framework only. It may give the court power to issue a witness summons in certain circumstances, or to rectify an earlier mistake. But any Act, however comprehensive, cannot always go into the nuts and bolts of how the power may be applied. For that, it is often necessary to look at subordinate legislation, which has been mentioned earlier – rules, regulations and orders made by Ministers pursuant to powers contained in Acts of Parliament.

The Criminal Procedure Rules

Most importantly for the magistrates' courts are the Criminal Procedure Rules, first promulgated in 2005 under the Courts Act 2003, and now consolidated and re-published annually. These rules deal with the practice and procedure of the criminal courts, including the magistrates' courts, and introduced the overriding objective that criminal cases are to be dealt with justly. This is defined as including:

- acquitting the innocent and convicting the guilty;
- dealing with the prosecution and the defence fairly;
- recognising the rights of a defendant;
- dealing with the case efficiently and expeditiously;
- ensuring that appropriate information is available to the court when bail and sentence are considered; and
- dealing with the case in ways that take into account the gravity of the offence alleged, the complexity of what is in issue, the severity of the consequences for the defendant and others affected, and the needs of other cases.

These few short sentences go to the heart of the criminal process and emphasise the principles which should be the focus of all concerned in it. All parties in a case are expected to further the overriding objective. In a case before the High Court, not long after the rules came into force, the court said that they had brought about a 'sea change' in how cases should be conducted, emphasising the court's duty to further the overriding objective by actively managing cases, and the need for early identification of the real issues. The days of ambushing the other side and making last-minute technical points – which had sometimes notoriously hindered cases and obstructed justice – were gone. The rules are considered further in Chapter 5.

The remaining provisions of the rules relate to preparations for trial and case management, the service of documents, and the keeping of court records.

Then there are provisions concerning preliminary matters, custody and bail, evidence, the trial, sentencing, confiscation of the proceeds of crime, contempt of court and appeals. Most of these are mentioned in more detail elsewhere in this book. From time to time, the Lord Chief Justice issues Practice Directions which supplement the rules.

That is not the end of the story. Statutes governing particular aspects of magistrates' powers often have their own subordinate legislation, to which the court may need to refer. Thus, for example, the Prosecution of Offences Act 1985 includes a part dealing with costs in criminal cases, and details the powers that the court may have in given circumstances. Anyone considering these provisions may well need to look also at the regulations made under the Act – the Costs in Criminal Cases (General) Regulations 1986 and the Costs in Criminal Cases (General) Regulations 1986 – Rates of Allowance. Not only that, but the original 1986 Regulations have since been amended a number of times. The Children Act 1989 provides a further example. That landmark piece of legislation (discussed in Chapter 7) has given rise to subordinate legislation to prescribe how it should work in practice. The most significant is the Family Procedure Rules 2010, which replaced a host of earlier rules. The 2010 Rules not only set out the details of the procedure in these courts, but, like the Criminal Procedure Rules, include an overriding objective of dealing with cases justly. The rules themselves may be further supplemented by Practice Directions made by the President of the Family Division of the High Court.

JURISDICTION OF JUSTICES' CLERKS

One of the most important pieces of subordinate legislation empowers justices' clerks to carry out certain functions. Justices' clerks may in turn authorise their assistants to carry out most of these functions. These are generally matters of a non-controversial, administrative nature and do not extend to making findings of guilty or not guilty, or to imposing sentence. They are set out in the Justices' Clerks Rules 2005, and include:

- laying an information, making a complaint or issuing a summons (these are all ways of starting a case, discussed further in Chapter 5);
- issuing an uncontested warrant of arrest if a defendant fails to come to court when required to do so;
- dismissing certain types of case where the prosecution offers no evidence;
- extending bail on the same conditions (if any) as those already in place;

- imposing or varying conditions of bail where both prosecutor and defendant agree;
- committing for trial a defendant who is on bail;
- giving, varying and revoking directions for trial;
- requesting a pre-sentence report on an offender who has pleaded guilty;
- remitting a case to another court for sentence;
- ordering a convicted offender to produce his/her driving licence;
- varying the arrangements for paying a fine by instalments.

All these functions are explained in more detail elsewhere in this book.

JURISDICTION OF MAGISTRATES

One of the characteristics of the magistracy through the centuries has been the concept of a locally based institution discharging its duties in its own areas. The idea is that justice at the lowest level can be sensitively and efficiently delivered from local roots. History has demonstrated the strengths of an enthusiastic and well-trained magistracy which is appointed from, and broadly representative of, the community which it serves. For many years – indeed centuries – magistrates were appointed to local areas, but they are now appointed to England and Wales as a whole. They are then assigned to a particular local justice area – usually the one in which they live or work. Although justices therefore have authority to act in any part of England and Wales, in practice they do not normally do so outside their own local justice areas. While the effect of these arrangements is that magistrates still act in their own areas, the twenty-first century view is that consistency of approach to decision-making and sentencing takes priority over customs and attitudes which may be special to individual areas. Thus the approach to sentencing offenders should be the same whether the offence is committed in Berwick-upon-Tweed or in Penzance. If a man pleads guilty to assaulting his wife, causing injury, should there be any difference in approach if the offence is committed in Carlisle rather than in London? Chapter 9 contains more about guidance on sentencing, designed to promote uniformity of approach.

As we have seen in Chapter 1, the Lord Chancellor is responsible for the appointment of the 27,000 justices for England and Wales. Advisory committees throughout the country, also appointed by the Lord Chancellor, recommend to him people who are thought suitable for appointment. At the time of writing (April 2012), moves are afoot to reorganise the advisory committee system to reduce the number to forty-nine, aligning them with the forty-nine justices' clerkships, and to transfer the administration of the advisory committees to HMCTS.

Each advisory committee may have a number of sub-committees to assist in its work. Advisory committee members include magistrates and non-magistrate representatives of the local community. In counties which have a lord lieutenant (the monarch's representative in the county), the lord lieutenant is usually the chair of the advisory committee.

The committees are voluntary non-governmental bodies, and their conduct is subject to the Lord Chancellor and Secretary of State's Directions for Advisory Committees on Justices of the Peace. The committees not only recommend candidates for appointment as magistrates, but also have a role in ensuring that training is completed satisfactorily, in ensuring that magistrates do not sit too frequently or too infrequently and in disciplinary matters. These other functions are discussed elsewhere in this book.

There is one specific restriction on the jurisdiction of magistrates, relating to magistrates who are also members of a local authority. The Courts Act 2003 provides that such a magistrate may not sit in a case where the local authority, or a committee or officer of the local authority, is a party to the proceedings, or if the case is an appeal from a decision of that local authority. Clearly, this is to avoid a situation in which the individual may have a conflict between the two roles. See also Chapter 12, on other examples of conflicts which are not covered by legislation.

The 2003 Act also provides that magistrates are immune from any legal action against them in relation to anything they do in the execution of their duties as magistrates and in relation to anything within their jurisdiction. On the other hand, there are provisions for the removal of magistrates from office – these are discussed in more detail in Chapter 12.

THE MAGISTRATE IN THE CROWN COURT

Magistrates do not sit only in magistrates' courts. After a minimum of two years on the bench, and having successfully undergone threshold appraisal, they become entitled to sit in the Crown Court, hearing appeals against decisions of the magistrates' courts (although obviously not in respect of decisions in which they personally participated). Appeals are dealt with in more detail in Chapter 9, but they may be appeals against conviction itself, or against the sentence imposed. Two magistrates sit with a judge or a recorder. They have an equal vote with the judge, but are expected to follow the judge's guidance on the law. Among the tasks of the magistrates' liaison judge are arranging for magistrates to attend the Crown Court as observers and ensuring that, when sitting there, they are treated as full members of the courts. Magistrates should take any opportunity that presents itself to sit in the Crown Court. They will find the experience invaluable.

RESIGNATION AND RETIREMENT

A magistrate is free to resign at any time, but must retire no later than his or her seventieth birthday. A chairman of a bench who attains seventy while in that office may, however, remain until the end of the term of office. Likewise, if the magistrate's seventieth birthday falls while hearing a case, the magistrate may complete the case before retiring. Upon retirement, a magistrate's name is entered on the 'supplemental list'. This list is maintained by the Clerk of the Crown in Chancery, and the names of retiring magistrates appear there in recognition of their years of service. A magistrate on the supplemental list may not sit as a justice and no longer has any of the powers of a justice.

JURISDICTION IN CRIMINAL CASES

Sections 1 and 2 of the Magistrates' Courts Act 1980 provide for the powers of the magistrates and the magistrates' courts to issue summonses and warrants and to try cases. Although magistrates are appointed to England and Wales as a whole, in practice, most cases they deal with arise in their own local justice areas and are against defendants living there.

There are limits on the powers of the magistrates' courts depending on the type of case before it. It will be remembered that charges and summonses before the court can concern indictable, either-way and summary offences. Indictable offences – the most serious – can be heard only in the Crown Court, although the magistrates often have the task of dealing with preliminary matters such as deciding whether the defendant is to be free on bail pending trial, or is to be in prison. Either-way offences are heard at either the Crown Court or the magistrates' court, depending on the views of the magistrates about its likely seriousness, and/or on the defendant's choice. More about this is said in Chapter 5. Summary-only offences are tried by the magistrates, although they may sometimes find their way to the Crown Court, as where the same defendant is charged with both a summary and an either-way or indictable offence arising out of the same set of circumstances. If the more serious case is to go to the Crown Court, the less serious offence may well go with it.

Normally, cases start in the court for the area where the offence is said to have been committed. Thus an offence of driving while disqualified alleged to have been committed in London would not normally be charged at Sheffield. The exception to that sensible rule arises where the defendant already faces other summary matters at, in this example, Sheffield. Then it is possible to 'marry them up' so that one court can deal with all matters. This power should be contrasted with the power to remit to another court for sentence. That power arises only where a defendant has been convicted at both courts and the receiving court consents. The summary offences at each court must carry either the power of imprisonment or the power to disqualify.

There are, on the other hand, certain situations in which it is wiser to bring a case away from the area where the alleged offence was committed. Where a crime has received much publicity in the area where it took place, the view may be that the defendant has a greater chance of a fair trial if the case is heard elsewhere in the country. Serious allegations arising out of acts of terrorism may be charged in a court with a high level of security many miles away from the venue of the incident. Again, there may have been a direction, such as that mentioned above in relation to the riot cases in 2011, that all cases of a certain type be heard at a specified court.

TIME LIMITS

There is no limit on the time within which prosecutions may be brought for indictable offences and either-way offences. There have been cases where a prosecution is started years after the allegations complained of, for example, cases of serious sexual offences or child abuse where the complaint has been made only after the child has attained adulthood.

The position is different in respect of most summary-only offences, which form the bulk of the magistrates' work. These are generally subject to a time limit of six months from the date of the alleged offence during which the prosecutor may start proceedings, unless a specific statute allows a longer period. Longer periods are allowed for certain road traffic offences. For example, in respect of driving without insurance, proceedings must be brought within six months of the date on which the prosecutor has sufficient evidence to warrant prosecution, but subject to an overall limit of three years from the date of the offence.

Time limits are not always a simple question of the date on which a person is charged or summonsed. There is an overriding need in the criminal justice system to ensure that the defendant has a fair trial, and a proper opportunity to dispute and defend the allegations made. Therefore the trial should take place as soon as is reasonably practicable and consistent with the need for both prosecution and defence to prepare their cases. It follows that if the prosecution does not proceed with due expedition, complying with directions for trial and serving documents in good time, the defendant could appeal to the High Court. In a recent case of being in charge of a motor vehicle when unfit through drugs, on the day set for trial, no prosecution witnesses appeared at court. It emerged that the prosecution had failed to disclose to the defendant the medical evidence of unfitness to drive, and had failed to arrange for the attendance at the trial of the medical practitioner who was going to give evidence of unfitness. Nor had it responded to ample notice that another vital witness would not be available on that date. There was no explanation for these failings. The magistrates granted the prosecution's application to adjourn the case and set a new trial date. The High Court ruled that the prosecution had been seriously at fault and the case should not have been adjourned. If the application for the adjournment had been refused, the prosecution would not have offered any evidence and the case would have been dismissed. This might have meant a guilty person was unconvicted, but the High Court ruled that the duty of the prosecutor to proceed diligently was more important.

POWERS OF SENTENCE

A most important limit on the powers of the magistrates concerns the sentence which may be imposed on a defendant who pleads guilty or is found guilty. These powers are limited in two ways. First, there are overall limits on the sentences which a magistrates' court may impose for any one offence. Secondly, the statute which creates an offence usually sets a maximum penalty for that offence. Any sentence passed must be within these limits, as well as being formulated in accordance with good sentencing practice, described in Chapter 9.

In general, the *maximum* penalty which a magistrates' court may impose is a fine of £5,000 and/or a term of imprisonment of six months. When sentencing for two or more either-way offences, the court may impose a term of imprisonment in respect of each, and make those terms either concurrent or consecutive, so that, if imposed to run consecutively, the aggregate maximum is twelve months. But for summary offences, the maximum aggregate prison sentence which may be imposed is six months, even if the sentence is for more than one offence.

These general maximum sentences do not apply if the statute which creates the offence provides otherwise. Many summary offences carry a lower maximum. For example, the maximum penalty for failing to surrender to bail is a £5,000 fine and/or three (not six) months' imprisonment. There is no power to impose a prison sentence for many summary offences. These include minor public order offences, and being drunk and disorderly, for which the maximum penalty is a £1,000 fine.

On the other hand, some offences carry higher maximum penalties. The maximum fines for certain offences under the environmental protection legislation go up to as much as £20,000 and £50,000.

The jurisdiction of the magistrates is strictly limited by these rules. It is important to remember that the sentences mentioned here are the most severe which may be imposed. As will be seen in Chapter 9, good sentencing decisions mean that in practice most penalties are well below the maxima.

In many courts the maxima are shown on the court lists handed to magistrates before going into court. If not, or if the information is unclear, the magistrates should always ask the legal adviser.

JURISDICTION OF SINGLE MAGISTRATE

A magistrate sitting alone has power to deal with certain matters. These powers are much the same as those of a clerk to the justices (listed earlier in this chapter), and include extending bail or imposing or varying conditions of bail, dismissing a case where the prosecution offers no evidence, asking for a pre-sentence report and giving directions for trial. In addition, a host of statutory provisions provide for individual magistrates to issue warrants and hear applications. While proceedings of this type often take place in court, and indeed often with more than one magistrate, they may nevertheless be done by a single magistrate, and, in an emergency, they may be done elsewhere than at court.

OUT-OF-HOURS DUTIES

Magistrates may be asked to deal with certain matters out of court hours, often at home. These matters may be applications by police for search warrants, perhaps to look for and seize illegal drugs, stolen property or firearms. Or the applicant may be an officer of a local authority who needs a warrant to deal with noise at night, whether loud music or a persistent burglar alarm. These applications should be heard out of court only where absolutely necessary. It is always preferable for applications to be heard in court, with the benefit of a legal adviser and all the usual facilities.

The routine for an out-of-hours application is that the person seeking to make the application first contacts a member of the legal team. It is not good practice for applicants to approach magistrates direct, and if this happens, the magistrate should refer the applicant to a legal adviser. The legal adviser takes responsibility for ensuring that the matter cannot wait until the next court sitting, and, if it cannot, contacts a magistrate to ask if the magistrate is able to deal with the application, explains the application briefly and gives any appropriate legal advice.

When hearing an out-of-hours application, the magistrate should act judicially and with a certain formality. When the applicant arrives, he or she must be asked for identification – a warrant card if a police officer, or other formal identification if not. The magistrate should not make do with a cursory glance but should check the identity carefully. If the application is for a warrant, the applicant must produce a written 'information' setting out the facts and the grounds for the application, and the warrant itself (with copies). The applicant must sign and date the information in the presence of the magistrate and confirm it by oath or affirmation. If a Bible or other appropriate holy book cannot be found, then the applicant, whether of any religion or none, can be asked to affirm. The precise wording is not crucial, but this is as good as any:

> I do solemnly sincerely and truly declare and affirm that this is my information, and the contents are true to the best of my knowledge and belief.

The magistrate should read the information carefully, and then ask the applicant to explain the reason for the application in simple terms. In this way the magistrate receives the information twice, allowing an opportunity to make a preliminary assessment of it. Informations and warrants must contain certain elements. For example, if the application is for a search warrant, it is vital that the place to be searched is clearly identified. The applicant must satisfy the magistrate that the preconditions for granting the particular application are met. To deal with this, many courts supply checklists and other information to their magistrates; otherwise, it may be necessary to have a further word by telephone with the legal adviser.

The magistrate usually has questions for the applicant. For example, have the premises been searched before, and, if so, with what result? Have any steps been taken to corroborate what is said in the application? The magistrate should make a note of the questions and answers. The magistrate must always act judicially. An application must never be rubber stamped. The grant of a warrant almost certainly affects the liberty or property of another citizen, and should be made only if there appear to be good grounds to do so. Further, the contents of applications should be treated as confidential and not disclosed to anyone else, to avoid, say, any risk of jeopardising a police investigation.

Finally, and most importantly, a magistrate must never be pressurised into granting a warrant if not happy to do so. Applicants often give the impression of being rushed. They may be. They often give the impression that the application is very important and urgent. It may be. They may imply that it is a matter of life and death. It may be, but that is more doubtful. However critical the application, the magistrate must reflect on the merits of the application. If the magistrate is not satisfied, then the application must be refused. Acting judicially requires taking proper care in evaluating the merits of it, suspending the application for a few minutes to take telephone advice from a legal adviser if necessary, and making a logical decision after the application has been made and, if necessary, clarified.

If satisfied, the magistrate signs, dates and times the information, and signs and dates all copies of the warrant. The signed warrant is handed to the applicant. The magistrate usually keeps the information, and should hand it in to the court office as soon as possible.

SIGNING DOCUMENTS

Apart from warrants and other documents resulting from an emergency application as described above, magistrates are often asked to sign many other types of document. These include oaths, affirmations, affidavits and statutory declarations. For example, a person may have been convicted of a road traffic offence without his knowledge – perhaps because the person was out of the country for a prolonged period which included the time when the documentation was sent to him. In circumstances such as this, the person may make a statutory declaration that he did not know of the proceedings. The declaration is formally made before a magistrate, who countersigns the document. The person can then take the declaration to the prosecuting authority and ask for the proceedings to be set aside. In cases such as this, where the document must be signed by a magistrate, the person must pay the court a fee for the service, and for this reason such matters are usually dealt with at court. The magistrate is not concerned with the contents of the document, only with verifying the person's identity and ensuring the person understands the penalties for making a statement which he or she knows to be false or does not believe is true.

A second category of documents – notably passport applications – is those where a magistrate signs as a person of good standing. In the case of a passport application, the magistrate must have known the applicant for at least two years, and, to check the identity of the counter-signatory, the application form asks for the magistrate's own passport number. No fee is levied for signing documents of this type.

When approached to sign any document the magistrate should pinpoint exactly what is being asked – to verify identity, to witness the document, to make some sort of judgment about the person or to say that the contents are true. The individual should be sure that he or she is in a position to do what is asked before going ahead. If signing a document which may be signed only by a magistrate, the suffix 'JP' should appear, and the fee should be paid.

The journal *Magistrate* listed some unusual examples in its November 2011 issue. They included certifying 'driving twenty-four shire horses in hand over a measured distance' to support an application for an entry in the *Guinness Book of Records.*

DISTRICT JUDGES (MAGISTRATES' COURTS)

As well as the magistrates, there is a bench of professional judicial officers who sit in the magistrates' courts – district judges (magistrates' courts). They are under the leadership of the Senior District Judge, or Chief Magistrate. A district judge (magistrates' courts) has all the powers of a bench of magistrates sitting in court, so it may be said that one district judge equals three magistrates. District judges are legally qualified and salaried. They usually sit on longer or more complex cases.

As noted in Chapter 1, there are now about 140 district judges (magistrates' courts) and 150 deputies. Some magistrates fear that district judges may take the most interesting cases, leaving the more routine work for them. Others fear an increase in the influence of professionals to the detriment of the magistracy. Recent research carried out for the Ministry of Justice may, however, allay such fears. The aims of the study included investigating the relative strengths and skills of magistrates and district judges, how each are best deployed in different types of case and the relative costs to the courts system of magistrates and district judges. The results are heartening for magistrates. They were widely perceived to have a greater connection with their local communities than district judges. Sitting as benches of three, they were perceived to be more democratic than a single district judge. Some also believed they are more open-minded in the sense of being less 'case-hardened'. District judges, on the other hand, deal with cases more quickly, which is not surprising given they have less need to consult the legal adviser, and can make decisions without having to retire or discuss with others. The study also confirmed that district judges tend to be allocated to complex, lengthy or serious cases. Finally, despite the fact that district judges deal with cases more quickly than magistrates, they are typically more costly per case than magistrates. Perhaps the magistrates are indeed 'a democratic jewel beyond price' – a description given them by the former Lord Chief Justice, the late Lord Bingham.

Chapter 5

Criminal Proceedings

INTRODUCTION

It has been seen in Chapter 4 that, under the Criminal Procedure Rules, the overriding aim of the criminal justice system is that criminal cases be dealt with justly, and that this comprises a number of fundamental elements intended to promote fairness and balance. The work of the magistrates' courts is but a part of the criminal justice system as a whole, in which the police, the CPS, the courts, the prison service, the Probation Service and others all have their roles. Over the last twenty years, successive governments have, in pursuit of greater efficiency, sought to increase co-operation between these bodies.

At a strategic level the three government departments that are jointly responsible for the criminal justice system and its agencies are the Ministry of Justice, the Home Office and the Attorney General's Office. The Ministry of Justice is responsible for the courts, prisons, the Probation Service and attendance centres. The Home Office has responsibility for drugs policy, crime, counter-terrorism and the police. The Attorney General is chief legal adviser to the Crown and has overall responsibility for superintending the prosecuting bodies.

At the local level, forty-two local criminal justice boards share responsibility for delivering criminal justice in their areas, bringing together the chief officers of the various bodies concerned to co-ordinate their activities. In a real sense, the court system is at the fulcrum, and although there are important functions in the criminal justice system which do not involve the courts in any way (for example, the process under which offenders are diverted from the courts when cautioned by the police), the vast majority of cases come into court for determination and conclusion. As will be seen, the courts have explicit powers and responsibilities to prevent delay and ensure that cases are dealt with speedily.

A criminal case usually begins by way of arrest, charge, summons or requisition.

ARREST

Without a warrant

A police officer may arrest without warrant anyone who has committed an offence, or whom the officer has reasonable grounds to suspect has committed an offence. There are similar powers of arrest in relation to suspected offences, and in relation to persons about to commit offences, or in the act of committing offences. These powers of arrest, however, are exercisable only if the officer has reasonable grounds for believing that it is necessary to arrest the person:

-   to enable the person's name or address to be ascertained;
-   to prevent the person causing physical injury (to himself or herself or someone else), suffering physical injury, causing loss or damage to property, committing an offence against public decency, or causing an unlawful obstruction of the highway;
-   to protect a child or other vulnerable person from the person in question;
-   to allow the prompt and effective investigation of the offence or of the conduct of the person in question;
-   to prevent any prosecution for the offence from being hindered by the disappearance of the person in question.

Particular statutes also confer specific powers of arrest without warrant in defined circumstances.

With a warrant

In addition, there are wide powers for the police to arrest suspects with a warrant, for example, where only a description of the offender was known at first, but evidence of the identity of the suspect is obtained later, or where a police officer is enforcing the attendance of a defendant before the courts. The officer seeking the warrant must lay before the court an information (brief details of the conduct complained of), and some evidence on oath or affirmation to substantiate the information. The grant of a warrant is a matter for the discretion of the court. It is a judicial act, and the court must never automatically grant an application.

Whether the power of arrest is exercisable with or without a warrant, from the moment of arrest, the procedure which the police are obliged to follow is the same.

Certainly from the moment of arrest and in some cases beforehand – for example where the police have searched the suspect or the suspect's property

– there are very strict provisions governing police conduct. Some of these are statutory and some are non-statutory but operate within a statutory framework. The most important are the Codes of Practice made under the Police and Criminal Evidence Act 1984 (PACE) which specify how the police (and other investigatory bodies, such as HM Revenue & Customs) should conduct themselves in given situations.

When an arrest is effected

The first requirement for the police on arresting a suspect is to tell the suspect the reason for the arrest, unless it is impracticable to do so. Plainly, if the police intervene to restore order in a disturbance and the suspect violently resists detention, it may not be practicable to explain the reason until later, although the reason may be obvious. The police are then required to take the suspect to a police station and put him or her before the custody officer, normally a police sergeant. The custody officer is independent of the investigation and has duties to protect suspects in detention and take steps to safeguard their welfare. That duty is a positive one, and all dealings with a detainee must be recorded in writing in a document known as the custody record. Thus, routine checks on well-being, the times refreshment is given, and the occasions of removal from the cells for any reason all have to be noted in the record.

TIME LIMITS

There are strict limits on the time a detainee may be held in custody without being charged with any offence. The police are required to charge as soon as they have evidence which, in their judgement, would sustain a case. Some evidence may be obtained after arrest, such as the detainee's answers to questions in interview conducted at the police station, but it would be manifestly unfair to hold a detainee endlessly while evidence is amassed in dribs and drabs. The police have some evidence against a detainee before arrest, but as the arrest is an infringement of liberty, PACE states that time in custody before charge should be limited. The limit is usually twenty-four hours, but that may be extended in the case of an indictable offence by a further twelve, to a total of thirty-six hours, on the authority of an officer not below the rank of superintendent. Strict criteria must be fulfilled before this power is exercisable.

If the police are still not in a position to charge when the additional twelve hours have expired, they may apply to a magistrates' court for a warrant of further detention, when similar criteria apply. In brief, the court must be satisfied that:

- the suspect's detention without charge is necessary to secure or preserve evidence relating to an offence for which the suspect is under arrest;
- an offence for which the suspect is under arrest is an indictable offence; and
- the investigation is being conducted diligently and expeditiously.

Such an application is heard by magistrates in a closed courtroom, but with the suspect and the suspect's lawyer present. The suspect or the suspect's lawyer may challenge the grounds on which it is sought to extend the period of detention. The magistrates, provided they are satisfied that the statutory criteria are made out, may extend the period for up to thirty-six hours, and there may be a further application for an extension to the warrant of further detention, subject to an absolute maximum of ninety-six hours. The vast majority of enquiries are over well within that period, and applications for warrants of further detention remain comparatively rare. Indeed, in the broad spectrum of cases with which the police have to deal, charges are preferred after just a few hours – a lengthy detention before charge is a relative rarity. It goes without saying that if the police do not have enough evidence to charge and the investigation is effectively at an end, they must release the detainee forthwith.

THE CHARGING PROCESS

It was noted in Chapter 3 that in most cases – about two thirds – it is for the police to decide whether or not to charge a suspect. In more serious or complex cases, the CPS decides whether or not a person should be charged. Whoever makes the decision, it is the police who actually bring the charge.

Where the charging decision falls to the police, and as soon as the police have enough evidence to justify charging a detainee, the detainee is taken before the custody officer. A printed copy of the charge is handed to the detainee on a form known as a charge sheet. The charge is then read out. Although detainees are cautioned on arrest, and again before any interview that may take place, a further caution is given at the charge stage, and the detainee is asked if he or she wishes to say anything in answer to the charge.

If the police do not have enough information to decide whether or not to charge the suspect, or if the case is one in which the CPS has the charging decision, the suspect is bailed to return to the police station at a later date. On that date, the police charge the suspect if they are in a position to do so. Otherwise, the suspect is released without charge.

BAIL

After charging a suspect, the police have to decide whether the defendant is to be bailed to court, with or without conditions, or whether bail should be denied, in which case the defendant must be taken to the magistrates' court as soon as is practicable. This means in any event within twenty-four hours, excluding Sundays, Christmas Day and Good Friday. The decision whether bail should be granted at this stage is wholly that of the police. PACE lays down the considerations that apply. The defendant may be a person whose name and address cannot be ascertained or verified. There may be reasonable grounds for believing that the defendant would fail to attend court, or commit an offence or offences if bailed. The circumstances of the current allegation and previous criminal convictions (if any) may provide some guidance. Are there reasonable grounds for believing the defendant would interfere with witnesses or otherwise obstruct justice? Should the defendant be kept in custody for his or her own protection? Would the imposition of bail conditions meet those fears?

If the police are of the opinion that the defendant can be safely bailed, they grant bail and the defendant signs a part of the charge sheet acknowledging the duty to surrender to the custody of a specified magistrates' court at a specified time on a specified date. If not bailed, the defendant is brought before the next sitting of the magistrates' court and the magistrates decide whether or not to grant bail, applying the criteria referred to in Chapter 8. Many suspects are advised at the police station by a duty solicitor, whose role is discussed in more detail below and in Chapter 11.

BETWEEN CHARGE AND COURT

Practice may vary in different parts of the country, but the interval between the time the defendant is charged at the police station and the first appearance at court is usually between seven and fourteen days.

During the period that the defendant is bailed by the police to attend court, the police prepare a file, which they must send to the CPS within forty-eight hours of the defendant being charged. A crown prosecutor scrutinises the charge and the available evidence to decide whether there is enough evidence to sustain a reasonable prospect of conviction, and whether it is in the public interest to proceed with the prosecution. The Code for Crown Prosecutors, a freely available public document, explains the criteria that a prosecutor applies in making this decision and is discussed in Chapter 3.

INITIAL DETAILS

The Criminal Procedure Rules provide that the prosecution must provide initial details (formerly known as advance information or advance disclosure) to a defendant in summary-only and either-way cases. In the case of summary-only offences, the purpose is to enable a defendant, on first appearance at court, and on advice if necessary, to enter a plea. If the offence charged is an either-way offence, initial details help the defendant (again with legal advice, if necessary) to decide whether to opt to have the case dealt with in the magistrates' court or in the Crown Court. These processes are explained in more detail later in this chapter.

Initial details usually consist of a case summary prepared by the police, a copy of the charge sheet, personal details about the defendant, a list of any previous convictions of the defendant, and copies of any witness statements that may have been taken. They are served on the defendant or on the defendant's solicitor if he or she has one.

LEGAL AID

A well-organised defendant will not be idle during the period between being charged and first appearing in court. He or she may instruct a firm of solicitors, or at least obtain legal advice concerning the charge, and will probably apply for legal aid. If so, forms must be signed and supporting information provided to enable the application to be considered in accordance with the legal aid regulations. This sometimes takes time, but there is an expectation that the court will deal with both plea, and (if appropriate) mode of trial, at the first hearing. More about legal aid is said in Chapter 11.

SUMMONSES

We have considered two ways in which a defendant may be brought before a court: an arrest with a warrant and an arrest without a warrant followed by charge. The third method of bringing a defendant to court is by issuing a summons. This is by far the most common form of process. In theory it may be used in any sort of case, but in practice it is confined to the vast majority of road traffic cases, minor criminal matters, most prosecutions by local authorities for breaches of planning and other environmental matters – in fact, the vast bulk of the work of magistrates' courts. The procedure is long-standing and arcane. The person seeking to bring the prosecution to court lays an 'information' in person, by post, or by electronic means at the court, and a justice of the peace or justices' clerk then considers it. An information should contain short particulars of what the defendant is said to have done, including the date and place, and identify the statute which has allegedly been contravened. If the breach is of subordinate legislation, that authority should also be cited. Only one breach may be contained in an information; more than one allegation in a single information will render it 'bad for duplicity', a concept explained in detail in a mass of case law. Charges, as well as informations in summonses, can be bad for duplicity.

The general rule is that an information must be laid within six months of the alleged offence, although certain statutes may grant longer. Again, the law attaches importance to proceedings being taken with reasonable expedition, and summonses have been refused where the prosecutor leaves the laying of the information to the last permissible day without good reason. Issuing a summons is a judicial act, and the justice or justices' clerk is required to scrutinise the information to ensure that all the required information is given and that it is in time. If so, a summons is issued, addressed to the defendant, containing details of the allegation and naming a date, place, and time when the defendant is required to attend court.

To be effective, there must be proof that a summons has been properly served, that is, that the defendant has received it. Good service is effected by:

- delivering the summons to the person to whom it is directed ('personal service');
- leaving it for the defendant with some person at the defendant's last known or usual place of abode;
- sending it by first class post in a letter addressed to the defendant at the defendant's last known or usual place of abode;
- in certain circumstances only, by sending it by document exchange, or transmitting it by fax, email or other electronic means.

Without proof of proper service, the court must assume the defendant does not know about the proceedings and is therefore unable to proceed in the absence of the defendant.

POSTAL CHARGING AND REQUISITIONS

The Criminal Justice Act 2003 introduced a fourth method of commencing criminal proceedings, under which a prosecutor issues a written charge, and at the same time issues a 'requisition'. A requisition is a requirement to appear before a specified magistrates' court to answer the charge on a specified date. These two documents are issued by the police without reference to the courts, and may be served either manually or by post. This effectively dispenses with the summons process and is intended to lead to an increase in efficiency, in that it is not necessary, under this procedure, to refer cases to the court before issuing the documents. The procedure is not yet available in respect of all types of case, or in all parts of the country, so far applying only to magistrates' courts in specified locations. It is available only to public prosecutors, for example, the police, the CPS and the Serious Fraud Office.

FIRST APPEARANCE IN COURT

The Crime and Disorder Act 1998 created a system of early first hearings and early administrative hearings, which enable the court to take control of cases straight away, and, in early first hearings, dispose of simple guilty plea cases on the first court day after charge. Early administrative hearings apply in more complex cases, and the courts adopt a regime of case management so that issues ancillary to trial can be identified and dealt with promptly. Case management may be conducted by a single justice, the justices' clerk or a full court. The arrangements for early first hearings and early administrative hearings may vary in different court areas.

When the defendant appears at court for the first time, the court expects that first hearing to be effective: that is, either the defendant will enter a plea, or the question of mode of trial (see below) will be dealt with. We have noted that the defendant will almost certainly have been told of the right to apply for legal aid, but even if the defendant has not done so, there is almost always a duty solicitor at court who is there for the express purpose of advising unrepresented defendants about their cases. Thus, for the sake of ten minutes' worth of advice, the defendant may have a clear idea of whether (in an appropriate case) to elect trial by jury or consent to trial in the magistrates' court, and if summary trial is chosen, how to plead. Duty solicitors are practitioners who take their turn in assisting the courts in this way. Some busy courts have more than one, and some have a custody duty solicitor for those appearing unrepresented from custody, and a bail duty solicitor to represent those who have been granted bail by the police to appear at court. An experienced duty solicitor is invaluable to a busy court. More is said about duty solicitors in Chapter 11.

ASSERTING CONTROL

The most important thing a court can do is to assert control over the progress of a case from the very first moment it appears in the list. It is the court – not the parties – which should control the proceedings. Proper case management, consistent with the overriding objective to deal with cases not only justly, but also efficiently and expeditiously, requires that at every appearance some progress towards the conclusion of the case should be made.

Before looking at the role of the court in dealing with case management, it is worth briefly reviewing the changes made in the last decade to restore magistrates' courts to courts of summary justice. During the latter years of the last century, a number of initiatives and legislative changes had led to magistrates' courts becoming slow and inefficient. There were too many unnecessary adjournments and too many delays in fixing trial dates. At trials, witnesses, particularly police officers, were being asked to attend court unnecessarily. Government initiatives to reduce these delays led to the codification of the various criminal procedure rules into a single set of rules for all criminal courts – the Criminal Procedure Rules. This in turn facilitated radical changes in the way that criminal cases were dealt with, including the introduction of active case management.

In 2006, another government report entitled *Delivering Simple, Speedy, Summary Justice*, set out plans to improve the speed and effectiveness of the magistrates' courts system. Pilot schemes of the CJSSS (Criminal Justice – Simple, Speedy and Summary) initiative showed dramatic reductions in the delays, and the initiative was rolled out across the country. A key factor in its success was that the various criminal justice agencies – the police, the CPS, the Legal Services Commission and the Probation Service – all supported its implementation. From the judiciary's point of view it meant that there had to be judicial management of first hearings and robust case management.

The key messages of CJSSS for magistrates are to ensure that:

- the defendant enters a plea;
- where a guilty plea is entered, sentence takes place on the same day where possible;
- where a not guilty plea is entered, the issues are identified and a date for trial – as soon as possible – is fixed.

Adjournments should be granted only where it is necessary in the interests of justice. This obliges courts to question – often with vigour – every application for an adjournment and, if an adjournment is unavoidable, to adjourn for the minimum time necessary to enable the purpose of the adjournment to be achieved. Often it is possible to do so in a significantly shorter timescale than the period of adjournment requested, with no detriment to any party. In many cases it can be achieved by setting the case back in the court list, for example, for advice to be given or documents considered. There is no such thing as an agreed adjournment between prosecution and defence. The court must always be convinced that it is in the interests of justice to delay cases. Deciding whether or not to grant a request for an adjournment is considered further in Chapter 10.

The Criminal Procedure Rules and the accompanying Consolidated Criminal Practice Direction assist the courts to achieve the key messages of CJSSS, and deal with case management in magistrates' courts. In furthering the overriding objective that criminal cases are dealt with justly, the court must actively manage the case. This was emphasised by Lord Justice Judge (as he then was) in the case of *Jisl* (2004) when he said that, 'active, hands-on, case management, both pre-trial and throughout the trial itself, is now regarded as an essential part of the judge's duty'.

The same judge, now the Lord Chief Justice, has used a footballing analogy to show how the role of the judiciary has changed with regard to case management:

> Dealing with it superficially, the judge or magistrates are referees. But until recently the role of this particular type of referee has been to wait on the pitch until the teams turn up. Wait for as long as they wished. That is no good. We need referees who will go into the changing rooms beforehand, tell each side how the game will be played, warn the players who may go offside that they are being watched, and as for those who foul, that they will be sent off. And the proceedings played once.

TAKING THE PLEA

The expectation is that the prosecution and defence are ready to make progress on the first appearance. What happens? When the defendant has been called and his or her name, address and age have been confirmed, the charges are read by the legal adviser. In other words, the legal adviser takes the court copy of the charge sheet or the information and reads the charge(s) aloud to the defendant.

Summary-only offences

If the matters are summary only, on each information being put, the defendant is invited to plead guilty or not guilty. The plea comes from the defendant personally, although it is not uncommon for an advocate to prompt the defendant. If the defendant pleads guilty, the court proceeds to review the facts of the case with a view to sentencing. This is considered further below.

If the defendant pleads not guilty, the court must commence its case management role. It must identify the real issues in the case, for example, is the matter in issue identification or self-defence? It goes on to consider what matters are not disputed; the types of evidence in the case (written evidence, CCTV); the number of witnesses to be called – whether their evidence can be agreed in writing, or whether they must come to court and give live evidence; whether special measures (see below) may be appropriate; whether interview tapes need to be played instead of a summary being read; whether there is a substantial legal argument; and any anticipated complexities. All these matters are reviewed, so that an appropriate amount of court time can be allotted.

To aid the process, a case management form is used. Where a defendant intends to plead not guilty the prosecution and defence must complete the relevant parts of the form before the case is called on. The form requires both prosecution and defence to identify the issues. It is then handed to the legal adviser. The court takes an active role in questioning the need for witnesses to attend court and the type and form of evidence each is to give. The prosecution and defence must assist the court in furthering the overriding objective by actively managing the case. The court also makes standard directions, which includes applying time limits, for example for the service of disclosure by the CPS upon the defence, or the making of a bad character application.

Special measures

Having taken a not guilty plea, it may be appropriate for the court, as part of its case management role, to consider whether special measures will be needed at the trial in relation to certain witnesses, for example children or other vulnerable persons, or adults who have been subject to intimidation. In such cases, the court may depart from the usual procedures for hearing evidence and make special arrangements to improve the quality of the evidence. These arrangements are called special measures, and include:

-   screening the witness from the accused;
-   giving evidence by live video link, accompanied by a supporter;
-   giving evidence in private;
-   evidence in chief being video recorded and played back to the court;
-   video recording of cross-examination and re-examination;
-   examination of a witness through an intermediary in the case of a young or incapacitated witness;
-   aids to communication for a young or incapacitated witness.

The measures apply to both prosecution and defence witnesses, but different provisions apply to the defendant. Either party may apply to the court for special measures to be put in place. Applications, even in cases where witnesses are automatically eligible (such as defendants under eighteen at the time of the hearing) must be in writing, and made within twenty-eight days after a not guilty plea in the magistrates court (fourteen days in the Crown Court).

The magistrates should themselves raise the question of whether special measures should be used if the party in question has not applied for them. Courts should be concerned that witnesses are enabled to give their best evidence, and should ensure that elements of the court process that cause undue distress to such witnesses are minimised.

Setting the trial date

Finally, a date is fixed for trial – the legal adviser allocates a date either using a computer in the courtroom, or by telephoning the listing section. The defendant is bailed to that date, or the case may simply be adjourned to that date for the defendant to attend again then.

Indictable-only offences

In the case of an indictable-only offence, the magistrates' court simply sends the defendant forthwith to the Crown Court for trial. The court's sole function is to decide whether or not the defendant is to have bail meantime. Bail is dealt with in Chapter 8.

Either-way offences

In the case of offences triable either way, the question of where the defendant is to be tried – at the Crown Court or at the magistrates' court – is dealt with once the defendant has been identified. The prosecution makes representations about where it believes the defendant should be tried. The defendant, through his or her advocate if represented, may then make representations in the matter, or may choose to make no representations. The defendant may, however, before the magistrates decide where the case will be heard, give an indication that he will plead guilty. If so, the magistrates proceed to deal with the matter, retaining their power to commit the defendant to the Crown Court for sentence if they consider their own powers of sentence are insufficient (see Pleas of Guilty, below).

MODE OF TRIAL

If the defendant is unable or unwilling to indicate a guilty plea, the magistrates decide where the case should be tried – the 'mode of trial' decision. There are both statutory provisions and detailed guidelines on how magistrates should make this decision, aimed at ensuring consistency of approach between benches in what may be a very important decision. Thus, the court is required by statute to have regard to:

- the nature of the case;
- whether the circumstances make the offence one of a serious character;
- whether the punishment which a magistrates' court would have power to inflict would be adequate;
- any other circumstances which appear to the court to make it more suitable for the offence to be tried in one way rather than the other;
- any representations made by the prosecution or the defence.

The guidelines include general observations, and guidance relating to specific offences. They apply to defendants aged eighteen and above, and include advice such as:

- the court should never make its decision on the grounds of convenience or expedition;
- the court should assume for the purpose of deciding mode of trial that the prosecution version of the facts is correct;
- the fact that the offences are alleged to be specimens is a relevant consideration; the fact that the defendant will be asking for other offences to be taken into consideration, if convicted, is not;
- in general, unless otherwise stated, either-way offences should be

tried summarily unless the court considers that the particular case has one or more specified features and that its sentencing powers are insufficient;

- the court should also consider its power to commit to the Crown Court for sentence if information emerges during the hearing which leads it to conclude that its powers of sentence are inadequate.

Further guidelines relate to specific offences. For example, in relation to theft or fraud, the court should take into account any of the following features which may be present:

- breach of trust by a person in a position of substantial authority, or in whom a high degree of trust is placed;
- theft or fraud which has been committed or disguised in a sophisticated manner;
- theft or fraud committed by an organised gang;
- the fact that the victim is particularly vulnerable to theft or fraud (for example, is elderly or infirm);
- the unrecovered property is of a high value.

The magistrates consider the representations of both prosecutor and defence in the light of the guidance, make their decision and announce it. If they decide that the matter is too serious to be dealt with before them, they adjourn the case for the preparation of committal papers (see below). If they consider the matter suitable for summary trial, that is not the end of the matter. The legal adviser then tells the defendant that he or she has the choice of where to be tried, and that if the defendant consents to be tried by the magistrates, the magistrates retain the right to commit the defendant to the Crown Court for sentence if, in the course of hearing the case, the magistrates consider that the offence seems to be more serious than it at first appeared. This occurs most often when a defendant's criminal record, which is never disclosed when the mode of trial is being decided, aggravates the criminal conduct under consideration. The defendant thus has a free choice: to elect trial by jury, or to consent to summary trial. If trial at the Crown Court is elected, the case is adjourned for the preparation of committal papers. If the defendant consents to summary trial, a plea is taken, although, as has been explained, the defendant may already have indicated that he or she will plead guilty. If the defendant pleads not guilty, the court proceeds to case manage the matter using the case management form, and a trial date is fixed at which the witnesses will be called. If the defendant pleads guilty, the court invites the defendant to sit down and the facts are then given.

If a person is remanded in custody at the end of a first hearing, the court must take into account the strict statutory limits on the time the person may remain in custody before trial or committal. Although those limits are capable of being extended if strict criteria are met, the Divisional Court has rightly construed applications to extend them very restrictively.

PLEAS OF GUILTY

Outlining the facts

If the defendant pleads guilty, the prosecutor gives the facts of the case to the court. It is rare that this is more than a brief summary of what the defendant is alleged to have done, including the defendant's reaction when arrested and/or questioned about the offence. It may well go to the credit of the defendant when sentence is decided if the defendant showed contrition at an early stage, and indicated readiness to admit responsibility for the crime. If the defendant wishes for other similar matters to be taken into consideration (TICs), those matters are then put before the court, and the legal adviser asks whether the defendant accepts responsibility for each TIC, and wishes the court to take them into consideration on sentence. The convention allowing a defendant the opportunity to have similar matters taken into consideration saves the police the expense of preparing a full prosecution file on each offence. There is no requirement for the defendant to accept the TICs, but the advantage of doing so is that it wipes the slate clean. If the defendant does not accept them, the police have a choice between bringing separate charges or taking no further action.

Compensation

Details of any financial loss arising from the crime are also given, for example, the cost of repairs to the window broken or the amount of money stolen from the employer's till. It is well established law that compensation is payable to cover loss, up to a theoretical maximum of £5,000 but, as is seen in Chapter 9, the court must always have regard to the ability of the offender to pay. If a compensation order is payable by instalments, then it should normally be capable of payment within about twelve to eighteen months, although payment may, in certain circumstances, be made over two or even three years. What is important is that payment should be made within a reasonable period of time. Compensation orders should be made only in respect of readily quantifiable amounts. If there is a real dispute between the offender and the victim either as to liability to pay compensation or the amount that should be ordered, and the dispute seems to be incapable of resolution after the hearing of brief evidence, it is preferable for the magistrates' court to make no order, and for separate proceedings to be brought by the victim in the county court to determine liability and amount. Chapter 9 contains more information about compensation orders.

Previous convictions

Finally, the prosecutor puts the defendant's previous criminal record before the court. It is for the court to determine whether any entries on the list of previous convictions aggravate the latest offence. It is helpful to all parties if the court gives an indication as to whether or not they are considered to be aggravating. It will certainly help the defence advocate in his plea in mitigation.

Mitigation

When the prosecutor has finished and sits down, the defendant has the opportunity to offer mitigation – arguments aimed at persuading the court to be lenient. But first, it is important that the court understands that the defence accepts broadly what the prosecution said in outlining its case. In many cases there are one or two minor facts which the defendant does not accept, but these are peripheral and do not affect sentence. There are some cases, however, where the defendant, although admitting responsibility for the crime, substantially disputes the facts. The defendant may accept that he or she assaulted the victim, but may say the assault consisted only of a punch or a slap with the flat of the hand. The victim may allege that the injuries were caused by a weapon. If there is a substantial discrepancy which is likely to have an effect on sentence, then the court must hold a special hearing after plea (a *Newton* hearing) in which witnesses are called on behalf of both prosecution and defence and the court makes findings of fact. It is on the basis of facts which the prosecution has proved beyond reasonable doubt that the court sentences the defendant. The *Newton* hearing is comparatively rare but of growing importance.

The first task of the defence is to try to gauge how the court will look at the prosecution facts, and whether to request the court to obtain a pre-sentence report. If the court is amenable to such a request, mitigation is usually left until the report is available. Otherwise, the defence advocate tackles the mitigation straightaway. This usually falls into two parts: mitigation based on the facts of the offence to try to show that it was less serious than might otherwise appear, and mitigation based on the personal circumstances of the offender. This may take the form of drawing attention to the defendant's usual good behaviour, excellent work record, or his or her community activities, or it may dwell on the defendant's sad personal circumstances – stress, illness, straitened circumstances, etc. The magistrates consider their sentence, often after deliberation in the retiring room, and come back into court to announce their sentence. The process of deciding which sentence is appropriate is described in Chapter 9.

SUMMARY TRIAL

If the defendant has pleaded not guilty, then a trial must take place. The Criminal Procedure Rules set out the procedure. Evidence is given before the court and, after speeches from the advocates, the magistrates decide whether the defendant is guilty of the matter before the court. The speeches of the advocates are not evidence, but should be of assistance to the court in identifying the issues in the case and directing the court (and the legal adviser) to matters of law which are likely to arise. In the magistrates' court, the prosecution has the first word by opening the case to the court. After the defence has closed its case, the prosecutor may make final representations in support of the prosecution case and then the defence has the last word in its final address to the bench.

The prosecution case

The prosecutor should tell the court simply and without repetition what the case is about and how it is said that the defendant is guilty of the offence charged. The prosecutor may then outline what evidence is to be called (or read) to try to satisfy the burden on the prosecution to prove the defendant's guilt. Although there are occasions when the defendant has an evidential burden in a particular case, the 'golden thread' in the English criminal law is that the prosecution must prove the defendant's guilt, and to a standard that the court is *sure* of his guilt. See Chapter 10 for the standard of proof required. The prosecution then calls its evidence. Evidence is something which tends to prove or disprove any fact or conclusion. In a trial it means the information which is put before the court to prove the facts or matters in issue. Evidence may take the following forms:

- oral evidence given by a witness in person;
- written statements served under s. 9 of the Criminal Justice Act 1967 – often simply known as 'section 9 statements';
- formal admissions under s. 10 of the Criminal Justice Act 1967;
- documents produced for the inspection of the court;

- real evidence.

Each of these is considered further below.

Submission of no case

Once the prosecution evidence is before the court, the defence assesses whether the defendant has a 'case to answer', and if not, may ask the court to dismiss the case at that point. The court may, of its own volition, find no case to answer; but, before dismissing the case, must ask the prosecution if it wishes to argue the point.

A hypothetical test applies to decide whether or not there is a case to answer: could a reasonable bench, properly directing itself as to the law, and in the absence of any contrary evidence, find the defendant guilty of the offence charged? If the answer is yes, the case goes on; if the answer is no, then the case is dismissed then and there. There are several authorities to which a legal adviser might direct the bench in consideration of a submission of no case, in particular the principles outlined in the case of *R v Galbraith*. Of course, the prosecutor may at any time up to that point offer no further evidence if the witnesses have not come up to expectation.

The defence case

If there is a case to answer, the defence may elect to call no evidence, and the bench then has to decide whether it is sure of the defendant's guilt. In other words, the theoretical test has now become specific to this bench's assessment of the evidence against this defendant in this case. Furthermore, there may be the power to draw an adverse inference against the defendant because of his or her failure to testify. More often the defendant does give evidence and, as with the prosecution witnesses, this evidence takes the form of examination in chief, cross-examination and re-examination (see below). Most witnesses are witnesses of fact, but there are exceptions, such as expert witnesses and character witnesses, who fulfil a different function from that of a witness of fact, but whose evidence is scrutinised by the court in exactly the same way.

At the end of the defence case, the prosecutor may make final representations in support of the prosecution case, and then the defence advocate addresses the court, perhaps drawing attention to the limitations of the prosecution case and inconsistencies between the witnesses. Just as it is valuable to have the first word at the beginning of a trial, it is undeniable that it is equally beneficial to have the final word before the bench goes out to consider whether or not the prosecution has proved the defendant's guilt beyond a reasonable doubt. How the magistrates make that decision is considered in Chapter 10.

TYPES OF EVIDENCE

Oral evidence

The most common form of evidence in the magistrates' court is oral evidence given from the witness box. Generally, after an incident has taken place, the police or other investigating authority take a statement from each witness, and it is those statements, sometimes supplemented by additional statements, which form the basis of the 'proof' from which the prosecutor examines the defendant. Evidence which is formal or uncontroversial is usually served or admitted (see below), so that oral evidence normally deals with issues of fact which are in dispute between the prosecution and defence.

Witnesses in criminal trials wait outside the courtroom before giving evidence, and are called in at the request of the advocates at the appropriate time. They are present to give their accounts of the incident in question, and it is considered that those accounts are more likely to be accurate if untainted by what an earlier witness may have said. The defendant, of course, remains in court throughout the trial and hears everything that is said. The general rule is, however, that if the defendant chooses to give evidence, he or she does so before defence witnesses, who remain outside until called. Occasionally it happens that a witness has remained in court before giving evidence and has heard the testimony of earlier witnesses. The court should not refuse to hear that witness's evidence, but, when assessing its accuracy, may take account of the fact that he or she has been in court and heard other witnesses.

All witnesses normally give evidence either on oath or affirmation, and indeed the prospective witness has the right to take the oath on the holy book of his or her choice. If the witness has no religion, or the taking of an oath is contrary to the witness's religion, or it is impracticable to administer the oath, for example because the appropriate holy book is not readily available, the witness instead affirms. An affirmation carries exactly the same authority as an oath. It is sometimes the case that through error a witness takes an oath on a book which may not be the holy book of the witness's religion, for example, a Sikh may have taken the oath on the Bible, but that does not in any way invalidate or cast doubt on the evidence given, provided that the witness in fact regarded himself or herself bound by the oath that was taken.

If a witness refuses to take either an oath or an affirmation, the witness is liable to be fined or imprisoned by the court. Such conduct is rare.

Any question as to whether a witness is competent to give evidence is determined by the court. A child witness may not be sworn unless aged fourteen or more, and must appreciate the solemnity of the occasion and the responsibility of telling the truth which is involved in taking the oath; this is a matter for the court to determine. A child below the age of fourteen gives unsworn evidence.

Each witness is first questioned by the lawyer for the party which called the witness. This process is known as examination-in-chief. It is followed by cross-examination – questioning by the lawyer for the opposite party. The first lawyer may then re-examine the witness on any points arising. Finally, the magistrates may have questions for the witness, though the court should ask questions only to clarify matters which are unclear. The court should not start a new line of questioning; there may be very good reasons why certain questions have been left unasked. The court should not 'enter into the arena', but should let the parties conduct the case. At the end of the evidence, it is a courtesy to thank the witness for giving evidence. The witness may then remain in the courtroom for the remainder of the case, although it is becoming more common for the party calling the witness to ask the court's permission to 'release' the witness. If the court agrees, the witness may leave the building, perhaps with a word of reminder not to discuss the case with anyone who may be waiting to come into the witness box. In the case of an unrepresented defendant the legal adviser or the court may ask any question necessary in the defendant's interests.

Section 9 statements

Written evidence in the magistrates' court is governed by s. 9 of the Criminal Justice Act 1967. It would be a very inefficient use of court time if, in every case, no matter how trivial and whether the defendant attended or not, all witnesses were required to attend to give oral evidence. It would be unsatisfactory both for members of the public who may lose time from work as a result of their civic-mindedness, and for police officers, ambulance personnel and others who could find themselves hanging round court buildings waiting to be called to give what might be uncontroversial evidence. Section 9 allows a copy of a signed statement in the prescribed form to be served on the other parties to the proceedings, and, by being read at the court hearing, to be admissible in evidence in the same way as oral evidence would be. This is subject to the proviso that none of the parties or their solicitors, within seven days from the service of the copy of the statement, serves a notice on the party proposing to adduce it, objecting to the statement being tendered in evidence under the section. If there is an objection, the prosecution should call the witness, or do without him or her. If there is no objection, then the evidence is read aloud by the party adducing it and the court considers that evidence along with all other evidence laid before it in the case. Although it is more often the prosecution which makes use of this procedure, it is available to any party to the proceedings.

Section 10 admissions

It is the general rule that the prosecution is obliged to prove every element in its case against the defendant, and indeed in some cases strict proof of all parts of the allegation is required. But in most cases it is very plain where the dispute between the parties lies. For example, in a case of careless driving, it may be that the defendant does not dispute that he was the driver, nor that he was driving on a road, but the issue is whether he drove without due care and attention. Or in a case of theft from a supermarket, it may not be in dispute that the defendant walked out of the store, nor that he failed to pay for the items the subject of the charge: the issue in dispute was whether he intended to steal.

Section 10 of the Criminal Justice Act 1967 allows for matters which are unlikely to be in dispute between the parties to be formally admitted. Certain conditions are laid down, but the gist is that any fact which could be the subject of oral evidence may be admitted and, if it is, the admission counts as conclusive evidence against the party making the admission.

In recent years greater use has been made of this provision, but in reality there are also a number of *informal* admissions that are made in almost any trial. Without them the wheels of justice would certainly grind to a halt.

Documents produced for the inspection of the court

Another kind of evidence that may be presented to the court is documentary evidence, for example, public and private documents, bankers' books, maps, plans, sound and video recordings, trade and business records. Documents are usually classified as private, public or judicial documents. Sound and video recordings fall into the category of documents because 'document' means anything in which information of any description is recorded. A party wishing to rely on the contents of a document must first prove it, but in most cases this is not an issue and documents are usually agreed.

Real evidence

Real evidence consists of material objects for the court to inspect, such as property which was stolen, a knife, a stolen cheque, clothing or photographs. Again, in order to adduce or introduce this evidence, a party must satisfy a number of requirements not detailed here.

COMMITTAL PROCEEDINGS

As mentioned earlier, offences which are indictable only are sent immediately and without further formality to the Crown Court for a preliminary hearing. In respect of either-way matters, where the magistrates have rejected jurisdiction or the defendant has elected trial by jury, a further stage – committal proceedings – take place before the magistrates. Such proceedings do not determine an accused's guilt or innocence, but are instead an examination to decide whether or not there is a *prima facie* (sufficient) case against the defendant. In essence, this means that there must be evidence on which, unless contradicted, a reasonable jury, properly directed as to the law, could properly convict. If there is a *prima facie* case, the court commits the defendant to the Crown Court for trial. If not, the defendant is discharged. Note that the charge is not dismissed and the distinction is not without importance. If further evidence comes to hand, a prosecution may be recommenced. If a charge is dismissed after a trial, the prosecution is almost always precluded from proceeding a second time. Committals take two forms: committal without considering the evidence, and committal after considering the evidence.

Committals without consideration of the evidence

Committals without consideration of the evidence are by far the more common form, and require the defendant to be represented for them to take place. The proceedings themselves are little more than a paper exercise, although ancillary applications, such as whether or not the person committed should be granted bail or committed in custody, require appropriate consideration. The basis of committal without consideration of the evidence is that the prosecution prepares a bundle of witness statements in a prescribed form and a copy is sent to defence solicitors. The defence has the opportunity to read the evidence and consider whether or not there appears to be a *prima facie* case. If there is, the defence consents to committal and, when the matter is listed in the magistrates' court, indicates that fact and that it does not wish to make submissions at that stage. The bundle of original statements is handed into the magistrates' court and the legal adviser checks the statements ready for dispatch to the Crown Court. The defendant is then formally committed in custody or on bail to the Crown Court to appear at a plea and directions hearing on a specified date, usually in four to six weeks.

The plea and directions hearing is what it says. The defendant is expected to indicate a plea, and in the event of a guilty plea, is dealt with as soon as possible. If the defendant indicates a plea of not guilty, the judge gives directions on a wide range of matters. It is outside the scope of this work to go into further detail on this, but the clear purpose is the control and management of the case by the court, just as in the magistrates' courts, making optimum use of court time and preventing unnecessary delay and expense.

Committals after consideration of the evidence

If the papers served by the prosecution and considered by the defence are thought not to contain a *prima facie* case against the defendant, the defence may make submissions that the evidence served, when taken together, is insufficient to put the defendant on trial, or that in law sufficient evidence of the offence alleged is not provided. If the defence submission succeeds, the defendant is discharged, subject to the power of the court at committal proceedings to commit for any indictable offence disclosed on the face of the papers. If the submission is rejected, the defendant is formally committed in the same way as if it were a committal without consideration of the evidence. There can be no doubt that, if used properly, these proceedings can be effective in identifying and throwing out inherently weak cases at an early stage.

Over the years, various measures have been taken to reduce the amount of time spent on committal proceedings, and there have been many proposals to abolish them altogether. In December 2011 the government announced that statutory powers already in place would be phased in at some time in 2012. These provisions will finally do away with committal proceedings, and extend to either-way cases the 'sending' procedure already used for indictable-only cases.

MEMORY-REFRESHING

Whether witnesses may refresh their memories from a document while giving evidence is a question which frequently arises. Traditionally, a witness could refer to a document made at the time and at the scene of an event, or so shortly after the event that the facts were fresh in the witness's memory. Statute has since intervened, and the rule now is that a witness may refer to a document made at *any* earlier time, as long as it represents the witness's recollection at the time it was made, and that the witness's recollection at that time is likely to have been 'significantly better' than at the time of giving oral evidence. This has made it easier for witnesses to give evidence, as their previous and original statements are now more widely admissible at trial. This measure applies to any person giving evidence, including the defendant, and witnesses may refresh their memories during both examination-in-chief and cross-examination.

Most police officers deal with a large number of matters between an incident leading to an appearance in court and the court hearing at which the officer is required to give evidence, often many months or sometimes even years later. It follows that the officer's memory of the incident concerned might be extremely sketchy without reference to a note made at the scene or shortly after. The court should not, though, assume that a police officer will take out the notebook and start to refer to it. An application to refresh memory should be made by the prosecutor, or defendant's lawyer, who should ask questions about the making of the note to satisfy the two conditions described above, and then seek the permission of the court to allow the officer to refer to it. What no witness should be allowed to do is to repeat verbatim what is written down. The notebook may be a potent weapon in the prosecution's armoury, but, as with many other aspects of the investigation process, detailed rules exist to protect the public. There was a danger, until the enactment of PACE, that a defendant might be 'verballed', that is, untrue admissions put into the mouth of a suspect by an unscrupulous police officer. There had no doubt been convictions secured in this way. Concerns about police powers led to PACE, which, as well as giving extra powers to the police, imposed codes of practice on them which they are obliged to follow.

CODES OF PRACTICE

Codes of practice are not themselves law, but are made under the authority of PACE – the Police and Criminal Evidence Act – and provide appropriate working standards for the police and other investigating agencies, to ensure that investigations are fairly conducted. There are eight codes, concerning:

- statutory powers of stop and search (code A);
- searching of premises and seizure of property (code B);
- detention, treatment and questioning of persons (code C);
- identification of persons (code D);
- tape recording of police interviews (code E);
- visual recording of police interviews (code F);
- statutory power of arrest by police officers (code G);
- detention, treatment and questioning under the Terrorism Act 2000 (code H).

Each of the codes is a public document and is freely available from the Stationery Office, and at www.homeoffice.gov.uk/police/powers/pace-codes/. Many trials turn on whether or not the provisions of the relevant code have been followed. A breach by a police officer does not of itself render the officer liable to criminal or civil proceedings, though it may lead to disciplinary proceedings. Equally important is the power of the court, in its discretion, to exclude evidence which is shown to have been obtained as a result of a breach of a provision of one of the codes. The court has considerable authority and discretion. The PACE Act itself contains sections dealing with the exclusion of confessions obtained unfairly or oppressively and prosecution evidence obtained unfairly. In addition to the provisions of PACE, the court retains common law powers to exclude evidence if it considers that it would be unfair to the accused to admit it.

The codes contain substantial written material and in some regards could be considered a counsel of perfection, so it may not be that every breach – however marginal – will lead to evidence being excluded. On the other hand, a breach or a number of breaches which are significant and substantial normally lead a court to decide to exclude that evidence.

PACE and the codes apply to all courts having criminal jurisdiction, and magistrates are obliged to consider and rule on these matters when raised in the course of a trial, but evidence cannot be excluded under these provisions in contested *committal* proceedings.

The prosecution or defence may, however, take the view that the matters discussed in this paragraph are often more felicitously dealt with in the Crown Court where there is a clear distinction between the roles of the judge and the jury. Issues of admissibility of evidence ('PACE points') are dealt with by the judge in the absence of the jury and any evidence which the judge decides to exclude is never put before the jury. In the magistrates' court, justices both determine facts and rule on law, so that the controversial material is put before them as part of the legal argument to exclude. If the evidence is excluded, they then have to perform mental gymnastics in putting it from their minds.

There are no doubt those who feel that the codes of practice err too much on one side or the other. Overall, however, they may be thought to provide a fair balance between the need for thorough and vigorous investigation of what may be serious crimes, and the need to safeguard suspects' rights and deal fairly with suspects according to open and verifiable procedures.

THE LEGAL ADVISER

It can be seen that the prosecution of offences and court hearings of criminal matters are subject to a vast body of law, and many magistrates do not expect to develop much more than a working knowledge of the rules under which the criminal process operates. On the other hand, magistrates have the great benefit of being able to turn to a legal adviser for advice on the law, and on the practice and procedure of the court. Most legal advisers are legally qualified as barristers or solicitors. The standards of all legal advisers have risen immeasurably during the last twenty years or so, and magistrates can generally have confidence that the adviser with them will know the answer to a point that crops up, or at any rate will know where to look, or failing that, enlist the help of the deputy justices' clerk or justices' clerk who is ultimately responsible for giving advice.

The role of the legal adviser was considered in Chapter 3. It is most important to keep the functions of magistrates and legal adviser separate. Magistrates are there to decide the facts of the matter, and make decisions on points of law that may arise, and in an appropriate case, determine sentence. The legal adviser is just that – the court's professional adviser. There is no point in a bench asking the adviser whether he or she thinks the defendant drove carelessly because that is not the adviser's function, and a good adviser would politely decline to offer a view. The legal adviser must play no part in making findings of fact. Similarly, it would be wrong for an adviser to tell magistrates what sentence should be imposed. By doing so, he or she trespasses on the bench's function. What an adviser may do, and he or she may volunteer the information without waiting to be asked, is to give advice on the range of penalties available and any relevant guidelines from the Sentencing Council, Court of Appeal, or the local Crown Court liaison judge on sentencing offences of the same type. While every court has a statutory duty to follow any sentencing guideline, it may choose not to follow the guideline if to do so would be contrary to the interests of justice.

The guidelines do not put the court into a strait-jacket; magistrates are free to depart from a guideline provided they give clear reasons for doing so.

Where issues of law arise in court during a trial or hearing, any advice given by the legal adviser should be given in open court. This enables the parties to hear the advice, and, in an appropriate case, to draw the court's attention to law or guidance that may have been omitted. When a court retires to consider its decision in a case, advice may be given by the legal adviser in the retiring room and thus will not be heard by the parties. If so, the parties must be informed of the advice given when the bench returns to court. Further, if an issue of law or procedure arises during the court's deliberations which has not been canvassed during the hearing, it is submitted that the bench ought to return to court to hear argument on that point. This avoids the obvious peril of a bench deciding a case on law which has not been canvassed and which may be subject to argument.

Experienced magistrates and legal advisers are well aware of the parameters in which they are permitted to operate. In practice, there are few problems or concerns. The ideal arrangement marries the common sense and skills of the trained magistrate to the professional expertise of the adviser. A good test of how it works is to look at the relationship through the eyes of the impartial observer in the public gallery. If that individual perceives that the bench is making the decisions, assisted where necessary by the concise advice of its adviser, then the relationship is probably right. If, however, the legal adviser is running the proceedings, with a stance so proactive that the bench hardly gets a look in, then the perception will be that it is not a magistrates' court, and the relationship is awry. Fortunately such a situation is rare indeed.

THE COMPLEXITIES OF THE LAW

The criminal law is wide and complex and only certain elements of it are touched on in this short book. While magistrates soon find themselves familiar with some of the most relevant provisions, they cannot be expected to know all the law. One consequence of this is the need to pay close attention to the reading of the charge. What is universally known in convenient shorthand as 'threatening behaviour' contrary to s. 4 of the Public Order Act 1986 is, in fact, a most complicated offence capable of being committed in different ways and with different mental elements. Magistrates should not hesitate to have the charge read aloud in full at the beginning of a trial, or to ask advice from the legal adviser as to precisely what the prosecution has to prove. For example, a defendant pleading not guilty to shoplifting cannot be found guilty unless the prosecution proves, so that the court is sure, that he or she 'dishonestly appropriated property belonging to another with the intention of permanently depriving the other of it'. Our convenient use of shorthand must not be allowed to obscure a precise, almost scientific, definition. A bench can discharge its duty only if it knows exactly what it is being asked to decide. The role of the legal adviser is invaluable, but the advocates too, whether barristers or solicitors, are under a duty to the court, and if an address or a submission obfuscates rather than simplifies, it is always permissible, through the chairman, for a magistrate to ask the advocate to clarify precisely what he or she is saying.

Chapter 6

Road Traffic Offences

INTRODUCTION

All magistrates deal with road traffic cases. Indeed more than thirty per cent of the workload in magistrates' courts is concerned with traffic, and this is despite legislation diverting many of the less serious traffic contraventions to the fixed penalty ticket procedure and away from the courtroom. The just enforcement of the legislation is important – its purpose is to protect the road-using public from the unsafe use of vehicles, whether through design, loading, maintenance or the manner in which they are driven. In Great Britain we have far fewer deaths on the road than in many other European countries, and the statistics show continuing improvements. Nevertheless, almost 2,000 people were killed on the roads in 2010, some 22,000 were seriously injured and almost 200,000 injured less seriously. We often refer to 'accidents', although in fact many road incidents are not accidents at all.

It is against that background that a magistrate should approach road traffic cases. The vast body of road traffic legislation and subordinate legislation (increasingly with its origins in Europe) has, as its principal aim, the protection of the road-using public from those who, deliberately or through inadvertence, put them at risk. Fines, community sentences, imprisonment, endorsement and disqualification are some of the tools in the magistrates' armoury for dealing with traffic offenders. In Chapter 9 we look at sentencing, but is important to note at this stage that there is a statutory obligation on every court to follow the *Magistrates' Court Sentencing Guidelines*, and to give reasons when imposing a sentence outside the guidelines. The guidelines cover many road traffic offences, from dangerous and careless driving, driving with excess alcohol and speeding, to construction and use offences.

USE/CAUSE/PERMIT

It is not always the driver or the owner of a vehicle who is responsible for it. Traffic law often penalises the 'user', or someone who has 'caused to be used' or 'permitted to be used' a vehicle on the road. It may not be necessary to look at those definitions in great detail, except to say that 'using a vehicle on a road' has a wide definition. In common parlance, if a person is referred to as having 'used a car in the High Street', it would be assumed that he or she was driving it. But the technical way in which 'use' is interpreted in the legislation covers conduct which the man or woman in the street might not consider amounts to use. For example, a man buys a car and parks it on the road outside his house. He has decided not to drive it until he has bought insurance and had the vehicle tested. That person is nevertheless guilty of the offences of using a vehicle without valid insurance, and using a vehicle without a current test certificate.

More than one person can be using a vehicle at the same time. For example, a driver of a company's lorry is travelling along a stretch of road when part of the load falls off. If proceedings are taken by the police for the use of a vehicle with an insecure load, the driver is regarded as a user, and so is the company as long as the lorry was being used on company business.

'Causing' and 'permitting' have similar technical definitions; indeed ownership of a vehicle is seldom of any relevance. A vehicle registration document deals with the 'keeper' of the vehicle, and it is the keeper who has various responsibilities when a vehicle is acquired or disposed of. As many private motor vehicles are owned by hire purchase companies or lease car fleet operators, it will be appreciated that ownership is usually unimportant.

For offences alleging bad driving, it is usually the driver, rather than the user or the owner, who is prosecuted. It is possible to prosecute the owner where, for example, a lorry belonging to a company has been driven dangerously because of the state of the vehicle and its unlawful condition. In many instances, the police see the driver at the scene of the incident in question, but there are occasions where the police are not called, or the driver has failed to stop at the scene, and the only known information is the registration number of the offending vehicle. In those circumstances, the police carry out a check on the Police National Computer, where details of registered keepers are held. A form is sent to the registered keeper, who is required to give particulars of the driver of the vehicle on the relevant occasion. If the information is not given, the keeper is liable to substantial penalties, including a fine, a mandatory endorsement of six penalty points, and, at the discretion of the court, disqualification from driving. This approach works adequately in relation to comparatively trivial offences, but is not fast enough to deal with an instance of failing to stop after an accident where it is suspected that the driver had been drinking. By the time the identity of the driver is discovered, evidence of drink-driving has long since disappeared. It is one of the reasons why both Parliament and the courts have taken an increasingly serious view of motorists who fail to stop and/or fail to report an accident. Originally, offenders could not be imprisoned for this offence, but, to denote its seriousness, the law was changed to provide a penalty of up to six months' imprisonment. It is hoped that the deterrent effect of this will persuade potentially errant motorists to face up to their responsibilities.

FIXED PENALTY NOTICES

Not all traffic contraventions come to court; it would be a waste of time and resources if the most trivial parking infringement saw the defendant required to attend and be dealt with by a bench of magistrates. But we have not reached a stage where the right – as opposed to the obligation – to attend court has been abolished altogether. Motorists issued with fixed penalty notices (or 'tickets') can reflect for a few days on whether they consider themselves guilty or not. If guilty, the motorist can pay the amount specified in person or by post. If the motorist wishes to contest the matter, he or she can request a court hearing. At such a hearing, evidence is called and the bench decides in the usual way whether the defendant is guilty or not. Just occasionally, a motorist may wish to have a hearing to bring out particular items of mitigation which might lead to the bench ordering some lesser penalty than a fine, such as an absolute or a conditional discharge.

The relevant law is contained in the Road Traffic Offenders Act 1988. Speeding is a classic example. Provided that the motorist stopped after a speed check has his or her driving licence to hand and gives it to the police (speeding is an offence for which the offender's licence is endorsed), the officer might be prepared to issue a fixed penalty notice. The police have a discretion in this situation; they are not obliged to issue a ticket. The speed alleged may be substantially over the limit and therefore too serious to be dealt with by ticket, or the motorist's licence may reveal that he or she has previous endorsements and could therefore be disqualified from driving at court. All fixed penalty notices issued for offences leading to endorsement of the licence carry three penalty points (except no insurance, which carries six points), but a case of speeding dealt with by the court carries a range of points between three and six, depending on the court's view of the seriousness of the offence.

The fixed penalty system would be efficient and successful if those issued with tickets either paid promptly or requested a court hearing so that the case could be determined in court. Unfortunately a great many people simply do nothing. The Transport Act 1982 brought in, for the first time, a system of what has been called 'guilt by inertia'. This gives power to the police, where the ticket remains unpaid and no hearing has been requested, to have the sum registered for enforcement against the recipient as a fine in the local justice area where the offender lives. The unpaid ticket is enhanced in value by fifty per cent, so that, for example, a £60 ticket becomes a £90 fine. Such fines can be enforced in exactly the same way as any other fines. This is a system which, by and large, works satisfactorily, although it depends – like much else concerned with the enforcement of traffic laws – on people who acquire or dispose of vehicles remembering to notify the Driver and Vehicle Licensing Agency of any relevant changes.

Where the fixed penalty procedure is not appropriate, for example, where several traffic offences are alleged from the same incident, the police have two courses of action – to arrest the suspect if there is power to do so, or report the suspect for consideration of prosecution (see below). A suspect who is arrested is taken to the police station and charged if the police believe they have enough evidence. The person may then be bailed. If not, the person must be brought before a magistrates' court as soon as reasonably practicable, and in any event within twenty-four hours, not counting Sundays and certaain bank holidays.

COMMENCEMENT OF PROCEEDINGS

Much more common in traffic cases is that the suspect is 'reported for consideration of prosecution'. This means that a report is prepared by the investigating police officer, and considered by a senior police officer, who decides whether or not to prosecute. Prosecution is not automatic. Leaving aside the informal warning or advice given by the police officer at the roadside, the police may write to the suspect saying that no further action will be taken, or warning the person about his or her driving conduct. If the suspect is to be prosecuted, the police lay an information with the magistrates' court for the local justice area where the offence is said to have taken place. Informations may be laid before a magistrate or a justices' clerk, and they are scrutinised to see whether the allegation is clearly stated and discloses an offence known to law. Judicial consideration has to be given, and although informations are for the most part reviewed in the absence of the prosecutor, the prosecutor may be asked to attend to clarify or justify the proposed prosecution. If the statutory requirements have been complied with, the justice or justices' clerk issues a summons, a document containing the allegations which the motorist will have to face, and giving the time, date and place at which he or she must appear.

The laying of an information is not a formality, and the High Court has drawn attention on a number of occasions to the importance of properly observing the procedure. But much of the work is now produced in computerised form

– the police prosecution department may lay hundreds or even thousands of informations in one computer print-out by direct link to the magistrates' courts administrative centre. The justices' clerk or legal adviser then carefully casts an eye over the print-out and, if all appears in order, issues the summonses. See Chapter 5 for more about how cases are commenced.

The summonses then have to be served. There is a wealth of law concerning the service of summonses, but perhaps it suffices to say here that the vast majority of summonses are served by being sent by ordinary first class post. An alternative method is for a summons to be 'personally served', that is, hand-delivered by a police officer or process server to the individual concerned. Another option is to leave it with an adult person at the individual's last known address. Again, Chapter 5 contains more information about service.

While the majority of road traffic prosecutions are begun by laying an information, the Criminal Justice Act 2003 introduced a new procedure which enables prosecutors to institute criminal proceeding themselves by issuing a written charge and a requisition (which replaces the summons), requiring a defendant to appear before a particular magistrates' court to answer the charge. This process dispenses with the need to lay an information. It is not yet universally available, but it is in operation for proceedings instituted by police forces in four London areas and in Essex and Gloucestershire (see Chapter 5, which deals with requisitions in more detail).

GUILTY PLEA IN ABSENCE

Although the summons (or requisition) requires the attendance of the defendant, it is ironical that there is almost certainly a wad of other papers telling the defendant that he or she need not, in fact, appear. This is the documentation relating to the 'guilty plea in absence' procedure, first introduced over fifty years ago, and now very well accepted. There will be a statement of facts, giving an outline account of what is alleged, for example:

> That at 09.30 on April 1st 2012, you were seen driving a motor vehicle in Whiteacre Road, Anytown. The speed of your vehicle was checked by police radar equipment and was found to be 65 mph. The speed limit for the relevant part of Whiteacre Road is 30 mph.

A recipient who intends to plead guilty signs a form to that effect, and has the opportunity to write down any mitigating features, and give details of his or her financial circumstances. Although there is nothing to stop the defendant attending court and speaking in person, the purpose of the procedure is to excuse the defendant from doing so. Some defendants still appear at the hearing, even though they have completed and sent back the relevant forms. If they do, they can take a normal part in the proceedings, and if they plead guilty, offer their mitigation, either by asking the legal adviser to read out what was written earlier or by substituting or supplementing the written plea by oral comments.

The prosecutor, in this instance normally a presenting officer or an associate crown prosecutor, may read aloud only the statement of facts, and no elaboration is permitted. The legal adviser must then read to the court the defendant's mitigation and financial details, so that the bench has adequate information on which to base its decision. If the offence is one for which the offender's driving licence must be endorsed, the defendant will have been asked to produce his or her licence, and the legal adviser gives details to the court – including any endorsements and disqualifications recorded on it – when the prosecutor has read the statement of facts. The bench may decide to disqualify the defendant, either for the offence in question, or because he or she has now accumulated twelve points and is therefore due for a 'totting up' disqualification (see below). The defendant must be given notice of intended disqualification. Most courts require the defendant to be physically present when a disqualification is imposed. Others do not, but in all cases the defendant must have received notice of the court's intention, giving the defendant the option to attend to 'show cause' why disqualification should not ensue. The court can enforce the requirement to attend by the issue of a warrant, either with or without bail.

In all cases, the defendant is notified of the outcome of a case dealt with under this procedure. Usually that means a fine notice, giving details of the fine and any costs imposed, and the rate of payment or the date by which it is ordered that the fine is to be paid. Where a licence endorsement has been ordered, details are sent to the Driver and Vehicle Licensing Authority, which later returns the licence to the defendant at the address shown on the licence.

COURT HEARING

There are, of course, cases in which a fixed penalty notice or the plea of guilty in absence procedure is thought inappropriate. Then the summons means what it says, that the defendant must attend at the time, date, and place specified, to answer the allegation. At one time the case would actually be heard on the date in the summons, and perhaps scores of witnesses would be waiting around on the off-chance that they might have to give evidence. If a defendant pleaded guilty, the witness's time was totally wasted. The treatment of witnesses and efficient use of expensive court time has now been improved, and in consequence the defendant is dealt with on the return date only if he or she pleads guilty. If the defendant pleads not guilty, a date is fixed for trial. An estimate is given of the likely length of hearing, the dates on which witnesses for the prosecution and defence are not available are considered, and a date fixed. On that date, evidence is heard and a decision is made. Chapter 5 gives more details about the procedure when a not guilty plea is entered.

BAD DRIVING OFFENCES TRIABLE BY MAGISTRATES

As with other offences, traffic offences are divided between those which may be dealt with on indictment only, those which are triable either-way, and the vast majority which are summary only, that is, they can be tried only in the magistrates' court. Examples are causing death by dangerous driving which is indictable only, and dangerous driving, which is an either-way offence and can be tried either at the Crown Court or in the magistrates' court. Speeding, careless driving, and construction and use offences may be tried only summarily.

Dangerous driving

If tried by the magistrates' court this offence carries a maximum of six months' imprisonment and/or a level 5 fine (currently £5,000). It also carries an obligatory disqualification from driving of a minimum of twelve months, and a disqualification until an extended driving test is passed. It follows that dangerous driving is concerned with really bad driving behaviour.

Section 2 of the Road Traffic Act 1988 provides that a person is guilty of dangerous driving if the person drives a mechanically propelled vehicle dangerously on a road or other public place. The test of dangerous driving consists of an objective assessment of the defendant's driving. It is to be regarded as dangerous, if:

- the manner of driving falls far below what would be expected of a competent and careful driver, and
- it would be obvious to a competent and careful driver that driving in that way would be dangerous.

'Dangerous' refers to danger either of injury to any person or of serious damage to property. The court must have regard not only to the circumstances of which the driver could be expected to be aware, but also to any circumstances shown to have been within the driver's knowledge. Further, a person is to be regarded as driving dangerously if it would be obvious to a competent and careful driver that driving a vehicle in its current state would be dangerous.

The Sentencing Council's *Guideline on Causing Death by Driving* gives examples of the type of driving which would lead to an accusation of dangerous driving. These include aggressive driving (such as sudden lane changes or cutting into a line of vehicles), racing or competitive driving, or speed that is highly inappropriate in the prevailing conditions.

Careless and inconsiderate driving

This offence is, as we have seen, triable only before magistrates. The relevant section of the Road Traffic Act 1988 creates offences of driving without due care and attention, and of driving without reasonable consideration for other road users. There is a slight overlap between the two, but the penalties on conviction are identical. The Act provides that if a person drives a mechanically propelled vehicle on a road or other public place without due care and attention, or without reasonable consideration for other persons using the road or place, the driver is guilty of an offence.

A person drives without due care and attention if the manner of driving falls below what would be expected of a competent and careful driver. In deciding what would be expected of a careful and competent driver, the court must consider not only the circumstances of which the competent and careful driver could be expected to be aware, but also any circumstances shown to have been within the knowledge of the defendant. For inconsiderate driving (technically, driving without reasonable consideration for other persons), there must be proof of a victim, that is, someone actually inconvenienced by the driving.

The Sentencing Council again provides some examples. Overtaking on the inside, or driving inappropriately close to another vehicle, may amount to careless driving, while flashing lights to force other drivers to give way and misusing a lane to avoid queuing could be inconsiderate driving.

These offences carry a maximum penalty of a fine on level 5 (£5,000), with a mandatory endorsement on the licence of between three and nine penalty points. The court also has a discretion to disqualify the driver.

The court must apply an objective test in deciding whether a person charged with careless driving departed from the standards of the competent and careful driver in all the circumstances of the case. That model driver always drives with an appropriate level of competence whether there is a blanket of freezing fog, or it is a bright sunny day, whether on city streets or in the depths of the country. There is no requirement that the defendant fall *far* below as in the case of dangerous driving.

In assessing dangerous driving, a court may legitimately look at the consequences of what happened, for example that the offending vehicle struck a stationary vehicle, causing damage. With careless driving, by contrast, the focus is primarily on the act of carelessness rather than on the consequences. But the court may now, when assessing the penalty to be imposed, give weight to the fact that a person was killed as a result of an accident in which the defendant was driving carelessly. In most cases, this would be considered an aggravating feature justifying a higher-than-normal sentence. This may go some way to alleviate the sense of injustice suffered by relatives of those killed or seriously injured in incidents involving careless driving.

DRIVERS

If the traffic legislation is there to protect and promote safety on the roads, then the physical condition of the driver must be an important focus. There are measures to guard against the old and infirm holding licences when, owing to their medical state, or their diminished eyesight, they are unsafe to drive. Full driving licences are granted until the holder attains the age of seventy; thereafter the licence is renewed every three years.

The Secretary of State has power to revoke licences, regardless of the age of the driver, for reasons of disability. Non-disclosure of relevant information about an individual's state of health is a serious offence. The courts too have power to disqualify a defendant until he or she has taken and passed a driving test if it is deemed necessary on the grounds of safety. The law in this respect is not directed exclusively at the elderly, but it is the elderly who are more often disqualified under this provision.

DRINK AND DRUGS

Over the last forty years, much more stringent action has been taken against those who drive, or are in charge of, a vehicle, with excess alcohol or while unfit to drive through drink or drugs. As a conviction for an offence of driving with excess alcohol or while unfit leads to a mandatory minimum twelve months' disqualification, it is hardly surprising that much of the litigation in road traffic law in this period has concerned the procedures for proving excess alcohol.

When roadside breath testing was first introduced, there was concern in Parliament and in the country about the interference with personal liberty that the drink-driving procedure implied. That fear has diminished, particularly in the light of some very well publicised examples of deaths arising from accidents where one or more of those involved was over the limit. Despite the huge publicity campaigns which are still promoted about the effects of drink and driving, it has been estimated that in 2010 drink was a contributory factor in five per cent of all road casualties, and that 250 people were killed in drink-drive incidents.

In the offence of driving while unfit, the test is whether the suspect's ability to drive properly was impaired through either drink or drugs. Sometimes that is proved by direct evidence of the driver's condition: that the driver was unable to stand unaided or slumped to the ground on getting out of the car, or that a doctor at the police station certified the person unfit. 'Drugs' includes not only illegal substances, but prescription and over-the-counter medicines. The offence of driving with excess alcohol is a different offence from driving while unfit, and does not necessarily have anything to do with being drunk. It means that when tested, the proportion of alcohol in the breath, blood or urine exceeded the prescribed level (35 microgrammes, 80 milligrammes, or 107 milligrammes respectively). A person may be unfit to drive through drink even when not over the limit.

Before a motorist can be tested at the roadside, the police must have grounds for making the requirement, for example, they believe that the motorist has committed a moving traffic offence or has been involved in an accident, or have reasonable cause to suspect that the motorist has consumed alcohol. In 2004 the government introduced a new statutory scheme for the testing of drivers of motor vehicles for drink or drugs. A constable may now require a person to undergo each or any of three specific kinds of preliminary test that is, a preliminary breath test (for alcohol), a preliminary impairment test (for unfitness to drive) and a preliminary drug test. The change was in part designed to assist the police in detecting drug-related offences.

If the roadside test is positive, or if the suspect fails or refuses to undergo a preliminary test and the police remain suspicious, then the suspect may be arrested and taken to the police station. It is there that the evidential procedure is carried out, usually by requiring two breath specimens, or if there is good reason for not asking for breath, then a specimen of blood (taken by a doctor or nurse) or urine. The suspect cannot choose what form of test to have, but can put forward medical reasons, such as the fact that he or she is suffering from asthma, which may make the provision of breath specimens impossible or dangerous. The police are obliged to take note of what the suspect says as to this, and if breath cannot be given, then the officer may request blood or urine.

The breath analysis equipment at the police station gives an instant result. If the suspect has given the two specimens and the lower indicates excess alcohol, then the suspect is almost certainly charged with the offence there and then, and usually bailed to court. If, however, the lower reading is in the range 35–50, the suspect can choose to have the breath specimen replaced by a specimen of blood or urine. If blood, a doctor or nurse is sent for and a sample of blood is taken. It is divided into two, which are placed in sealed containers, and the suspect may choose to take one of the two. The suspect can then have the sample separately analysed if he or she so wishes. The portion retained by the police is sent for forensic analysis. The suspect is normally bailed to come back to the police station on a date when the results of the test are known. In the case of urine, a doctor is not involved. The suspect is required to provide two specimens within one hour. The first is discarded, the second – after being duly divided – is sent off for analysis.

There is increasing public concern about motorists who drive while unfit through drugs. In 2008, 168 people were convicted of drug-driving, and the proportion of people killed in road accidents found to have illegal drugs in their blood rose from three per cent in 1988 to eighteen per cent in 1998. This has led the Coalition Government to indicate an intention to create a new offence of driving with more than a specific level of an illegal drug in the body, bringing the drug-driving legislation partly into line with the drink-driving legislation. The Home Office is currently testing six different 'drugalyser' devices in laboratories using different drugs at varying levels, but as of July 2012 no firm date has been given for their introduction.

Failure without reasonable excuse to provide a preliminary test at the roadside is an offence carrying a fine on level 3 (currently £1,000), a mandatory endorsement with four points, and disqualification at the discretion of the court.

Failure to provide a specimen without reasonable excuse is punishable in the same way as driving with excess alcohol or unfitness through drink or drugs, with a maximum term of six months' imprisonment and/or a fine on level 5 (£5,000). This means that there is absolutely no advantage to a suspect who refuses to provide specimens. There is also a mandatory endorsement and a mandatory disqualification of a minimum of twelve months. If the offender is convicted of driving with excess alcohol, driving while unfit through drink or drugs, or failure to give a specimen, and committed another offence in this category within the previous ten years, the minimum period of disqualification is three years.

There can be no doubt that these laws have made a substantial contribution to the safety of the road-using public, if not because of the fine that is the normal sentence passed by the court, but because of the disqualification that is the usual consequence of conviction. It is only in a very narrow range of cases, where the court finds that there are special reasons relating to the offence (not the offender), that it may exercise its discretion and not disqualify. As a large number of motorists need their licences for work, the risk of being caught and then disqualified provides some deterrent. There is also now a high level of general disapproval of drink- and drug-driving. In the case of high readings of twice or three times the legal limit, courts consider a community order or even imprisonment. If there are aggravating features such as an accident with damage and/or personal injury, a term of imprisonment – though short – is often called for. If the court is considering making a community order, it could add an alcohol treatment requirement of at least six months during which the offender would be required to attend treatment (residential or non-residential) with a view to reducing or eliminating dependency on alcohol. A supervision requirement is usually appropriate to provide additional support, except in cases of low seriousness, when orders with a single requirement may be more suitable. Individuals are expected to confront their behaviour and participate fully in the programmes to which they are assigned. (Chapter 9 deals with community sentences in more detail.)

Many drivers who are convicted of drink-drive offences are offered, by the convicting court, the opportunity to reduce the period of disqualification if they satisfactorily complete a drink-drive rehabilitation course. These are courses approved for the purpose by the Department for Transport, and usually involve between sixteen and thirty hours' attendance. The offender must pay the fee for the course and complete it at least two months before the end of the reduced period of disqualification.

CONSTRUCTION AND USE OFFENCES

This rather uninspiring title covers a great many offences again intended to protect the road-using public. Increasingly, subordinate legislation in this branch of traffic law has its genesis in Europe where there is now considerable standardisation in the minimum specifications for many motor vehicle components. Several times each year, measures are passed importing into English law the latest weight restrictions on vehicles, technical specifications on brakes, or the approved dimensions of brake light clusters. Much of it is highly technical and is not of day-to-day importance to magistrates' courts.

More important than the construction of vehicles is the manner in which they are used, and, in particular, the law requires components of vehicles – brakes, lights, tyres, steering, etc. – to be properly maintained in good and efficient working order. It also requires loads and fittings to be safely secured. The law is flexible enough to cater for matters of growing environmental concern; for example, prosecutions for exceeding prescribed exhaust emissions may be brought.

Offences under the Road Vehicles (Construction and Use) Regulations 1986 are all triable summarily only, and can be divided into several categories.

Danger

It is an offence to use, cause or permit a motor vehicle to be on a road, when:

- the condition of the vehicle,
- the purpose for which it is used,
- the number of passengers carried or the manner in which they are carried, or
- the weight, position, or distribution of its load or the manner in which it is secured,

is such that the use of the vehicle involves a danger of injury to any person.

An offender's licence is endorseable with three points, and, at the court's discretion, the offender may be disqualified from driving. The maximum fine is on Level 5 (if committed with a goods vehicle or a vehicle adapted to carry more than eight passengers); otherwise level 4.

Brakes, steering, tyres

For failing to comply with a requirement relating to brakes, steering and tyres, an offender's licence may be endorsed with three points, or, at the court's discretion, the offender may be disqualified from driving. Such offences usually feature matters such as bald tyres, or brakes which do not work properly.

Weight

Failing to comply with a construction and use requirement concerning the weight applicable to a goods vehicle – usually overloading – is an offence which does not attract endorsement or disqualification. The maximum fine is on level 5.

The remainder

The remaining offences relate to matters such as defective warning instruments (horns). They do not attract endorsement or disqualification. The maximum fine is on level 4, if committed in respect of a goods vehicle, and level 3 in any other case.

Mobile phones

With the growth in the use of mobile phones, a new provision was introduced in 2006, to make it an offence to drive a motor vehicle on a road while using a hand-held mobile telephone, or hand-held device. For such an offence, the driver's licence is endorseable with three points, or, at its discretion, the court may disqualify the offender from driving. The maximum fine is as for defective warning instruments above.

DRIVING WHILE DISQUALIFIED

One of the great problems facing courts dealing with the road traffic legislation is to ensure that their orders are followed. Non-payment of fines can be dealt with by enforcement procedures (see Chapter 9), but a substantial problem exists where motorists fail to respect an order of disqualification. Any flouting of the order of a court is to be deprecated, but the more so with driving while disqualified, because, automatically, the offender's insurance is of no effect during the period of disqualification, putting the public at still greater risk.

The offence of driving while disqualified is common. At one time it was tried only at the Crown Court, but for many years now it has been triable summarily only. At one time custody was almost inevitable, nowadays it is common, but often a community sentence is imposed. Proving the offence requires proof of the disqualification (and there can be difficulties in proving that the defendant before the court is the same individual as the one who was disqualified at a particular court on a particular date for a particular offence), and proof of driving. The offence carries a maximum sentence of six months and/or a fine on Level 5. The driving licence may be endorsed with six points, or the court may decide to disqualify.

ENDORSEMENT AND DISQUALIFICATION

Some offences, like highway obstruction, and using a vehicle in contravention of the lighting regulations, do not carry endorsement or disqualification, but for very many offences the court must endorse an offender's licence and has the discretion to disqualify. In respect of other offences, the court must both endorse and disqualify. It is important to remember that the principal purpose of road traffic legislation is to promote road safety, and the power of courts to endorse licences and impose disqualifications gives effect to the requirement that persons convicted of serious offences, or those convicted of several less serious offences over a period of time, should forfeit their right to drive for a fixed period.

Assuming that the court has convicted an offender of an offence of exceeding the speed limit, the next task is to look at the licence, which the defendant should have brought to court. Alternatively, the court can often itself obtain a printout of the driver's record direct from the Driver and Vehicle Licensing Agency. The justices decide whether the circumstances of the case require that the offender be disqualified for the offence. The offender may have driven at a very high speed in a built-up area, at a time of day when the roads and pavements are busy, and the court may decide, in addition to imposing an endorsement on the licence, to use its discretion to disqualify the offender. This power is available whether or not the offender has previous endorsements, and, subject to the statutory maximum, the period of the disqualification is wholly within the discretion of the court. Often for a first offence of this type, a disqualification of one month or less might suffice. The road-using public is protected from the offender's driving for that period of time. On the other hand, it may be that the speeding offence does not raise any particular concern, and a disqualification is not called for. In this situation, the court is obliged to endorse points on the licence. The court has a discretion to endorse a number of points in a range of between three and six.

Let us suppose that the court determines that four is the appropriate number. Those points are endorsed on the licence, and the Driver and Vehicle Licensing Agency is notified of that fact. The points stay on the licence for four years, but are effective for three. If the offender receives twelve or more points within a three-year period, he or she must be disqualified from driving for a minimum of six months under the 'totting-up' provisions. The original four points act as a warning to the offender to maintain good driving conduct or face the consequences of a ban. If, on requiring production of the licence, the court sees that in the three years before the date of the commission of the offence before it, the defendant already has, say, nine points, the addition of the four that the court has decided to impose for the new offence means that it must impose a minimum six months' disqualification. That period is, however, increased to one year if the defendant has had a previous disqualification for a fixed term of fifty-six days or more within the last three years, and to two years if there has been more than one such disqualification during that period. The purpose of this is to increase the penalties for cumulatively bad driving.

If the offender is convicted of an offence which carries obligatory endorsement and obligatory disqualification, the court does not impose points, but endorses the licences and goes on to disqualify the offender for a minimum of twelve months. If the offender has a previous similar conviction within a ten-year period, an enhanced period of disqualification applies.

SPECIAL REASONS AND MITIGATING CIRCUMSTANCES

Special reasons for not endorsing

If the court is obliged to order the endorsement of a driving licence, it may, in certain rare circumstances, decide not to endorse where it finds there are special reasons for not doing so. In general terms, these must be clear mitigating features which do not amount to a defence to the charge, but which a court ought properly to take into account when arriving at a sentence. An example may be where a father broke a speed limit in rushing a sick child to the accident and emergency department of the local hospital. There is no defence to the charge, but there is a genuine reason which a court ought properly to reflect in sentencing. If such a reason is accepted, the court does not have the power to endorse, and that means the offender receives no penalty points for that offence. If the offender would otherwise be liable to totting up, there is no disqualification.

Special reasons and drink-driving

Special reasons for not disqualifying may be pleaded in offences carrying obligatory disqualification, and these also are very tightly construed. In many instances they arise in cases of excess alcohol and the defendant often says that his or her drink was laced, so that the defendant did not realise how much alcohol he or she was consuming. Medical evidence to support the plea is almost certainly needed, and the law is not uncomplicated. In such a case the bench will need careful advice from its legal adviser, and it is outside the scope of this work to consider this in greater detail.

Mitigating circumstances and totting up

An offender who is liable to be disqualified for accumulating twelve points may be able to escape a totting-up disqualification if he or she is able to convince the court that there are mitigating circumstances to justify not disqualifying at all, or disqualifying for less than the period which would otherwise be appropriate. The law requires that before a court finds such mitigating circumstances, it must be shown that the offender would be caused *exceptional hardship* by the disqualification. The phrase is important. All disqualifications result in some hardship to the defendant, but the hardship to be considered here must be exceptional. Unlike the plea of special reasons, which relates to the offence, exceptional hardship can relate to the defendant's personal circumstances – more often than not, the defendant would lose his or her job if disqualified. It is important that the court scrutinises the evidence carefully. Does the plea depend on the defendant's own evidence? Has the employer come to court to give evidence about the potential loss of employment? If exceptional hardship is found, the court then has to determine whether there should be no disqualification at all, or whether the term should be abbreviated. The legal adviser should note in the court register the precise findings of the court, because the offender will not be able to argue the same mitigating circumstances, should he or she be liable for totting up again within the three-year period.

CONCLUSION

It can be seen that, far from being dull and routine, road traffic work can be important and stimulating. The least satisfactory aspect concerns the small number of motorists who ignore summonses, adjournment notices, and often warrants with bail. It can be months or even years before the court catches up with them, and thus in serious cases, persons who may represent a danger to the public and who should be disqualified are still driving.

The fault does not lie with the substantive law, which has developed with logic and certainty, but rather with anachronistic procedural methods of securing attendance. Although opposed by the civil liberties lobby, the legal requirement for drivers to carry their driving licences would be of considerable assistance in tightening up the enforcement of traffic laws, with consequent benefits to road safety.

Chapter 7

Special Jurisdictions

INTRODUCTION

Strictly speaking, what we examine in this chapter is not 'special' at all, but an integral part of the jurisdiction of the magistrates. The principal focus of this chapter is the youth court and the family proceedings court, but many other matters come before the magistrates which do not involve the police or the CPS. It was noted in Chapter 3 that other bodies may bring prosecutions before the magistrates, and there remains the power of ordinary citizens to institute and prosecute cases. HM Revenue and Customs and the UK Border Agency may appear, particularly if the magistrates' court is near a major airport or seaport. HM Revenue and Customs is responsible for the administration and collection of VAT, and accordingly VAT frauds may be prosecuted in a magistrates' court. More traditional customs work might consist of prosecution for evasion of excise duty on large amounts of liquor or tobacco imported into the United Kingdom. The UK Border Agency deals with cases involving the illegal importation of drugs. Both agencies may detect drugs couriers or intercept parcels containing drugs. All prosecutions start in the magistrates' courts, and most of the importation cases proceed through the usual committal procedure to the Crown Court as outlined in Chapter 5.

Local authorities frequently bring cases before the courts. In the discussion of the family proceedings court (below) the role of local authorities in public law cases is considered, but in the magistrates' courts generally, local authorities often appear. They may bring prosecutions for unlawful harassment of a tenant, for the burgeoning problems of noise nuisance, benefit fraud and enforcement of council tax arrears and non-payments. Breaches of planning regulations are brought to court by local authorities. HM Revenue and Customs, perhaps surprisingly, is entitled to come before the magistrates' court (rather than the county court) to recover as a civil debt amounts of income tax due and payable, provided they amount to less than £2,000. Other regular prosecutors include bus and railway companies, bringing cases for non-payment of fares or breaches of by-laws.

It is also worth mentioning the right of gas and electricity suppliers to apply for warrants of entry. These are usually for the purpose of reading meters where access has not been possible in the usual ways, but also for disconnection of the supply where there is a history of non-payment, or to replace the meter with a pre-payment meter. These are powers which need to be exercised with the greatest care, and although there may be applications for perhaps forty or more similar warrants, it is important that individual attention is given to each application. Both gas and electricity suppliers operate according to codes of practice, and when magistrates are hearing an application it is important to confirm that the relevant code of practice has been followed. If not, or if there is doubt whether it has, then the application should be refused. Although there is an obvious desire to move through a list of applications in a business-like way, it is important that time is taken to consider each application with appropriate care. The need to do justice is always more important than the battle against the clock.

This note of non-police prosecutors is not in any way exhaustive. A magistrate might turn up to a sitting to find that he or she is hearing a prosecution brought by the Information Commissioner, the Federation Against Copyright Theft (FACT), or the RSPCA. All this adds to the scope and interest of the work of these courts. It also confirms the need for magistrates to prepare properly for their work. This does not usually mean advance reading – although in the family proceedings court it frequently does – but it does mean arriving at court in good time to be briefed by the legal adviser as to what unusual features the list might contain. Magistrates are almost all busy people with a range of commitments, and sitting in court is just one, but to be at court at least fifteen minutes before the sitting of the court is always time well used.

We have spent most of our tour through the work of magistrates and magistrates' courts considering the adult courts, and we must now turn our attention to magistrates' roles in other jurisdictions, to enable us to complete our picture of the vast amount of work they undertake.

CHILDREN AND YOUNG PERSONS

Children and young persons have been treated separately by the courts for over a century. The Children Act 1908 established separate courts for children and introduced a 'children's charter' which allowed them to be dealt with according to their needs, which may be very different from those of adults. Youth courts deal with children aged between ten and seventeen. The age of criminal responsibility below which a person is irrebuttably presumed incapable of crime is ten (raised from eight to ten in 1963, but still low when compared with other European countries), and so the youngest person liable to be dealt with by magistrates exercising their criminal jurisdiction is aged ten years. Between that age and their fourteenth birthdays, they are known as children, and from their fourteenth to their eighteenth birthdays they are young persons.

A child, as defined above, was for many years rebuttably presumed incapable of crime, which meant that in order to secure a finding of guilt against a child, the prosecution was required to prove to the court's satisfaction not only that the defendant did the act with the necessary intent, but that in doing so, knew that what he or she was doing was seriously wrong. It was not sufficient for the Crown to show that the child knew he or she was merely naughty or mischievous. This rebuttable presumption has, however, been abolished and now all children and young persons are treated similarly. The only presumption remaining is that a child under ten is still irrebuttably presumed incapable of crime.

Many of the provisions regulating the manner in which youths are dealt with by the courts are found not in a single statute, but in a series of statutes enacted over the last seventy years. It was only in 1998 that the Crime and Disorder Act established for the first time that the principal aim of the youth justice system is to prevent offending by children and young persons, and that it is the duty of all those working in the youth justice system to have regard to that aim. In addition, courts must have regard to the welfare of children and young persons as provided by the Children and Young Persons Act 1933 as amended:

> Every court in dealing with a child or young person who is brought before it, either as an offender or otherwise, shall have regard to the welfare of the child or young person and shall in a proper case take steps for removing him from undesirable surroundings and for securing that proper provision is made for his education and training.

THE YOUTH PANEL

Any young person appearing before the *adult* court appears before a bench of magistrates for that local justice area. The bench may include one or more magistrates who are, in fact, members of the youth panel, but that will be a coincidence and not a requirement. The circumstances in which young persons appear before an adult court are dealt with below. More usually, children and young people accused of criminal offences appear before a youth court, where the bench *must* comprise magistrates appointed to the youth panel. Each sitting of a youth court must include a man and a woman if possible, although there are provisions allowing for an exception in an emergency.

Appointment to the youth panel

There are rules under which youth panel members are appointed and the Judicial College prescribes a discrete syllabus for youth panel training. Eligibility for appointment to the youth panel is not especially onerous, applicants have to demonstrate that they understand the nature of the work of the youth court, have an aptitude for the role and are able to devote the time to carry it out. That does not imply formal qualification, but may include those especially interested in the youth of the country, whether from professional or social contacts, or indeed from bringing up families of their own.

Magistrates who wish to be authorised to sit in the youth court must have sat in the adult court for two years and have undertaken their threshold appraisal (described in Chapter 3), and must have observed a youth court in session on at least two occasions. Each local justice area must have a youth panel. The BTDC is responsible for authorising magistrates to sit as members of a youth court. The BTDC, assisted by data from the justices' clerk, first assesses the volume of business that is likely to arise and the number of youth panel members who are soon to retire. When numbers have been determined, volunteers may be sought, and magistrates may make written applications to the BTDC. If the local justice area is small, with little youth work, one or more neighbouring local justice areas may form a joint panel. This enables persons appointed to sit in a full range of cases and build up experience. One of the important features of youth (and indeed family work) is the need to sit regularly to gain and maintain expertise, always remembering that there is the normal adult court work to do as well. Once authorised to sit in the youth court, membership continues until a magistrate resigns or retires, or, less commonly, until authorisation to sit in the youth court is revoked.

Members of the panel should meet at least twice a year to discuss matters of interest with regard to their work, and after the principal part of such a meeting is over, they may well have a speaker who may lead a discussion on a particular aspect of youth work or youth sentencing. The purpose of this arrangement is to stimulate interest and expertise. At one of these two meetings, known as the 'youth election meeting', held between September and November, the members of the panel elect a chairman and one or more deputy chairmen for a term of one year. Each youth court must be chaired by a magistrate who is on the list of approved youth court chairmen kept by the

BTDC. The BTDC must ensure that there are sufficient chairmen to enable each youth court to sit with a chairman.

Upon appointment to the youth panel, the magistrate undertakes youth induction training in accordance with the Judicial College's National Training Programme for Magistrates. This is a one-day course, and those attending are requested to read certain material in preparation for it. Two observations of the youth court in session also have to be undertaken. The course provides a foundation for the new youth panel magistrate and its aim is to provide an opportunity to consolidate what the individual has learned from the advance reading and from observations of the youth court. The course looks at the culture of the youth justice system. Its principal aim is, as already noted, to prevent offending, and its key objectives are:

- the swift administration of justice;
- confronting young offenders with their offending behaviour;
- intervention that tackles particular factors that lead youths to offend;
- punishment proportionate to the offending;
- encouraging reparation; and
- reinforcing the responsibility of parents/guardians.

The roles of parents or guardians, the Youth Offending Service and other agencies are also covered in the training, as are the court's powers and procedures relating to remands, jurisdiction and sentencing. The programme must be completed before the new youth panel justice starts to sit. Visits to establishments dealing with young offenders, such as an attendance centre and a young offenders' institution, are also arranged for the new youth magistrate.

After the magistrate has been sitting in the youth court for between nine to eighteen months, it is time for a one-day consolidation training programme. The aim is to reinforce and build on the original induction course and on what the magistrate has learned from sitting in the youth court, enabling the magistrate to reflect on experience, and to consolidate his or her knowledge. It also prepares the magistrate for a first appraisal in the youth court. The course looks at structured decision-making and at provisions relating to venue, grave crimes and dangerous offenders. Other agencies such as the youth offending team, the CPS, the youth panel chairman or an experienced youth court magistrate, provide specialist input. Continuing training to develop and sustain the competences achieved makes a valuable and important contribution to the effective working of the courts. If this training is conducted imaginatively and draws fully on the expertise of the relevant agencies, the youth panel magistrate should feel confident in his or her ability to discharge these important duties.

After a number of years, youth magistrates who wish to become youth chairmen are eligible if they are on the BTDC's list of approved adult court chairman, have been a youth magistrate for at least two years, and have been successfully appraised in the youth court. They will then be able to undertake a youth chairmanship programme followed by a number of appraisals.

Sentencing

How should courts sentence youths, what principles should they take into account and what guidance is available? In 2009, the Sentencing Guidelines Council (now the Sentencing Council – see Chapter 9) published a definitive guideline entitled *Overarching Principles – Sentencing Youths.* This guideline provides that when sentencing a young person under eighteen the court must have regard to the aims mentioned above – to prevent offending by children and young persons, and the welfare of the offender.

The fact that an offender is young calls for a different, and more individualistic, approach from that in the adult court. The expectation is that a child or young person is to be dealt with less severely than an adult offender. Sentences therefore differ according to the age and maturity of the offender, although the sentence must always be proportionate to the seriousness of the offence. In determining the sentence, the key elements are the age of the offender (chronological and emotional), the seriousness of the offence, the likelihood of further offending and the extent of harm likely to result from any further offences. The court should have regard to the mental health and capability of the offender, and to any relevant learning disability, learning difficulty, speech and language difficulty or other disorder. It has to balance all these factors in coming to a determination. In addition to the guidelines, the legal adviser has access to sentencing guidance from the Court of Appeal. It is also important that the chairman of the youth court engages with the young person in a productive and meaningful way; this is a vital part of the sentencing process.

The range of penalties available in the youth court is also somewhat different from that in the adult court. It includes a referral order, under which the offender is referred to the youth offender panel. This panel consists of members of the local community, supported by a member of the youth offending team. A meeting of the panel is held at which the offender and his or her parent(s) attend, and the panel members review the offence and its consequences. The victim(s) may attend, or have their views put before the panel. The panel works on the principle of restorative justice, encouraging offenders to be aware of and take responsibility for what they have done, and to have the opportunity to make reparation to victims and to the community. At the end of the meeting, a contract is agreed, comprising elements of reparation or restoration, and a programme of activities to address the risk of further offending. If the offender does not agree to the contract, or does so but then fails to comply, the offender is referred back to the court which may then revoke the order and impose a different punishment.

Alternatively, a youth rehabilitation order may be made, including one or more requirements aimed at punishment, the protection of the public, reducing reoffending or reparation. A fine may be imposed, although this is rarely appropriate because offenders are unlikely to be able to pay. In an extreme case, the court may decide to impose a custodial sentence. The Legal Aid, Sentencing and Punishment of Offenders Act 2012 will, when implemented, make some changes to sentencing in the youth courts.

There can be no doubt that the youth court remains a jurisdiction of great interest and importance, despite the fact that some of the ethos behind the creation of separate courts for young people has become less important with the passage of time. One of the main reasons for this separate summary jurisdiction was to mitigate the rigours of the adult courts as they then existed, and, as we have seen, to provide a welfare basis for the treatment of the young and to prevent offending. Youth courts were to be kept separate from adult sittings to prevent young people from mixing with and being influenced by adult offenders. Today, young people are beginning to offend earlier – at thirteen and fourteen – and peaking between the ages of sixteen and seventeen. The transition into adulthood can be the determining factor between maturing and diverting from offending, or developing a more entrenched lifestyle of offending which continues significantly into their adult years. Many young offenders face charges of crimes of the greatest magnitude in the youth court, and move on to the adult court at eighteen with the relative sophistication of some years of offending behind them.

As noted above, statute provides that the principal aim of the youth justice system is to prevent youth offending, and local authorities, in partnership with other relevant agencies, are required to establish a local structure of teams and services to deal with young offenders. All this is overseen by a Youth Justice Board, which monitors the operation of the youth justice system as a whole. For all that, the welfare ethos of the youth court remains as it did nearly eighty years ago. It must be right that society approaches the young in a way which places the greatest emphasis on reform and welfare. There are many young people who have had a brush with youth courts and have been grateful for the measured and constructive response shown by that court in helping to turn them away from offending towards a law-abiding life. Such individuals are seldom mentioned by the media, but social workers and probation officers attest to their existence. The youth panel performs a service which is seldom straightforward, but which nonetheless can bring its own rewards.

Relationship between the adult court and youth court

It would be simple if all criminal matters involving persons under eighteen were dealt with in the youth court, but a moment's reflection reveals that that is impossible. What happens when a crime is alleged to have been committed jointly by an eighteen-year-old (an adult) and a seventeen-year-old (a young person)? What happens if a young person is alleged to have committed an offence of a serious nature such as murder, rape or robbery where it is obvious that magistrates' courts powers, whether exercised in the adult court or in the youth court, would be wholly inadequate? What should happen when a person is seventeen when proceedings are commenced, but reaches the age of eighteen at some point before the proceedings have been concluded?

Some of these issues are solved by reference to the Magistrates' Courts Act 1980, which regulates the circumstances in which young people can be dealt with by the Crown Court rather than summarily. It provides that a person under the age of eighteen should be tried and sentenced in the youth court, unless the youth:

- is charged with an offence of homicide;
- is charged with possession of a firearm and at the time of the offence has attained the age of sixteen years;
- is charged with what is called a 'grave crime' (see below) and a youth court has determined that, if convicted, a sentence beyond its powers should be available. In such circumstances a young person may be sentenced by the Crown Court to long term detention;
- is jointly charged with an adult and the court considers it necessary in the interests of justice to commit them both for trial (to the Crown Court);
- is charged with one of certain violent or sexual offences, and a sentence under special provisions relating to dangerous offenders is likely to be needed.

A 'grave crime' for these purposes is:

- an offence that, in the case of an adult, is punishable with fourteen years imprisonment or more (for example, robbery, wounding with intent);
- one of various offences in relation to firearms, ammunition and weapons; and
- one of various sexual offences under the Sexual Offences Act 2003.

The court has to decide the appropriate venue before the accused enters a plea. Does the offence call for a greater punishment than the youth court has available to it? The maximum custodial sentence the youth court may impose is a two-year detention and training order. In order to decide whether to commit the case to the Crown Court as a grave crime, the magistrates take into account the facts of the offence, the age of the defendant, the defendant's previous convictions, the Sentencing Council's guidelines, and any specific guideline cases. The court also has to consider whether a custodial sentence exceeding two years is a realistic possibility. The legal adviser will be able to give advice on the guidelines and any cases to assist the court in making that judgment.

Having dealt with the assignment of cases between the Crown Court and the magistrates' courts, we will now consider assignment between the adult court and the youth court.

The general rule is that charges against persons who have not attained their eighteenth birthdays are to be heard in the youth court, but there are exceptions where an adult and a young person are charged jointly with an offence, or an adult is charged with aiding, abetting, etc. the young person in the commission of an offence. Problems may arise where, in a joint charge, the adult consents to be tried summarily and pleads guilty, and the young person pleads not guilty. Where should the trial of the young person take place? The magistrates have a discretion in these circumstances. They can either direct trial before the adult court, or direct that the young person be remitted for trial to the youth court. Before making a decision, the court hears representations made on behalf of the parties.

If a young person has pleaded guilty or been found guilty after a trial in the adult court, then he or she must be remitted for sentence to the youth court, unless the adult court is satisfied it can deal with the case by way of an order requiring the young person's parents to enter into a recognisance to keep proper control of the young person, or by imposing a fine, or by an absolute or conditional discharge. The court to which the young person is remitted is the youth court for the area in which the young person lives.

The other jurisdictional issue between the adult court and the youth court concerns the young person who reaches eighteen at some point after the proceedings have been begun. There has been much litigation over the years on a number of aspects of this seemingly trivial point, most of it concerned with the right of an individual to elect trial at the Crown Court, which is available as a right only for those of eighteen years and over. The key date is the date on which the charge is put. If, on that date, the defendant has attained the age of eighteen, the defendant has the right to trial by jury and the matter should be heard in the adult court. If the defendant has not reached eighteen on that date, then he or she is treated as a young person and the youth court goes on to deal with the case even if the accused becomes eighteen before the trial takes place. If the defendant is convicted, the court proceeds to sentence in accordance with the powers of the youth court.

Occasionally the youth court may have to deal with an itinerant child, without parent or guardian, whose age cannot be verified. In those circumstances, the court may itself determine how old the individual is, by considering matters such as the child's height, size and understanding. If satisfied that he or she is a young person, the court can deal with the case even if information later becomes available showing that the person was, in fact, an adult. This may happen where a birth certificate is produced at a subsequent hearing. Where the dispute as to age is material, the court has the option of adjourning the matter for further enquiries to be made.

A defendant who has been given a conditional discharge in the youth court, but who breaches it after attaining the age of eighteen, should be dealt with for the breach by the youth court. On the other hand, if a defendant was given a supervision order in the youth court and, after reaching the age of eighteen, is alleged to be in breach of its requirements, he or she is brought before the adult court.

FAMILY PROCEEDINGS AND THE FAMILY PANEL

Of the changes to the magistrates' jurisdiction over the last twenty years or so, none has been more significant than the reform and revival of the court's family jurisdiction. Since the Children Act 1989, family proceedings courts take their place in a unified system of courts dealing with family matters. As well as the family proceedings court, this includes county courts and the Family Division of the High Court. Proceedings can be allocated between the different courts in accordance with subject matter, length and complexity, so that disputes are dealt with in a court having the appropriate level of expertise. Although family proceedings courts do not determine property issues, which may have complex legal foundations, their local base as part of magistrates' courts sitting in towns and cities throughout the country make them a suitable forum for dealing with a range of private and public law disputes in relation to children. The principal legislation relating to the family proceedings courts is the Children Act 1989, supplemented by the Family Procedure Rules. These courts may also make non-molestation and occupation orders under the Family Law Act.

More and more courthouses have dedicated family court facilities, separate from the criminal courts, so that parties to family proceedings use a separate entrance and wait in an area which is away from the other work going on in the building. The atmosphere in the family proceedings court is very different from that of the criminal court. In the family proceedings court the parties remain seated, and the procedure is less adversarial and less formal than in the criminal court.

Appointment to the family panel

We have seen that the magistrates sitting in youth courts must be authorised to do so and must be presided over – except in an emergency – by a chairman whose name is on the list of appointed court chairmen maintained by the BTDC. Similar provisions apply to the family panels.

Two or more local justice areas may constitute a single family panel, consisting of magistrates from both local justice areas. Family panels are made up of magistrates authorised by their Family Training and Development Committee (FTDC) on the basis of their aptitude and personal suitability. The prospective family panel magistrate must have been sitting as a justice for a minimum of two years in the adult court, must have been appraised at least once as competent, and must have observed a family proceedings court on at least two occasions.

Arrangements for the election of a chairman and deputy chairmen of the family panel are similar to those for the youth panel, and the family panel must meet as often as necessary, but not less than twice a year. Family proceedings courts should be chaired either by a district judge, who is *ex officio* a member of the panel, or a chairman who is on the FTDC's list of approved family court chairmen, although in an emergency another member of the court may preside.

All magistrates appointed to the family panel must receive training before they sit and throughout their membership of the panel. If they aspire to take the chair, there will be further training, and, although the burden may appear heavy, it is necessary. Sitting in family proceedings courts requires particular skills and insights which are not needed in relation to other magisterial duties. As with training to sit in the adult and youth courts, magistrates must demonstrate certain competences in key areas of the jurisdiction and powers of the family proceedings court. The newly appointed magistrate undertakes a two-day family court induction training programme. It focuses on the key principles of the Children Act, the powers available in private and public law family cases, structured decision-making, giving reasons, and the roles of the different parties, agencies and officers in family proceedings – the local authority, the Children and Family Court Advisory and Support Service (CAFCASS), and the guardian, for example.

As with the youth court, about twelve to eighteen months after appointment to the family panel, and prior to first appraisal in the family proceedings court, the magistrate undertakes a one-day family court consolidation training programme. The objectives include ensuring the magistrate is able to apply structured decision-making not only when reaching final decisions in public and private law cases, but to case management issues, and to articulate reasons for decisions.

After two years as a family magistrate, and having undertaken an appraisal in the family proceedings court, the magistrate may undertake a two-day family chairmanship training programme. Unlike the position in relation to the adult and youth courts, in the family proceedings court, the FTDC may itself select magistrates for chairmanship training.

Public law

The family proceedings courts deal with both 'public law' and 'private law'. Public law in this context means proceedings brought by the state, that is, a local authority, in connection with the protection of children. One of the disturbing aspects of modern day living is the number of children who are at risk of significant harm through one or more of a number of types of abuse, including neglect.

Much of the work in the family proceedings court is care proceedings. Such cases arise where the local authority's social services department has reasonable grounds to believe that a child has suffered significant harm (or is likely to suffer significant harm), and that the harm (or risk of harm) arises because the care given by the child's parent(s) is not what it would be reasonable to expect a parent to give. In these cases the court appoints a solicitor to act on behalf of the child. The court also appoints a guardian, who is an officer of the court and advises the bench on the child's welfare. Before it may make an order in relation to the child, the court must be satisfied that the threshold described above is met – that the child has suffered significant harm, or is at risk of such harm, and the harm or risk arises because the care given to the child is not what it would be reasonable to expect a parent to give. If that test is met, the court must decide what kind of order is appropriate. The rights of the parties and the child may be competing with each other, but the court must balance the rights of all parties, while being mindful that the welfare of the child is paramount. There is also a statutory provision in favour of non-interference unless essential – the court should make an order only if it is better to make an order than to make no order at all. Care orders may be interim (that is, of limited duration), or final (that is, until the child is eighteen). Interim care orders are often made where further investigations are needed before deciding on whether or not a final care order should be made.

Applications for emergency protection orders are also heard by family panel magistrates. This is the mechanism under which a court (or single magistrate) authorises a social worker to take a child into protection where the court has reasonable cause for believing that there is significant harm to the child's welfare, or the child is at risk of such harm. As its name suggests, this is an emergency measure, which lasts for a maximum of eight days, although it can be extended for a further seven. It is an extreme step, and a child should be removed only if in immediate danger. Following an emergency protection order, the social services department then decides whether care proceedings need to be instituted or, if the situation has stabilised, whether the child can safely be returned.

Private law

Private law cases concern disputes between family members, and do not usually involve a public body such as the police or social services. These are often disputes between a mother and father or family members, in relation to where a child is to live and how and when parents are to see the child(ren). Gone are the days when it was thought that parents had 'rights' to custody or access, almost as if the children were items of property to be fought over. Thanks in large measure to the Children Act, children are seen as *the* important people caught up in what may be a rather depressing saga of disharmony. The Children Act requires that the court puts the welfare of the child at the heart of its deliberations, and the welfare checklist set out in the Act requires that the views of the child or children concerned should be considered in the light of their age and understanding.

In a disputed case about where a child should live and the contact he or she should have, the case is first listed for a mediation appointment and directions. If that does not bring resolution, it is likely that the court will require a welfare report. This is prepared by a court reporter employed by CAFCASS, who may provide a report with recommendations. In many cases the contents of the welfare report take the heat out of the dispute and the application may cease to be contested, perhaps with some fine tuning of specific issues between the parties. A good welfare report is of inestimable benefit to family proceedings courts.

Case management

In Chapter 5 the role of the criminal court in managing criminal cases was considered. So too in family proceedings, both private and public, the courts take an active role in ensuring that cases are dealt with expeditiously and fairly. For public law proceedings a Practice Direction (Guide to Case Management in Public Law Proceedings, 2010) sets out the main principles underlying case management and the procedure to be followed. The overriding objective of the case management process is to enable the court to deal with cases justly having regard to the welfare issues involved. This includes, as far as possible, ensuring the case is dealt with expeditiously and fairly, in ways which are proportionate to the nature of the issues, and saving expense. The court must give effect to the overriding objective and the parties are required to assist the court in so doing. This means that the court has actively to manage cases, give directions to the parties and set a timetable for each stage of the child's case. The Practice Direction is the judiciary's greatest effort so far to address the serious problem of delay in public law family cases.

Allocation

In view of the importance of avoiding delay, one of the principles applying in the family courts is that any unjustified delay may be inimical to the welfare of the child concerned. The need to avoid delay may also influence where the case should be heard. Depending on the complexity of the case and/or the likely length of the final hearing, a case may be transferred from the family proceedings court to a county court or the High Court. Cases can also be transferred laterally – from one family proceedings court to another, or from one county court to another – to prevent delay. This is simply a question of managing a case to make the best use of available resources. As we have seen before, there is no national family court, but a common jurisdiction under the Children Act between the family proceedings court, county court and High Court, and these courts now work together as never before. There are provisions setting out the mechanics for allocating proceedings to the appropriate level of court to reduce delay and ensure that they are heard at the appropriate court.

All emergency protection order and care proceedings begin in the family proceedings court. Proceedings may be transferred from the magistrates' court to the county court because:

- it would reduce delay;
- of the complicated or conflicting evidence about the risks involved to the child's physical or moral well-being or about other matters relating to the welfare of the child;
- there is a real possibility of a conflict in the evidence of two or more experts;
- there is a novel or difficult point of law or public policy;
- of a conflict with the law of another jurisdiction, or there are international law issues;
- there are ongoing criminal proceedings against one or more adult parties;
- the proceedings are likely to last more than four or five days;
- there are mental health issues.

Each magistrates' court has a county court to which such proceedings are transferred. In the London area, public law proceedings are transferred to the Principal Registry of the Family Division and private law proceedings to a local county court.

There are also provisions dealing with transfers downwards from a county court to a magistrates' court, and upwards from the county court to the High Court.

The orders which the family proceedings court may make

The family proceedings courts have wide powers to make orders to settle the matters which come before them. The most usual orders which may be made in public law matters – emergency protection orders and care orders (both interim and final) – have been considered above. The court may also make certain supervision orders, again either interim or final, placing a child under the supervision of a local authority or a person such as a social worker or probation officer.

In both public and private law, there may be orders concerning when and where contact between a child and a specified person is to take place; concerning with whom, or where a child is to live; concerning specific issues arising; or prohibiting certain things from taking place. The court can make a parental responsibility order in favour of a father who is not married to the mother of his child, or to some other person. This confers on the person in whose favour the order is made, all the rights, responsibilities and authority of a parent relating to the child or the child's property. The court may make placement and adoption orders under the Adoption and Children Act 2002, or make special guardianship orders, which provide a legally secure placement for a child who cannot live with his or her birth parents, but for whom adoption is not appropriate.

In private law, the court can make a non-molestation order prohibiting a person from molesting another person and/or a child. 'Molestation' is not defined but it has been held to imply deliberate conduct aimed at a high degree of harassment. The court also has powers in relation to the enforcement of maintenance orders.

Reasons

Justices sitting in family proceedings courts must give written reasons for their decisions. These should be carefully prepared in consultation with the legal adviser.

After the evidence has been concluded and speeches made, the bench retires, either with the legal adviser, or the legal adviser joins the bench fairly soon thereafter. The legal adviser may assist the bench to identify the issues, if these remain unclear, but it is a matter for the magistrates alone to determine what facts have been found on the evidence heard. In other words, the facts which are agreed between the parties are identified, then the relevant facts which are in dispute. The magistrates then make decisions, on the evidence, about each of the disputed facts. There is a structure to the process of writing reasons which assists magistrates in coming to their decision. It sounds more complicated than it is, but the legal adviser is there to assist the magistrates and there are some very helpful pro formas available. Writing reasons is a skill that can be honed with practice.

When the reasons have been completed, the bench returns to court and the chairman announces the court's decision and reads the reasons. Copies of the reasons are given to the parties, who then have full details of what has been decided and why. They can then consider how the judgment affects them and what they must do to comply. The written reasons also provide a basis for considering whether or not to appeal against the decision.

Reasons have to be given not only at the final hearing, but also at interim hearings, and this includes decisions made at a preliminary stage when the facts may be unclear. For example, reasons have to be given for the grant (or refusal) of an emergency protection order or an interim care order, but these need not be extensive. They should cover only the evidence which has persuaded the court to make the decision it has, without more, and the aspect(s) of the evidence which persuaded the court that the statutory requirements for making the order were, or were not, made out. Findings of fact should not be made at interim hearings.

The future of family proceedings

The family justice system is under strain, with increasing numbers of cases, longer cases, and more delay. The cost to the state is now around £1.5bn each year. Long and complicated legal processes are emotionally and financially draining for parents and distressing for children. A Family Justice Review panel, appointed by the government to review the whole of the family justice system in England and Wales, reported in 2011. In response, the government has announced plans to introduce legislation to implement the panel's recommendation to impose a six-month time limit in care cases, to reduce delays.

The family courts have also been the subject of widespread criticism for what is perceived to be the secrecy of their proceedings. There are, of course, good reasons for maintaining the confidentiality of sensitive and difficult issues concerning children. Nevertheless, there have been changes to allow certain representatives of the media, but not the general public, to be present at many family cases. The court also has power under the Family Proceedings Rules to permit persons to be present in many instances, and magistrates are unlikely to refuse anyone who, in good faith, asks to observe the proceedings and has a *bona fide* reason to do so.

REWARDS AND BURDENS

It must not be forgotten that appointment to the youth or family proceedings panel heralds a considerable extra burden in terms of both sittings and training, although most panel magistrates could rightly expect some diminution of their sittings in the adult court. It is unlikely that magistrates are able to sit in adult criminal courts and in the youth and family proceedings courts – the burden would be too great. Although there is no legal prohibition on serving on both panels, at one time the Lord Chancellor disapproved of magistrates sitting on both panels at the same time. Some benches have adopted an informal rule that a magistrate wishing to serve on one of the panels may be appointed either to the youth panel or to the family proceedings panel, but not to both. In areas where there is a shortage of family magistrates, however, this convention has been relaxed to enable magistrates to serve on both panels. There are also some magistrates who sit exclusively in the family jurisdiction.

LIQUOR LICENSING

For many years, magistrates were responsible for the licensing of pubs and clubs, and for granting bookmakers' permits, betting office licences, bingo hall and casino licences, and for authorising certain types of gaming by machines. These were examples of the administrative jurisdiction of magistrates which was a large part of their work until the creation of local authorities in the nineteenth century. Before then, magistrates had even been responsible for matters such as the maintenance of highways and bridges.

The Licensing Act 2003 transferred responsibility for the licensing of alcohol in premises open to the public and qualifying clubs, from the magistrates to licensing authorities, that is, the local authorities – district councils, unitary authorities, and London boroughs. But the magistrates' courts deal with appeals against the various decisions made by licensing authorities under the Act. It also has jurisdiction to deal with a number of new offences created by the Act.

The 2003 Act extended the powers of the police to close licensed premises on the spot for up to twenty-four hours where they are associated with disorder, or give rise to noise nuisance. The police may also apply to the magistrates' court for a closure order to close a licensed premises, or a number of licensed premises within a geographical area, in anticipation of disorder. Interestingly, under different legislation, magistrates may make closure orders to close premises for up to three months where Class A drugs are being used or dealt, and there is serious nuisance or disorder associated with the premises, or where the premises are used for activities related to specified prostitution or pornography offences.

CONCLUSION

This chapter illustrates that any general perception that magistrates spend their sittings dealing with minor thefts, assaults and speeding cases is a gross over-simplification. Much of the important work of the bench consists of specialist matters, and magistrates develop particular interests and skills in tackling these duties. In different ways, the informed decisions taken in balancing competing arguments about whether or not a baby should be made the subject of a care order, or whether a young person should be sent to a young offender institution, show not only the diversity, but also the importance, of work in the specialist jurisdictions open to magistrates.

Chapter 8

Bail

INTRODUCTION

We have seen that, for many reasons, criminal cases are not always completed on the day the defendant first appears before the court. This gives rise to the question of what is to happen between court appearances, up to the time of conviction and punishment or acquittal. Should bail be granted so that the defendant is free to go home and carry on with normal life, or should the defendant be confined to prison? The court often has to make important and difficult decisions about a defendant who is unconvicted and who may be innocent of the offence charged, or who has been convicted but not yet sentenced. The statutory provisions are robust, providing for a presumption in favour of bail, and restricting the circumstances in which bail may be denied.

The decision whether or not a court should grant bail in criminal proceedings, and if so whether with or without conditions, is one of the more difficult decisions faced by magistrates and regularly causes concern. The reason is plain: most decisions taken by courts are in respect of events that have actually happened in the past. For example, a defendant has pleaded guilty to an offence of theft from a shop and is sentenced for that offence, for something that he or she has accepted actually happened. Again, a court hears evidence in a contested case and makes findings of fact in determining whether the prosecution has proved the defendant's guilt. The court bases its decision on what it finds actually happened in the past.

The bail decision, however, is not about what happened in the past, but about what might happen in the future, although what has happened in the past may be a helpful factor in the court's judicial deliberations. In deciding whether or not to grant bail, a court may be assisted in predicting whether the defendant is a good bail risk by considering whether he or she has previously failed to surrender to bail, or whether he or she has committed an offence while on bail. On adjourning a case, the court has to make a decision about bail. It is emphasised elsewhere (see Chapter 5) that a court must carefully consider all applications to grant adjournments, and grant such an application only where it is just to do so. It is then that the bail decision comes into play.

THE BAIL ACT 1976

The Bail Act 1976 (as amended) provides the framework for the bail decision. It creates a statutory right or rebuttable presumption in favour of bail for any person who is accused of an offence, when he or she:

- is before a magistrates' court or the Crown Court in connection with the offence; or
- applies to a court for bail in connection with the proceedings.

It also applies to a person who has been convicted of an offence and whose case is adjourned for enquiries or a report to be made to assist the court in dealing with that person for the offence. It extends to a person who has been convicted and sentenced, but is back before the court accused of breach of the requirements of a community order. A person charged with murder may be bailed only by a Crown Court judge, not by magistrates.

INSUFFICIENT INFORMATION

Before we examine the circumstances in which bail may be withheld, and a defendant remanded in custody, there is a helpful provision which deals with the common situation where a court feels it has inadequate information to make a bail decision. There may be serious doubts about a person's identity or address and community ties, or perhaps a check on his or her criminal history is awaited. The defendant need not be granted bail if the court is satisfied that, owing to lack of time since the commencement of the proceedings, it has not been practicable to obtain sufficient information to make a decision on bail. The court may therefore remand the defendant in custody for a period to enable these matters to be resolved. Although a court may sometimes be justified in remanding for the maximum permitted eight clear days, this is rare. Often the information needed can be made available in a day or two, and the court should remand for the shortest period necessary so that the interests of the defendant can be protected by a full bail application as soon as practicable. This power is a useful one, but it must not be abused. As in all decisions involving bail, the liberty of the subject is the central issue, and in most cases the defendant is unconvicted.

POWER TO WITHHOLD BAIL

Schedule 1 to the Bail Act sets out different grounds for withholding bail, depending on whether the offence charged is an either-way offence for which an offender may be imprisoned, a summary-only offence for which an offender may be imprisoned, or a summary-only offence for which an offender may *not* be imprisoned.

Either-way offences for which an offender may be imprisoned

In these cases, the three most important grounds on which a court may withhold bail are that the court is satisfied that there are substantial grounds for believing that the defendant, if released on bail (whether subject to conditions or not), would:

- fail to surrender to custody; or
- commit an offence while on bail; or
- interfere with witnesses or otherwise obstruct the course of justice, whether in relation to him- or herself or any other person.

It can be seen from the outset that a high degree of certainty is required before bail can be withheld. 'Substantial grounds' means precisely what it says. If, for example, some grounds exist but they are not substantial then bail must be granted, although it may be appropriate for that bail to be conditional. It is not a ground for withholding bail that the defendant faces a serious charge, or has a bad criminal record. Persons facing serious charges are regularly bailed and answer to their bail in accordance with the law, and persons with bad criminal records often manage to survive their bail periods without offending.

In applying the test described above, the court must have regard to a number of non-exclusive factors. These may seem fairly obvious, but it is helpful that they are included in the Act because it enables courts to approach any bail decision in a structured way. The factors to be considered are:

- the nature and seriousness of the offence and the probable method of dealing with it if the defendant is convicted;
- the character, antecedents, associations and community ties of the defendant;
- the defendant's record of answering bail in the past;
- the strength of the evidence against the defendant;
- the risk that the defendant would commit an offence while on bail by engaging in conduct that would be likely to cause physical or mental injury to a person or persons other than the defendant.

Consideration of these factors may mean that a defendant with a substantial criminal record, but who has always surrendered in the past and who has never committed an offence on bail, may not have the presumption in favour of bail displaced. The question of the strength of the evidence may be troublesome, because at an early remand hearing the evidence may still be being collated. In some cases forensic analysis of items seized is not available and may not be so for many weeks. Or perhaps the case depends entirely on identification evidence which cannot be tested before the trial. By contrast, there is the situation where a defendant is caught 'red-handed' committing the crime, and the evidence is overwhelming. Strength of the evidence is only one factor, however, and the court is required to perform a balancing exercise in determining whether the strong presumption in favour of bail has been displaced. Other exceptions to the presumption in favour of bail include where:

- the defendant has previously been released on bail in the same proceedings and has been arrested for absconding while on bail or breaking the conditions of bail;
- the defendant should be kept in custody for his or her own protection, or, if a child or young person, for his or her own welfare;
- the defendant is in custody in pursuance of a sentence of a court;
- the defendant is charged with murder, in which case bail may not be granted unless the court is of the opinion that there is no significant risk that the defendant will cause physical or mental injury to another person.

In 2003 the Bail Act was further amended to include a new exception to the right to bail, applicable to drug users in certain circumstances. It applies where a defendant over eighteen provides a positive drugs test for specified Class A drugs pursuant to powers of the police to test people arrested for certain offences associated with drug use. If the person is charged with possession or supply of a Class A drug, and a link is established between the defendant's drug misuse and offending, the court may not grant bail unless the defendant agrees to drug treatment, or the court is satisfied that there is no significant risk that the defendant will commit an offence while on bail. If the defendant agrees to drug treatment then that becomes a bail condition (see below) throughout the proceedings, unless the court later becomes satisfied that there is no significant risk of further offences. A failure to comply with this condition is treated in the same way as any other breach of bail.

Summary-only offences for which an offender may be imprisoned

The Criminal Justice and Immigration Act 2008 amended the Bail Act so as to limit the grounds upon which a court may refuse bail to a defendant accused of a summary-only offence for which, if convicted, a person may be imprisoned. Examples of such offences are common assault and criminal damage cases where the cost of repairing the damage is £5,000 or less. The court may withhold bail if:

- the offence before the court was committed while the defendant was on bail, and the court is satisfied that there are substantial grounds to believe that if released on bail the defendant would commit an offence while on bail;
- there are substantial grounds to believe that if released on bail the defendant would commit an offence while on bail by engaging in conduct that would, or would be likely to, cause physical or mental injury to somebody else or cause somebody else to fear such injury;
- the defendant should be kept in custody for his or her own protection, or if a child or young person, for his or her own welfare;
- it has not been practicable to obtain sufficient information to make a bail decision; or
- the defendant is in custody in pursuance of a sentence of a court.

Summary offences for which an offender may not be imprisoned

The grounds on which bail may be withheld in the case of someone charged with an offence for which, if convicted, the defendant may not be imprisoned, are much more limited. Bail may be refused only if:

- the defendant has previously failed to answer bail, and the court believes that if released the defendant would again fail to surrender;
- the court is satisfied that the defendant should be kept in custody for his or her own protection, or, if a child or young person, for his or her own welfare;
- the defendant is in custody in pursuance of a sentence of a court;
- having been released on bail, the defendant has been arrested for failing to attend court or for breaching a condition of bail, *and* the court is satisfied that there are substantial grounds for believing that, if released on bail, the defendant would fail to surrender, commit an offence on bail, interfere with witnesses, or otherwise obstruct the course of justice.

CONDITIONAL BAIL

In the lead-in to the enactment of the Bail Act 1976, it was widely thought that a defendant appearing before the court, to whom the presumption in favour of bail applied, would be dealt with in one of two ways. If the court was satisfied that a substantial ground or grounds existed for withholding bail, then the defendant would be remanded in custody, but if not, unconditional bail would be granted. The power to impose conditions on bail existed in the Bail Act from the beginning, but the architects of the legislation would surely be surprised at the frequency of conditional bail, and the tendency of courts to use conditional bail as a 'halfway house' between withholding bail on the one hand, and granting unconditional bail on the other.

Before imposing conditions, a court must find that unconditional bail is inappropriate but that there are no substantial grounds which would justify withholding bail altogether. Conditions have to be imposed for good reason, and not on mere whim. In a decision arising from the 1984 miners' strike, Lane LCJ held, in *R v Mansfield JJ, ex parte Sharkey* (1984), that magistrates were not obliged to have substantial grounds for imposing conditions, but that conditions should be imposed to meet a real (rather than a fanciful) risk, and they must be imposed to help meet one of the three grounds listed above (substantial grounds for believing that if bailed, the defendant would fail to surrender, commit an offence while on bail, or interfere with witnesses). This means that if a court finds no substantial grounds for withholding bail on the basis that the defendant *would* abscond, yet it is satisfied that there is a real risk that he or she *might* abscond, conditions designed to meet the risk may be imposed on the defendant's bail. For example, taking a surety before granting bail, together with a condition of residence once released on bail, may be appropriate.

Alternatively, a defendant may be made subject to a curfew as a condition of bail. This means that the defendant must remain at a specified address (usually the defendant's home) between specified hours. The defendant's compliance with the curfew may be monitored by electronic tagging. This is a system operated by specialist companies under contract to the Ministry of Justice. It involves attaching an electronic device to the defendant's wrist or ankle, and installing monitoring apparatus at the address in question. If the defendant is not at the address during the required hours, that absence is immediately transmitted to a central control room and action can be taken.

A court may order that a defendant must present himself or herself to a police officer on request at a given address. This is usually known as a 'doorstep condition', and allows the police to check that the defendant is living at the address the court specified as a condition of bail, or is complying with a curfew condition.

There is a danger that a defendant's bail may be overloaded with conditions, and magistrates must remember that any condition imposed restricts the liberty of a defendant. Only the minimum necessary conditions should be imposed. As a useful rule of thumb, magistrates considering the imposition of conditions should remember the three Es: conditions should be exact, efficient and enforceable. A condition, for example, 'not to enter the Wembley area' fails the first of these tests; it is inexact in that it does not set out a precise geographical area. The same criticism can be levelled at a condition 'not to contact prosecution witnesses' unless the names of the witnesses are specified precisely so that the meaning of the condition is clear not only to the defendant, but also to the police. A condition of 'reporting to X police station each Saturday at 8 pm' is almost certainly ineffective to meet the risk of a defendant absconding. A defendant could report within the terms of the condition this Saturday, and be at the other side of the world well before next Saturday. The idea that reporting will enable the police 'to keep an eye on the defendant' is unrealistic. The imposition of a surety in an appropriate amount may be a better bet, as may the deposit of a security (that is, a cash sum with, or to the order of, the court). If there are real fears that the defendant will leave the jurisdiction, a condition may be imposed requiring the surrender of the defendant's passport to the police with a prohibition against applying for a new passport or other travel document.

A defendant may apply to the magistrates' court to vary the conditions of bail, and may appeal to the Crown Court against the imposition of certain bail conditions, but only if the defendant has first unsuccessfully applied to the magistrates' court for the conditions to be varied.

ABSCONDING

The Bail Act creates an offence of absconding when on bail. This may take one of two forms. The first, and the more common, is where a person released on bail fails without reasonable cause to come to court on the appointed date, at the appointed time. The second is where a person has a reasonable cause for not surrendering on the appointed date at the appointed time, but then fails to surrender as soon as reasonably practicable thereafter. Both these offences carry the same maximum penalty: on summary conviction, imprisonment for up to three months and/or a fine of up to £5,000; or on conviction by the Crown Court as a criminal contempt of court, by up to twelve months' imprisonment and/or an unlimited fine.

A defendant who says he had a reasonable cause for failing to surrender is not required to prove it beyond reasonable doubt, but on the balance of probabilities (the distinction is explained in Chapter 10). The cause for failing to surrender must be reasonable and courts regularly have to examine reasons for non-appearance to see whether they provide a defence. Illness which is certificated is a common cause, although doctors' certificates or notes should be carefully scrutinised for it does not necessarily follow that a defendant who is unfit for work is unfit to attend court. Defendants who have mislaid charge sheets, bail forms or other notices, or have simply forgotten the date on which they are due to surrender have, it is submitted, no reasonable cause, although the court will have to consider each case on its own merits.

The commencement of proceedings for absconding depends on whether the defendant was bailed to court by a police officer from a police station, or bailed by a court. In the former case, the proper procedure is initiated by charging the defendant or, more usually, by laying an information to which the defendant enters a plea. In the latter case, the defendant has, on the face of it, defied a court order and the court may initiate proceedings of its own motion. The prosecutor nonetheless conducts the proceedings and, in a disputed case, calls evidence.

THE APPLICATION FOR BAIL

It is often assumed that bail is only ever granted after a spirited application by the defendant's advocate, but the Bail Act imposes a duty on the court to approach a bail decision in a way which is quasi-inquisitorial in nature. This means that the court must actively consider whether bail should be withheld, and, if so, on what grounds, even if there is an indication from the defence that there is no application for bail. Of course, it may be that the grounds for withholding bail advanced by the prosecution can be put before the court much more concisely than if there were a full application, but the court must still make findings as to the legal grounds for withholding bail and give reasons for its decision. The Act states that, on subsequent applications, it is the court's duty to consider whether the defendant ought to be granted bail. The general rule governing the hearing of applications for bail must always be viewed in the light of that duty. But a defendant does not have a right to make bail applications on appearance after appearance, rehearsing the same points each time without success. Full applications may be made on the defendant's first two appearances before the court. After that, a further application may be made only if some new aspect has arisen, whether of fact or law, which the court has not heard previously. The precise wording of the Act needs to be considered:

> At the first hearing after that at which the court decided not to grant the defendant bail he may support an application for bail with any argument as to fact or law that he desires (whether or not he has advanced that argument previously). At subsequent hearings the court need not hear arguments as to fact or law which it has heard previously.

The onus of showing that a further bail application should be allowed lies with the defendant, but in a marginal case the court should probably err on the side of hearing an application. Failure to do so may result in the defendant remaining in custody for many weeks. It is submitted that at the stage of committal to the Crown Court, the committing court should carefully review bail, although there is no need to hear a full bail application again. The reason is that, after committal, the case passes out of the control of the magistrates' court, and it may be a matter of some weeks before the defendant appears before the Crown Court. In addition, where the defence has conceded at committal stage that there is a *prima facie* case (see Chapter 5), the court has the first real opportunity to assess the strength of the evidence against the defendant. Although this is generally statements in written form only, at least some sort of assessment can be made, and that may lead to the grounds for withholding bail being confirmed or modified. As mentioned in Chapter 5 above, the Lord Chancellor has indicated that committals for either-way offences will be abolished on a phased basis beginning in 2012.

Any court hearing a bail application must comply with the principle that both sides of the argument must be heard. Typically the Crown is asked to state its objections or observations about bail. The prosecutor describes the offence(s) and the circumstances under which the defendant came to be arrested. Details may be sketchy, particularly if the defendant is appearing for the first time, or was arrested the day before and has been held overnight. In other cases the evidence may appear strong, but it must be remembered that it is highly exceptional to hear evidence at remand hearings, so the court must make what it can of the prosecutor's representations. After detailing the allegations, the prosecutor puts before the court particulars of the defendant, what is known of any community ties, and the defendant's previous criminal record (if any). The prosecution concludes by giving its views about bail, and, if the prosecution feels bail should be withheld, the reasons.

The defence then applies for bail, perhaps first commenting on the allegation, any apparent weaknesses in the evidence, and so on. Information is given to the court on behalf of the defendant. The intention is to set the magistrates' minds at rest. For example, it may be said that the defendant is a local person with strong community ties who has always answered bail in the past; that despite a criminal record the defendant has never committed an offence while on bail; that despite convictions for violence, the defendant has never approached or interfered with witnesses before previous trials. The defence may concede that if bail were to be granted conditions should be imposed to meet the risks which concern the court, and then go on to list suitable conditions with which the defendant would be able to comply.

The court then makes its decision, applying the tests laid down in the Act and adopting a structured approach (see below).

REASONS

The Bail Act provides that where a court grants conditional bail it must give its reasons for imposing those conditions, and if it refuses bail, it must state the grounds, and the reasons for applying those grounds. In either case, a note of the reasons is made in the court's records, and the prosecution and defendant are given a copy of that record.

If the court imposes conditional bail, it must explain the conditions carefully so that the defendant fully understands them, and explain that if the defendant breaks any of the conditions, he or she is liable to be arrested and to lose bail.

APPEALS

If bail is withheld from a defendant after a court has heard full argument, the defendant may well wish to consider appealing against that decision. If he or she is unrepresented, the court, on withholding bail, must tell the defendant of the right to appeal to the Crown Court. In any event when bail is withheld after full argument, the court is obliged to issue a 'full argument certificate', which sets out in writing the grounds on which bail has been withheld and the reasons for applying those grounds. This document is vital to the appeal process, and must be lodged with the Crown Court before an appeal can be entertained. The appeal is heard by a judge in chambers, and usually in the absence of the defendant who is not brought from prison or the remand centre for the appeal. The judge, having heard both sides, has a free hand to grant unconditional or conditional bail, or to remand the defendant in custody as the magistrates' court had done, on the same or on other grounds. If bail is granted, the magistrates' court is sent a notice detailing any conditions imposed on the bail.

The prosecution has a right to appeal against the decision of magistrates to grant bail, but only where the defendant is charged with, or convicted of, an offence punishable by imprisonment. At the time of writing, the right of appeal against bail is available only where the prosecution is being conducted by the CPS, or certain other bodies specified in legislation. Further, the prosecution must have made representations against the grant of bail in the first place.

The prosecution must comply with various procedural requirements. Oral notice of appeal at the time of the decision must be followed by a written notice within two hours thereafter. If written notice has not been served at the conclusion of the two-hour period, the right of appeal lapses and the defendant must be released on bail in accordance with the magistrates' original decision. If the notice is served, however, the magistrates are then obliged to remand the defendant in custody pending the determination of the appeal by the Crown Court. This is treated as a matter of urgency, and must be heard within forty-eight hours, excluding bank holidays and weekends. The appeal at the Crown Court is by way of rehearing, and the judge has a discretion to grant bail, with or without conditions, or to remand the defendant in custody in line with the provisions of the Bail Act.

STRUCTURED DECISION-MAKING

A positive benefit of the Act has been the requirement for courts to approach the potentially difficult decisions of whether bail should or should not be granted according to a clear, statutory structure. Courts that carefully apply the tests laid down in the Act certainly make better informed decisions, and the risk of injustice is reduced. Relevant issues remain at the forefront; hunch, whim and suspicion are seen to have no place in the courts' deliberations. See also Chapter 10, on the bail decision.

Chapter 9

Sentencing

INTRODUCTION

The sentencing of offenders is at the very heart of magistrates' work, and the process by which an offender is sentenced deserves the greatest possible attention. At first glance, this may seem a fairly straightforward matter of applying the relevant guideline, but once a magistrate sees at first hand the almost infinite variety of factors that can influence the sentencing decision, it can seem not only problematical, but sometimes almost impossible to get right. It is true to say that no two cases are alike. Sentencing is neither an art nor a science, although it may contain elements of both. The more experience magistrates gain, then the more confidence they have in exercising their powers, and applying the appropriate criteria. The new magistrate should hope to gain a working knowledge of the framework of sentencing, and of the guidance that is readily available, but even for experienced magistrates, the advice of the legal adviser is often vital, because of the many pitfalls. There are, as we shall see, a sentencing framework, definitive guidelines for various offences, guideline cases, and a great many statutes which govern the powers of magistrates' courts in this field.

THE PHILOSOPHY OF SENTENCING

Since the Second World War there has been increasing parliamentary intervention in the sentencing framework. Criminal Justice Acts used to come about once every five years, but in the last couple of decades they have appeared with even greater frequency. One of the aims has been to reduce the courts' use of prison because prison places are expensive, and because research shows that imprisonment does not prevent re-offending. The best that can be said for prison as a sentence is that for the period that the offender is detained, he or she is not out committing offences. This is an important consideration where the offender is a danger to the public, as in bad cases of violence or burglary, but is a pretty limited goal for many less serious offenders. The depressing feature of penal policy is that the prison population has never been higher. The more attractive feature is that a number of imaginative sentences have been introduced which do not deprive offenders of their liberty by locking them in a prison cell; instead, they are deprived of their free time rather than their liberty. Magistrates, as citizens, know of the publicity given to the prison population and the cost of incarceration, but it is most important that their sentencing decisions are not motivated by cost, or achieving value for money. In accordance with their judicial oath, they must endeavour to do justice according to the law in all cases that are listed before them. Sometimes this inevitably leads to imposing sentences of imprisonment. Much more often it enables them to sentence offenders in the community. Of course, it is unrealistic to say that cost should never enter the minds of the court, but it should not be the motivating or deciding factor in passing a sentence.

THE SENTENCING FRAMEWORK

The Criminal Justice Act 2003 introduced extensive reforms to court procedure and sentencing, and the current law in relation to the sentencing of adults is largely contained in this Act, although it has been amended several times. The Act contains a staggering 14 parts, 339 sections and 38 schedules, and is by far the most wide-ranging statute of its kind in recent times. It contains numerous provisions dealing with sentencing, many of them based on the recommendations of the *Review of the Sentencing Framework for England and Wales* (2001), commonly known as the Halliday Report.

The 2003 Act created a new sentencing framework, intended to be clearer and more flexible than the regime that was in place before. It set out, for the first time, the purposes of sentencing adults, and the matters that should be considered by a court in determining the seriousness of an offence. It deals with aggravating factors which increase the seriousness of an offence and which may increase the severity of the sentence. Such factors include that the offender has recent and relevant previous convictions, or committed the offence while on bail in respect of something else. A Sentencing Guidelines Council was created, which may issue to all criminal courts guidelines on sentencing, which must now be followed by sentencing courts. The Act also replaced the former range of community orders by a single generic community order, to which may be attached any one or more of a series of requirements, tailored to meet the needs of the offence and offender

PURPOSES OF SENTENCING

Until the 2003 Act, the objectives of sentencing in the adult court were sometimes said to be confused. There was no provision relating to the sentencing of adults which was the equivalent of the simple principle of the youth justice system – to prevent offending by children and young persons (see Chapter 7). This was remedied by a new provision which requires the court, when passing a sentence on an adult, to have regard to five purposes of sentencing. These purposes apply in relation to offenders who are eighteen or over when convicted. They are:

- the punishment of offenders;
- the reduction of crime (including its reduction by deterrence);
- the reform and rehabilitation of offenders;
- the protection of the public; and
- the making of reparation by offenders to persons affected by their offences.

The Act provides that no one of these purposes is more important than any other. It is for the court to determine the manner in which they apply, and the weight to be attached to a particular purpose.

SENTENCING GUIDELINES

The Sentencing Guidelines Council has now been replaced by the Sentencing Council for England and Wales. It has a statutory duty to prepare sentencing guidelines. Courts are required by statute to follow any sentencing guidelines, unless satisfied that it would be contrary to the interests of justice to do so. The guidelines are intended to promote consistency of approach to the sentencing exercise, by assisting judges and magistrates in coming to the correct sentence. The great advantage of the guidelines for any court is that they facilitate a structured approach to sentencing.

THE SERIOUSNESS OF THE OFFENCE

While the court must have regard to the five purposes of sentencing, it begins the sentencing process by considering the seriousness of the offence. Its decision about seriousness enables the court to go on to determine whether the threshold for imposing a prison sentence or a community sentence has been passed. There are two threshold tests: for a prison sentence, and for a community sentence. Before passing a prison sentence, the court has to be of the view that the offence or offences were *so serious* that only a sentence of imprisonment is justified. In the case of community sentences the test is whether the offence or offences were *serious enough* to warrant such a sentence. Thus, for example, if an offence does not meet the 'serious enough' threshold for a community sentence, the court is restricted to imposing a fine, or an absolute or conditional discharge.

Culpability and harm

In determining the seriousness of the offence, the court must consider two criteria – the *culpability* of the offender in committing the offence, and any *harm* which the offence caused, was intended to cause, or might foreseeably have caused.

Culpability refers to the offender's blameworthiness or fault: did the defendant intend to cause harm, or was the defendant reckless or negligent as to whether any harm would be caused. The harm may be to individual victims (physical injury, financial loss or psychological harm), or to the community (the loss to the taxpayer of a fraudulent benefits claim, for example).

In addition, there are four situations when, in assessing seriousness, a court is required to treat an offence as more serious than it would otherwise have done, resulting in a more severe penalty. These statutory aggravating features are where:

- the offender has recent and relevant previous convictions;
- the offender was on bail at the time of committing the offence under consideration;
- the offence involved racial or religious motivation; or
- the offence involved hostility based on the sexual orientation or disability of the victim.

A host of other factors may indicate higher culpability. These are matters for the discretion of the court, and include:

- failure to respond to previous sentence;
- the degree of planning that went into the offence;
- offending in groups or gangs;
- an attempt to conceal the evidence;
- deliberately targeting a vulnerable person;
- using a weapon to frighten the victim;
- abusing a position of trust.

Other factors may indicate a degree of harm which is greater than usual, for example:

- multiple victims;
- a sustained assault, or repeated assault on the same victim;
- the fact that the offence was committed against a victim providing a service to the public – a bus driver, for example;
- the presence of others, notably children, at the scene.

Once the court has considered any aggravating factors, it turns to any matters personal to the offender which may go to reduce the seriousness of the offence. These may include the age of the offender, mental illness or disability, provocation, or the fact that the offender played only a minor role in an offence.

Offenders are entitled to a reduced sentence if they plead guilty, but the extent of the reduction depends on when the guilty plea is entered – the sooner the better for these purposes. The reduction is one third if the plea is entered at the first reasonable opportunity (for example, at the first hearing), but goes down to one tenth if the guilty plea is not entered until the day of trial.

PRE-SENTENCE REPORTS

An important tool in assisting a court to reach an appropriate sentence is the pre-sentence report or PSR. The court usually already knows enough about the offence, for either the defendant has pleaded guilty or has been found guilty, but even with help from a skilled and experienced defence representative, more background information about the defendant may be necessary. For this, the court turns to the Probation Service, which is under a statutory duty to investigate and prepare a written report for the court. The Criminal Justice Act 2003 defines a pre-sentence report as a report to assist the court in determining the most suitable method of dealing with an offender, and the type of information to be included is also prescribed.

When to ask for a pre-sentence report

The court must obtain and consider a pre-sentence report before deciding to impose a custodial or community sentence. The court has a discretion, however, to dispense with that requirement where it appears to be unnecessary. Examples of this include where an offender has recently been sentenced by the court for a similar offence and the court decides to use the pre-sentence report which was before the court on that occasion, or where the court is minded to impose only a fine. Again, it would be inappropriate to ask the Probation Service to use its hard pressed resources to advise a court dealing with an offender convicted of speeding. In the case of a juvenile, the court must order a pre-sentence report, or have before it a copy of the most recent report prepared on the youth.

Commissioning a pre-sentence report

When adjourning a case for a report, magistrates should not bind the hands of the magistrates who will later consider the report and decide the sentence, unless they are absolutely certain that is is right to do so. In *Nicholas v Chester Magistrates Court* (2009), the High Court disapproved of adjourning for a report and, in so doing, giving an indication of the type of sentence which would be appropriate, unless the same magistrates are coming back to decide the sentence, or it is absolutely obvious that a certain type of sentence should, or should not, be considered. In the usual case where the court commissioning the report has no firm view about the appropriate sentence, it should make clear that all sentencing options remain open, so that a defendant cannot complain that a particular sentence was implied, but a more severe sentence is later imposed. The legal advisor notes on the court papers any remarks made by the bench when ordering the report, and they are, in due course, brought to the attention of the sentencing bench.

A number of different types of report are available to the court.

Standard delivery report

A standard delivery report (SDR) is usually appropriate in the most serious offences, such as sexual offences, domestic violence or offences against children, or where there are serious mental health issues, and the court is considering a custodial sentence. It must be completed within fifteen working days when an offender is on bail, or ten working days if remanded in custody.

Fast delivery report

A fast delivery report (FDR) may be used for cases of low or medium seriousness where the court has indicated that it is considering a community order, or where the court has indicated that a custodial sentence may be appropriate but extensive information and analysis is not required. Fast delivery reports must be completed within five working days of the request.

Oral reports

An oral report may be provided instead of a written pre-sentence report for an offender aged eighteen or over where the court requires only a limited amount of information. For example, the court may take the view that the offence is less serious and that a single requirement – such as an attendance centre order, unpaid work or a curfew – as part of the community order might be appropriate. An oral report might be sought where an offender is already subject to a community order, or where there is a recent pre-sentence report (prepared within the last twelve months). In these circumstances, the probation officer may provide an oral update on the report, and/or a report of progress under the order already in place. These reports are provided on the day.

Preparation of reports

In order to prepare the report, the allocated probation officer interviews the offender, reads the prosecution papers, previous probation reports and reports from other agencies, and makes an assessment of the likelihood of reconviction and any risks posed by the offender. The components of the pre-sentence report are laid down as national requirements. A report contains an analysis of the offence and the offender's attitude to the offence; the reason for committing the offence; any genuine remorse and the offender's attitude towards the victim; and the offender's background, offending history and pattern of offences. It also refers to any personal problems of the offender, such as whether the offence is rooted in domestic disharmony or in alcohol, drug or solvent abuse; previous compliance with supervision; the risk of reoffending; and risk of harm to the public. In the final paragraph of the report, the writer usually provides a sentencing proposal to assist the court in coming to a determination. This proposal is in no way binding on the court, although it is often followed.

As noted in Chapter 3, magistrates elected to the probation liaison committee have regular meetings with local probation officers. These meetings underpin the relationship between the magistrates and the Probation Service, keeping the magistrates up-to-date with developments in sentencing and the resources available, and keeping the Probation Service up-to-date with the needs of the courts. For an extremely helpful and more detailed guide to the work of the Probation Service for the courts, see the London Probation Trust's Bench *Guide to Community Sentences* (3rd edn, September 2011 at www.london-probation.org.uk).

VICTIM PERSONAL STATEMENTS

The purpose of victim personal statements, introduced in 2001, is to give victims a more formal opportunity to say how a crime has affected them, and assist in identifying whether they have a particular need for information, support and protection. The court may take such a statement into account when determining sentence.

When a police officer takes a statement from a victim, the victim is told about the scheme and given the chance to make a victim personal statement. The decision is entirely a matter for the victim. The statement may be made or updated at any time before the disposal of the case.

Guidance on how courts should treat victim personal statements has been set out in a Practice Direction and by the Court of Appeal. The court should consider and take into account such a statement, and any evidence in support, before passing sentence. Evidence of the effects of an offence on the victim should be in a proper form, and a formal witness statement or expert report should be served on the defendant or the defendant's solicitors before sentence. If the offence has had a particularly damaging or distressing effect on the victim, this should be made known and the court should take it into account when sentencing. A sentencer must not make assumptions unsupported by evidence about the effects of an offence on the victim. The court should pass the appropriate sentence, having regard to the circumstances of the offence and the offender and, so far as is appropriate, the impact on the victim. The opinions of the victim or the victim's relatives as to the appropriate sentence are not relevant. The court should consider whether it is desirable, in its sentencing remarks, to refer to the evidence provided by the victim.

THE MORE USUAL SENTENCES

We now consider the sentences most commonly passed by magistrates, assuming that the offender is eighteen years or over. Many of these sentences apply equally to young persons, but, as discussed in Chapter 7, a number of distinct sentencing options are open to those sentencing in the youth court. The magistrates' court does retain some powers to sentence young persons who have appeared jointly charged with an adult. The first duty for the court is to remit the offender for sentence to the youth court, but the adult court may proceed to sentence if it feels it can do so by way of a fine, a discharge or a recognisance.

DISCHARGES

Absolute discharge

An absolute discharge is an acknowledgement that the defendant has pleaded guilty to, or been found guilty of, an offence, and yet the circumstances are such that the court has no need to impose any penalty. The defendant is still guilty of the offence, however. It is not the same as being found not guilty. An absolute discharge places no obligation on the offender. It is available to all courts whatever the age of the offender.

Conditional discharge

A conditional discharge discharges the defendant for a period of up to three years, on the condition that the defendant does not commit a further offence during that period. It is not necessary for the defendant to consent to the order. All criminal courts may impose a conditional discharge, whatever the offender's age.

If a person subject to a conditional discharge commits another offence within the period of the discharge, and is brought before the court, then the defendant can be dealt with again for the offence for which the conditional discharge was imposed, as well as for the new offence. If the conditional discharge was imposed at another magistrates' court, then the consent of that court has to be obtained first. Magistrates cannot, though, deal with breaches of conditional discharges imposed by the Crown Court, unless they were imposed at the hearing of an appeal from magistrates, when they are regarded as being the magistrates' court's own decision. Otherwise, the magistrates commit the offender to the Crown Court to be dealt with for the breach there.

NO SEPARATE PENALTY

A number of offences may arise from a single incident, none of which, taken alone, materially aggravates the seriousness of the incident overall. A classic case is where a motorist driving an 'old banger' is stopped by the police. Numerous offences under the Construction and Use Regulations may be evident, relating to dangerous parts, dangerous condition, defective tyres, defective steering, lights, indicators and so on. Defendants in this type of case are often young and impecunious. On guilty pleas being entered, or on convicting the defendant, the court considers the defects overall. It then generally imposes fines for the more serious matters, and makes an order of no separate penalty or absolute discharge in relation to the remainder. The use of an order of no separate penalty in respect of offences committed on the same occasion has been expressly approved by the Court of Appeal.

FINES

The fine is by far the most usual sentence in magistrates' courts. It is sometimes thought that fines may be unlimited but, with the exception of specific statutory provisions (often, though not exclusively, concerned with environmental protection), fines are subject to statutory maxima. A magistrates' court may impose a fine of up to £5,000 for any either-way offence, but in the case of summary-only offences, the maximum fine for a particular offence is expressed by reference to a scale from 1 and 5. At the time of writing, level 1 is not exceeding £200; level 2, £500; level 3, £1,000; level 4, £2,500; and level 5, £5,000. For example, the Public Order Act 1986 provides that the maximum fine for the offence of threatening behaviour under s. 4 is six months' imprisonment and/or a fine on level 5.

These maxima are, however, only part of the story. As will be seen, if the offender has caused injury, loss or damage to the victim, and an amount to measure that loss, etc. has been quantified, then a compensation order must take priority over other financial impositions. Further, when imposing a fine, the court must have regard to a number of statutory principles. When fixing the sum it must reflect the seriousness of the particular offence, but the court must take into account the financial circumstances of the offender so far as they are known, or appear to the court. All defendants must complete a means form when first appearing before the court, and cases are not called on until that has been done. The amounts which may be ordered to be paid in fines are also constrained by the fact that the magistrates must follow the guidelines issued by the Sentencing Council unless, unusually, it is contrary to the interests of justice to do so.

Guideline fines are expressed in terms of bands, which relate to the offender's relevant weekly income. A band A fine has as its starting point one half the offender's weekly income; a band B fine, 100 per cent of the offender's weekly income; and a band C fine, 150 per cent. Courts may set the fine within a range, and so the fine may be lower or higher than the starting point. The range for a band A fine is from one quarter to three quarters of weekly income; for band B, 75 per cent to 125 per cent; and for band C, 125 to 175 per cent. For example, for the offence of possessing a small amount of cannabis, the starting point is a band B fine, and the range is 75 per cent to 125 per cent. If the offender has a weekly income of £400, the range is therefore £300 to £500. An offender whose only source of income is state benefits is deemed to have a weekly income of £110. If the court has no information about the offender's income, it is taken to be £400.

There is an expectation that a fine is payable in full on the day it is imposed. Where that is not possible the court may allow time for payment, or order payment by instalments, and the fine should normally be paid within twelve months. Where an immediate payment is not made, an attachment of earnings order or a deduction from benefits order may be made. The consent of the offender is required if the offender is not already in default in paying a fine.

Whenever the court imposes a fine or a compensation order (see below), it must also make a collection order, which enables a court fines officer to enforce the order if it is not paid. Such enforcement may take the form of issuing a distress warrant, or making an attachment of earnings order or a deduction from benefits order. In addition, where a defendant is fined, the court must order payment of the controversial victims' surcharge (see Chapter 12).

COMPENSATION

One of the developing principles of sentencing is the importance of considering the needs of the victim. Traditionally, the criminal justice process involved the state on the one hand, and the defendant on the other. Offenders, who either pleaded guilty or were convicted after trial, were punished by the courts and that was the end of the matter. It is surely a wholly welcome development that victims, though not formally parties to the proceedings, can now not only make victim personal statements (described above), but may claim monetary compensation for the wrongs done to them.

A compensation order may be made for any personal injury, loss or damage which results from an offence in respect of which a defendant is convicted, or any other offence taken into consideration by the court. Compensation may be a sentence in its own right, or it may be awarded by an order ancillary to a sentence. A court must always consider compensation for the victim, and where the court has the power to make a compensation order but decides not to do so, it must give reasons in open court. Compensation may be awarded for an actual loss, for example, to compensate for the cost of repairing criminal damage, or for the pain and suffering resulting from an assault.

Two important limitations may prevent complete satisfaction of the victim's loss. The first is that the magistrates' court is subject to a limit of £5,000 on the amount it can award in respect of each offence for which the defendant is convicted, and, more importantly, before a court can make a compensation order it must have regard to the ability of the offender to pay. Where an offender has insufficient means to pay a fine, the court is required to give preference to the order of compensation. It is generally desirable for financial orders to be paid within a year, but periods of up to two or even three years have been accepted where there is a real likelihood that the sum will be paid. The *Magistrates' Courts Sentencing Guidelines* contain suggested starting points for compensating the kinds of physical and mental injury commonly encountered in a magistrates' court. For example, £125 is suggested as a starting point for compensating a black eye, and from £1,250 to £1,750 for the loss of a front tooth.

COMMUNITY SENTENCES

The Criminal Justice Act 2003 introduced a new community sentence – the community order – which replaced all the earlier community sentences for adults. A community order can be made up of one or more of twelve possible 'requirements', but must consist of at least one requirement. As mentioned above, a court must not pass a community sentence unless it is of the opinion that the offence is serious enough to warrant it. In addition, when imposing a community sentence the requirements(s) imposed must be the most suitable for the offender, and the restrictions on the offender's liberty which they entail must be commensurate with the seriousness of the offence. Importantly, community orders can be made only in respect of offences for which an offender may be imprisoned.

The Sentencing Guidelines Council (as it was then), in its guideline *New Sentences: Criminal Justice Act 2003* (http://sentencingcouncil.judiciary. gov.uk/docs/web_new_sentences_guideline1.pdf) provides a framework to help sentencers decide on the most appropriate use of the community sentence. It identifies three sentencing ranges within the community sentence band: low, medium and high. It suggests that the low range is for offences only just crossing the community sentence threshold. The medium range is for offences that obviously fall within the threshold. The high range is for offences that only just fall below the custody threshold, or where the custody threshold is crossed but a community sentence is more appropriate in all the circumstances.

What follows is a brief outline of each of the twelve requirements that may form part of a community order.

Unpaid work requirement

The idea of an offender making compensation to the wider community for criminal behaviour is long-standing and deep-seated; yet it was not until the Criminal Justice Act 1972 that pilot schemes for community service (as it was known then) were set up in four parts of the country. In the rather gloomy world of penal policy, it provided a genuinely bright light. Unpaid work requires the offender to work for nothing on a 'community payback' project for a total number of hours specified by the court. Provided the court is of the opinion that the offence is serious enough for a community sentence and there is work available, then it can make an order of between forty and three hundred hours. The work must be completed within twelve months (unless the court extends the order). Community payback sessions are usually seven hours in duration. There is no specific requirement that the offender should be suitable for community service, but it is as well that a pre-sentence report addresses that issue. It would be quite wrong for a court to set up a defendant to fail, as, for example, where there were doubts about his or her physical state of health; but a general lack of motivation is no reason for not making such an order.

Activity requirement

An activity requirement is a requirement that an offender presents himself to a specified person, at a specified place (such as a community rehabilitation centre), on a specified number of days up to a maximum of sixty, to take part in specified activities. These orders may feature a wide range of activities, including attendance at a day centre, education, basic skills assessment and training, and making reparation to victims or persons affected by the offending. A supervision requirement (see below) may be appropriate to provide additional support in cases of medium to high seriousness. The consent of the offender is not necessary.

Programme requirement

A programme requirement requires the offender to participate in an accredited group or individual programme, at a specified place, on a certain number of days. Programmes are designed to address attitudes and behaviour that contribute to offending, and fall into a number of categories such as general offending, violence, sexual offending, substance misuse and domestic violence. A supervision requirement (see below) is, as a matter of practice, usually imposed to provide additional support, including, for example, preparing the offender for the programme.

Prohibited activity requirement

Under a prohibited activity requirement, the court can require an offender to refrain from taking part in certain activities on a specified day or days, or over a specified time up to thirty-six months (or twenty-four months for a suspended sentence order – see below). Examples include a prohibition on entering licensed premises or attending any football match.

Curfew requirement

A curfew requirement is a requirement that the offender must remain at a place specified by the court for certain periods of time (between two and twelve hours in any one day, up to seven days a week). A curfew requirement must not last for more than six months. The curfew may be at different places and/or for different periods on different days. Where the court makes a community sentence which includes a curfew requirement, it must normally also impose an electronic monitoring (tagging) requirement, unless the court considers it inappropriate to do so. Such a requirement works in the same way as electronic tagging as a condition of bail, explained in Chapter 8.

Exclusion requirement

An exclusion requirement prohibits an offender from entering a specified place or places, or area, during the period specified in the order, which may be up to two years. It may be used for keeping the offender away from a specified person. Where a court makes an exclusion requirement it must normally also impose an electronic monitoring (tagging) requirement, unless the court considers it inappropriate to do so.

Residence requirement

Under a residence requirement, the offender must reside at the place specified in the order, which is either an approved premises (probation hostel) or private address. This is for high or very high risk offenders, and a supervision requirement (see below) is usually appropriate to provide additional support and contact.

Mental health treatment requirement

A mental health treatment requirement is a requirement that the offender must, for a period or periods specified in the order, undergo mental health treatment. Treatment may be provided in an independent hospital or care home, or a hospital, or as a non-resident patient at a place specified in the order, or as directed by a registered medical practitioner or chartered psychologist.

A mental health treatment requirement can be made in relation to any mental health issue, including personality disorder. Before making such a requirement, the court must, however, be satisfied, on the written or oral evidence of a registered medical practitioner approved for the purpose, that the mental condition of the offender is such as requires and may be susceptible to treatment, but does not warrant the making of a hospital or guardianship order. An assessment is normally given by way of a psychiatric report which is commissioned by the court.

Drug rehabilitation requirement

Under a drug rehabilitation requirement, the offender must undergo treatment, and provide samples at the times and in the circumstances set out, to determine whether there are drugs in the offender's body during the period of the order. Before imposing such a requirement, the court must be satisfied that the offender is dependent on, or has a propensity to misuse, drugs and that that dependence or propensity is susceptible to treatment. It must also be satisfied that treatment is available and can be arranged, and that the offender is willing to comply with the requirement. The requirement must be for a minimum of six months and a maximum of three years. The court may review the progress of the requirement at intervals of not less than one month, and ask the offender to attend review hearings at which the responsible officer provides written reports for the court. Reviews are optional for orders up to twelve months, and mandatory for orders over twelve months. A supervision requirement (see below) is usually appropriate to provide additional support to an offender subject to this requirement.

Alcohol treatment requirement

Before making an alcohol treatment requirement, the court must be satisfied that the offender is dependent on alcohol and requires, and may be susceptible to, treatment. The offender must express his willingness to comply with the order and the court must be satisfied that treatment can be arranged. The requirement must be in effect for at least six months, during which time the offender is required to attend treatment (residential or non-residential) with a view to reducing or eliminating dependency on alcohol. A qualified or experienced person to deliver treatment must also be specified. Again, a supervision requirement may be appropriate to provide additional support.

Supervision requirement

A supervision requirement requires the offender to attend regular appointments with the responsible officer allocated to the offender, or another person nominated by the officer, to promote rehabilitation. During the period of supervision, the Probation Service works with the offender to change attitudes and behaviour, and may refer the offender to other agencies for help with housing, health, financial management and other social issues. A supervision requirement is often used to support other requirements that may form part of the community order, and is rarely ordered as the only requirement attaching to a community order.

Attendance centre requirement

An attendance centre requirement may be inserted into a community order, but is normally available only for those aged eighteen to twenty-four. Under such a requirement, the offender must attend an attendance centre for not less than twelve and no more than thirty-six hours, with a maximum of three hours per attendance and one attendance per day. While the main purpose is punishment, the instruction and activities undertaken by the offender at the attendance centre are designed to improve the offender's lifestyle and attitudes, and to assist in diversion from reoffending. At the time of writing, the London Probation Trust is also running senior attendance centres for women – the first of this kind in the country.

SUSPENDED SENTENCE ORDER

A magistrates' court which passes a sentence of imprisonment for a term of at least fourteen days but not more than six months may order that the term of imprisonment is not to take effect unless the offender fails to comply with a requirement imposed by the court, or commits another offence during the period specified in the order. The court specifies a supervision period, during which the offender has to undertake at least one specified requirement selected from the same twelve options available for a community order (see above). It also has to fix the overall length of the order, known as the operational period of the suspended sentence. Both periods must be not less than six months and not more than two years.

A suspended sentence cannot, however, be ordered unless all the statutory requirements for the imposition of an immediate sentence of imprisonment have been met, that is, the offence must have crossed the custody threshold described earlier: the court must find that the offence is so serious that a period of imprisonment is the only appropriate penalty. The court should decide the length of the sentence before going on to suspend it and attach at least one requirement. Because a suspended sentence acts as a powerful deterrent, it is good sentencing practice for the requirements imposed to be less onerous than those imposed as part of a community sentence.

IMPRISONMENT

Imprisonment is the only custodial sentence for offenders of twenty-one years and over. Young adult offenders, that is, persons who are at least eighteen and under twenty-one, can receive a custodial sentence, but that will be detention in a young offender institution. Imprisonment is the most severe sentence available in the magistrates' court. It can be passed only if the court is satisfied that the custody threshold has been met, in that the offence was so serious that neither a fine nor a community sentence can be justified. The court must give its reasons for finding the custody threshold has been met. This does not imply a lengthy judgment, but it does require the court to articulate why it finds custody is inevitable, and to identify any definitive sentencing guidelines relevant to the offender's case. If the court has reduced the sentence as a result of a guilty plea, it must indicate that it has done so. The court must also explain to the defendant the early release and licence provisions, that is, persons sentenced to imprisonment have to serve only one half of the sentence before being released back into the community, though they may be recalled to prison if they offend during the unserved part of the original custodial term. The legal adviser records the basis for finding that custody is inevitable.

There is of course a limit to the period of imprisonment that may be imposed. As a general rule, the maximum is six months for a single offence, but if the maximum provided by statute for the particular offence is less, then obviously that specific maximum applies. For example, the offence of obstructing a police officer in the execution of the officer's duty carries a maximum of one month's imprisonment, and no term in excess of that can lawfully be imposed. An offence of theft carries a maximum of five years when dealt with in the Crown Court, but a maximum of six months when dealt with in the magistrates' court. When two or more offences are sentenced together, if they are both summary, or if one or more is summary and one is either-way, then the maximum remains at six months. If, however, there are at least two either-way offences, such as a theft and an obtaining by deception, then the maximum is two consecutive terms of six months – a total of twelve months. The minimum term that a magistrates' court can impose is five days' imprisonment.

As mentioned elsewhere, a person who has been remanded in custody prior to sentence and is then sentenced to a term of imprisonment, is given credit for the period of time spent on custodial remand. Likewise, where an offender has been subject to a curfew with an electronic monitoring condition before sentence, the number of curfew days is divided by two and the time the offender must serve in prison is reduced by the resulting number. These factors, together with other provisions, have the effect that the person sentenced rarely actually serves the time imposed, and it often takes quite a sophisticated series of calculations for the prison authorities to work out the earliest date of release. One matter should be stressed, however. It is not the business of a court to try to compensate for the fact that the defendant will be released soon by increasing the sentence. The defendant is sentenced to the just deserts for the offending behaviour, and if that means almost immediate release, then so be it.

OTHER SENTENCES AND ORDERS

In this general work it is not possible to deal with all the sentences and ancillary orders at the disposal of the court, but the overview of the sentencing decision and the range of sentences available given above should assist a justice in understanding the broad range of powers available, and the circumstances in which they are normally used. Other sentences and orders which may be imposed include:

- orders to pay the prosecution's costs or a contribution towards those costs;
- orders for one day's detention in lieu of paying a fine. Such detention may be in the court itself on the day;
- anti-social behaviour orders;
- orders for the forfeiture and destruction of drugs;
- binding over a person to keep the peace (mentioned in Chapter 4);
- orders excluding a person from licensed premises;
- restraining orders, prohibiting specified behaviour.

STRUCTURED SENTENCING DECISIONS

In deciding its sentence, the court should adopt a structured approach to ensure that it takes account of all the relevant factors, and gives each of them appropriate weight. Structured sentencing decisions are discussed in detail in Chapter 10.

The legal adviser is available at all times to advise on the law and on the practice and procedure of the court, and to bring to the attention of the magistrates any Sentencing Council guidelines, or guideline cases in relation to the sentencing decision. Despite all these sources of help, the sentence which is passed is the responsibility of the court alone. While magistrates should take full and careful account of the legal advice given to them, and any guidelines, there may nevertheless be instances when it is in the interests of justice to move away from the guidance, in which case the court may do so, and must give its reasons.

ANNOUNCING THE SENTENCE

When passing sentence the court has a statutory duty to state in open court, in ordinary language and in general terms, its reasons for choosing the particular sentence, its effect, and what will happen if the offender does not comply with the sentence. If the court departs from the Sentencing Council's guidelines, it must state the reason for the departure. If the offender is sentenced to a term of imprisonment, any days spent on remand in custody or subject to an electronically monitored curfew are taken into account as explained above, and the calculation must be explained to the offender. The court can, though, decline to give full credit where it is in the interests of justice to do so, and must give its reasons.

The Judicial Studies Board (now the Judicial College) has produced a series of suggested forms of words for announcing various sentences. For example, when sentencing an offender to a community order, the court must first state that the threshold has been made out – either the offence is serious enough for a community order, or it is so serious that a prison sentence could have been imposed but that the court is instead making a community order. The period of the order and expiry date are given. Then the requirement(s) attaching to the order, and the length of each, are explained. The offender is warned that breaking any of the requirements, or committing an offence while subject to the order, would lead to the sentence being increased, or a different sentence being imposed. The offender is warned to notify his or her supervisor, and the court, of any change of address and that if he or she cannot attend any appointment through illness a medical certificate will be required. The offender can ask the court to review the order if his or her circumstances change. Finally, the court gives its reasons for making the order, and may refer to the aggravating and mitigating circumstances, any personal mitigation, the purpose of the sentence, the reasons for a treatment requirement, the sentencing guidelines and the pre-sentence report. Any reduction for a guilty plea is also explained. This may seem long and complicated, but it is in the interests of transparency, consistency and fairness that all the points which went into the sentencing decision are properly explained to the defendant and to those present in the court.

COMMITTALS FOR SENTENCE

There may be circumstances in which the court considers that its maximum sentence (normally six months) is inadequate. Such circumstances may arise where a defendant has given an indication of a guilty plea at the plea before venue stage, but, when the facts are outlined, it becomes clear that the offence is far too serious to be sentenced in the magistrates' court. It may be a bad case of unlawful wounding leaving the victim gravely wounded, or it may be a theft in breach of trust of many thousands of pounds. By way of another example, the case may appear suitable for summary trial on the basis of the facts outlined, but the defendant's previous convictions may show a pattern of offending of the same type which aggravate the offence under consideration. Another example may be where, on pleading guilty, the defendant asks for a number of other matters to be taken into consideration, again aggravating the criminal conduct. The mechanism to deal with these situations is to commit for sentence to the Crown Court. This power should not take a defendant by surprise, because it will have been explained during the plea before venue or mode of trial procedure.

If the court makes a finding that the offence or offences are so serious that greater punishment should be inflicted than the court has power to impose, it may commit the offender to the Crown Court for sentence. The Crown Court maximum sentences then apply, for example, three years for affray and five years for theft. There is, however, no requirement whatever for the Crown Court to impose a sentence in excess of the maximum which the magistrates could have imposed. The Crown Court may view the offence in a less serious light, or some telling mitigation may appear which persuades the judge to impose a sentence which would have been within the magistrates' powers. That is immaterial. It is the flexibility afforded by this power which is important.

The defendant may have been accused of other offences at the same time which were summary only and could not therefore be committed to the Crown Court. Generally, if those offences are either punishable with imprisonment or carry the power to disqualify, they may be committed to the Crown Court too, but then the sentencing powers of the Crown Court are limited to the magistrates' court maxima.

Magistrates also have power to commit a defendant for sentence to the Crown Court where, at plea before venue, the defendant pleads guilty and has already been committed for trial for one or more related matters which are based on the same facts, or which form part of a series of offences already committed to Crown Court.

DEFERMENT OF SENTENCE

A relatively little-used power is that of deferring sentence. This may be done only with the consent of the defendant, who must also undertake to comply with any requirements concerning his or her conduct during the period of deferment. Sentence may be deferred for a maximum of six months. The purpose is to monitor the defendant's conduct after conviction to see whether the specific aims of the deferment are met. It may be, for example, that the offender has expressed remorse for causing criminal damage to a neighbour's fence, and at the date of the court appearance has already started to save money towards the cost of repair. The court may decide to test this goodwill and defer sentence, to enable the offender to save the balance and pay it over. A defendant whose offending has been drug-related may have just started a detoxification and rehabilitation programme which offers fresh hope. An initial report from the clinic might speak of good progress. Here again, the court may consider deferring sentence for the course to be completed. The court may also appoint a supervisor, who may be a probation officer, to monitor the defendant's compliance.

The court deferring sentence must be clear about the purpose of deferment. If the court is vague in its aims, or is tempted to defer rather than take a difficult sentencing decision, then it would be quite wrong to defer. Deferment should not be used as a way of putting off making a decision. If, however, the court has clear aims and deferment is appropriate, it must decide how long the deferment should last to allow those aims to be fulfilled. It must then spell out those aims to the offender and secure his or her consent to the deferment. The offender is given the date on which to return for sentence. The court should ask its legal adviser to write down the aims, and, ideally, a copy is given or sent to the offender. Certainly, the court papers should be clearly noted.

At the end of the period, the Probation Service prepares a pre-sentence report, informing the court of the extent to which the purpose or purposes of deferment have been met. If the aims of deferment have been achieved or substantially achieved, the court almost certainly imposes a less severe sentence than might otherwise have been the case, and so there is a real incentive for the offender to do what was agreed at the time of deferment.

If the defendant offends again during the period of deferment, the deferred sentence can be brought forward and dealt with at the same time as the new matter. Similarly, if at the end of the deferment the aims have not been met, then there is no obligation on the court to treat the offender in a more lenient manner than would have followed a successful deferment.

It can be seen that deferment works best in cases where there is a very specific aim or objective in mind, and success in achieving that can be measured easily. Deferring sentence 'to stay out of trouble' or 'to try to find work' is arguably insufficiently targeted and deferment on such vague grounds is to be avoided.

A magistrates' court cannot deal with a deferred sentence imposed by the Crown Court.

MENTALLY ILL OFFENDERS

One of the great problems for all those working in the criminal justice system is the number of offenders who are suffering from one or another form of mental illness. The Mental Health Act 1983 provides for intervention by magistrates' courts in closely defined circumstances. Some offenders who may have behaved apparently irrationally may not be suffering from mental illness at all as defined in the Act.

The magistrates do have power to remand a defendant to a hospital, under an interim hospital order, for an assessment of the state of the defendant's mental health in order to decide whether the defendant is suitable to be made the subject of a hospital order under the Act. Such an order can be made only where a defendant is convicted of an offence punishable by imprisonment, or has been found to have performed the act or omission which, save for the absence of the mental health element, constitutes the offence. Two psychiatrists approved by the Secretary of State must have reported to the court that the person is suffering from a mental disorder. A mental disorder is defined as any disorder or disability of the mind. The court must also be satisfied that a bed is available in a hospital, or will be available within twenty-eight days of making the order. The court can make a hospital order only if the above conditions are fulfilled and it is of the opinion that, having regard to all the circumstances, including the nature of the offence and the character and antecedents of the defendant, it is the most suitable way of dealing with the offender. A hospital order made by the court lapses after six months but may be renewed by the hospital authorities themselves. The patient may be discharged by the responsible medical officer, the hospital managers or a mental health review tribunal.

Rather than make a hospital order, magistrates may commit a defendant to the Crown Court with a view to the Crown Court making a restriction order under the 1983 Act. Such an order may be made only by the Crown Court. Unlike a hospital order, it does not lapse after six months, and powers to transfer or discharge a patient are exercisable only with the consent of the Secretary of State. A restriction order is usually made where the court is of the view that if the offender reoffends there is a risk that the public will suffer serious harm.

Many courts operate a psychiatric diversion scheme, to which it refers defendants in custody or on bail. These schemes involve psychiatrists and nurses being available on a certain day(s) of the week at the courthouse to screen defendants who appear to have mental health problems. The doctors then provide assessments to the court as to whether the person is suffering from a mental disorder. In 2009 Lord Bradley produced a review of people with mental health problems or learning disabilities in the criminal justice system (available at www.dh.gov.uk) and made recommendations to government. He argued for the organisation of effective liaison and diversion arrangements and the services needed to support them. He reaffirmed that there are more people with mental health problems than ever before, and that there is a growing number of defendants with learning difficulties in the criminal justice system who are not being identified.

ENFORCEMENT

It is an unfortunate fact of magisterial life that many court sentences are not complied with. Fines are not paid, unpaid work is not performed, supervision appointments are missed. In respect of each sentence of the court, there are powers to bring offenders back to court so that the court can assess whether there has been a default or breach, and decide what to do about it.

Default in payment

As far as fines and compensation are concerned, the powers available to the court fines officer under the collection order made when the penalty was imposed are first invoked if the offender does not pay as ordered. These are:

- making an attachment of earnings order, requiring the offender's employer to deduct specified sums of money from the offender's earnings and send them to court;
- making a deduction from benefits order, which has the same effect in relation to state benefits;
- issuing a distress warrant, under which bailiffs are authorised to seize and sell goods belonging to the defendant;
- registering the sum owing in the register of judgments, orders and fines. This is a statutory public register run on behalf of the Ministry of Justice, and anyone can inspect it;
- making an order to clamp the offender's vehicle; the court can order that the vehicle be sold if the sum outstanding is not paid within a month of the clamping;
- taking enforcement procedures in the civil courts.

If none of the above steps is successful, the fines officer refers the case back to the court. The court has power to take any of the steps listed above, or to:

- vary the payment terms, perhaps allowing further time to pay;
- increase the fine by up to fifty per cent if satisfied that the failure to pay is a result of wilful refusal or culpable neglect; or
- discharge the collection order and proceed as set out below.

If the collection order is discharged, the court conducts a means enquiry. The defaulter is required to complete a means form, which is handed to the bench. The defaulter is examined on oath or affirmation to determine income and expenditure, and the court listens to any reasons advanced for failure to pay as ordered. The legal adviser should outline the history of the account and the payment record. At the end of the examination, the court may:

- remit part or all of fine if the offender's circumstances have changed since the date of conviction, and the court finds that it is just to do so;
- if satisfied that there has been wilful refusal or culpable neglect to pay, make an order committing the defaulter to prison for a certain number of days (related to the outstanding balance). Such a term of imprisonment may be immediate, or suspended on terms, for example, that so much per week is paid.

Imprisonment is, however a last resort as a method of dealing with defaulters. A court must first consider all other methods of enforcing payment and give reasons for deciding that only imprisonment is appropriate. The High Court has intervened on several occasions to quash magistrates' decisions to impose imprisonment when inadequate reasons have been given.

If a defaulter is imprisoned, but the outstanding money is paid by or on behalf of the defaulter, the defaulter is released from custody at once. The debt has then been paid. In the rare instance that the defaulter actually serves the term of imprisonment, then the debt is wiped out.

Breaches of community orders

Proceedings relating to breaches of the requirements of community orders are brought in the magistrates' court if the original order was made there. They may be brought in the Crown Court if the Crown Court made the order in the first place and directed that any failure to comply with any of the requirements should be dealt with by the Crown Court. If, however, a breach of a Crown Court order is brought before the magistrates' court, rather than the Crown Court, the magistrates' court has no power to revoke the order and the offender is usually committed to the Crown Court to be dealt with there.

A magistrates' court dealing with a breach first ascertains whether or not the offender admits the breach. If not, it has to be proved, and the matter is adjourned for a hearing. When dealing with a breach, the court must amend the terms of the original community order and impose more onerous requirements, or revoke the order and deal with the offender in any way which would have been available to the court if the offender had just been convicted. If the latter course is adopted, the court must take account of the extent to which the offender has complied with the requirements of the order. If the offender has wilfully and persistently failed to comply, the court may pass a custodial sentence, whether or not the offence is punishable by imprisonment.

APPEALS

There are well-established mechanisms for appealing against decisions of magistrates. In fact, such appeals are relatively rare, which may mean that parties are broadly satisfied with the way they are dealt with, or at least do not consider it worth going to a higher court. It is important for magistrates to appreciate that the fact that their decisions are appealed against does not imply any sort of slight on their ability. If they have followed the advice given by their legal adviser, adopted structured decision-making, and taken into account all appropriate guidance, they have no reason to worry about appeals. For more on this aspect of appeals, see Chapter 12.

Appeals to the Crown Court

If the appeal is against conviction, the appeal is normally to the Crown Court and takes the form of a rehearing by a judge (or recorder) sitting with magistrates, though obviously not the magistrates who took part in the original decision. It follows that the prosecution and defence (or appellant and respondent as they have now become) can call the same, or different, evidence from that which was brought in the lower court. The Crown Court can affirm the decision of the lower court, or allow the appeal.

If the appeal against conviction is dismissed, then the sentence imposed by the magistrates stands unless the appeal is against both conviction and sentence. If that is the case, the Crown Court goes on to consider the appropriate sentence in the light of the information put before it. Again, sometimes material is put before the Crown Court which was not available below, and the Crown Court is fully entitled to consider everything before it in deciding whether or not the appeal against sentence should be allowed.

Sometimes the appellant complains only about the sentence, and if so the Crown Court looks at that aspect only; the conviction has not been appealed against, probably because the appellant pleaded guilty or, having pleaded not guilty, concedes that the weight of evidence was against acquittal and the magistrates' finding of guilty was correct.

Judicial review

Where objection is taken to the manner in which the proceedings were conducted in the magistrates' court – perhaps it is said that the magistrates showed bias in some way, or refused to hear defence evidence, or that the continuation of the hearing constituted an abuse of process – then the appellant may make an application to a Divisional Court of the High Court for judicial review. This is a widely-used process designed to allow the High Court to keep under review the procedures of subordinate courts and tribunals, and to intervene where there has been a breach of the rules of natural justice. The outcome of an application for judicial review is a matter for the discretion of the High Court. There have been instances where, although one or more grounds in the application have been made out, the High Court has not granted the order requested, perhaps because it was felt that the applicant has not been prejudiced by the outcome, or had brought the matter on himself or herself.

Appeal by way of case stated

The other method of appeal that deserves mention is an application for a case stated. This route of appeal is available not only to the defendant; anyone aggrieved by a decision of the court, whether Crown Court or magistrates' court, may appeal by requesting the court which made the decision to state a case for the opinion of the Divisional Court of the High Court. This procedure is, however, appropriate only where the matter at issue is a point of law on which the Divisional Court's ruling is sought. It is not appropriate where the issue is one of fact.

The party seeking to apply for a case stated makes the request to the justices' clerk for the court which made the decision, identifying the question on which the opinion of the High Court is sought. The magistrates can refuse to state a case if they consider the application frivolous, which is narrowly construed. A member of the legal team prepares a draft of the case after consultation with the adjudicating magistrates. The draft case is submitted to the parties for their written representations and the final case is prepared and signed by, or on behalf of, the magistrates. It is then submitted to the Divisional Court of the High Court, which in due course pronounces on the matter, indicating whether or not the magistrates came to the correct decision on the point in issue. These decisions are binding on the lower courts, under the principle of precedent, described in Chapter 2.

All appeals have to be pursued within strict time limits, although there is power for the time limits to be extended in certain circumstances. The normal period for appeal to the Crown Court is twenty-one days from the date of the decision complained of. Similarly, an application for the court to state a case must be made within twenty-one days of the disputed decision.

AMENDING DECISIONS

A magistrates' court has power under s 142 of the Magistrates' Courts Act 1980 to vary or rescind its decisions under certain circumstances. There is no time limit on this power. In essence, a court may vary or rescind a sentence or other order made by it, if it appears in the interests of justice to do so. This includes the power to replace a sentence or order, which for any reason appears to be invalid, by another order which the court does have power to make. If a court has convicted a defendant and it subsequently appears to the court that it would be in the interests of justice that the case should be heard again by different justices, the court may so direct. Obviously the court may not exercise the power in respect of any question, conviction, sentence or order arising in the proceedings if an appeal on the same point has been determined by the High Court or the Crown Court.

This power provides an expedient and effective method of correcting errors that may have been made by a magistrates' court or, short of error, where information has come to its notice after the hearing to suggest that the decision made may have been unfair in some respect. It might cover a situation where a bench was found to have acted in excess of its power to sentence; where it went on to hear a case in the (unexplained) absence of the accused, only to receive a medical certificate in the post after the hearing indicating that he or she was too ill to attend; or where a number of driving documents not produced by the defendant at the hearing came to light shortly afterwards. In each of those situations, the court may be persuaded to reopen the case in order to do justice. The decision to invoke the power is for the court, and there is no right for the defendant to insist that the decision complained of be set aside. There are many instances when it would be appropriate to proceed under s. 142, and others when the better course is to appeal to a higher court.

Chapter 10

Making Decisions

INTRODUCTION

At the core of the magistrate's work is the task of making decisions. Did defendant A drive in the way the police said? If so, did that amount to careless driving? If so, what punishment is commensurate with that offence? Is there anything about the defendant which makes it appropriate to reduce that penalty? If defendant B is released on bail, how sure can we be that B will turn up next time? Whom do we believe – PC X or defendant C, who are giving conflicting versions of events?

THE STANDARD OF PROOF

First, let us look at what has to be proved – how much evidence is needed to reach a particular decision. This is known as the 'standard of proof'.

The presumption of innocence

In criminal cases it has long been a fundamental principle that a person is innocent until proved guilty – the 'presumption of innocence'. This is viewed by many as an important civil liberty fundamental to our constitutional system, and now enshrined in the European Convention on Human Rights. Article 6(2) provides that everyone charged with a criminal offence must be presumed innocent until proved guilty according to law. In a 1935 appeal to the House of Lords from a conviction for murder, it was put like this:

> Throughout the web of the English criminal law one golden thread is always to be seen, that it is the duty of the prosecution to prove the prisoner's guilt.

One consequence is that the guilty may go free. The police may simply not be able to find enough evidence to enable the CPS to secure a conviction, with the result that no case is brought at all, or the case fails for lack of convincing evidence. On the other hand, the principle operates to protect defendants from the immense power of the state. It is for the prosecutor to prove the case, not for the accused to disprove it, or to establish innocence.

The introduction of the power for courts to draw inferences from an accused person's silence – to conclude that a person said nothing in order to conceal the truth – was widely criticised as an erosion of the presumption of innocence, but has nevertheless passed into law. The criminal law contains many other exceptions to the principle. If a defendant believes he is not guilty of an offence because he falls within an exception or exemption contained in the statutory definition of the offence, the defendant usually has the task of proving that the exception or exemption applies. Some examples of this are given below. Where it falls to the defendant to prove a matter such as this, the standard of proof is, as we shall see, lower than the usual standard of proof on the prosecution.

None of this means that it is necessarily wise for a suspect not to contradict what is said against him. If he was in the pub with Fred at the time of the offence, he would be well advised to say so straight away. If Fred confirms it, that may well be the end of the matter.

Beyond reasonable doubt

In a criminal case, the prosecution must, if it is to succeed, prove to the magistrates or to the jury *beyond reasonable doubt* that the accused committed the offence charged. Lord Sankey, in the appeal case mentioned above, went on to say that:

> If, at the end of and on the whole of the case, there is a reasonable doubt, created by the evidence given by either the prosecution or the prisoner, as to whether the prisoner killed the deceased with a malicious intention, the prosecution has not made out the case and the prisoner is entitled to an acquittal. *No matter what the charge or where the trial*, the principle that the prosecution must prove the guilt of the prisoner is part of the common law of England and no attempt to whittle it down can be entertained. *(emphasis added)*

In another case, in 1947, Lord Denning said of the standard of proof that:

> It need not reach certainty, but it must carry a big degree of probability. Proof beyond reasonable doubt does not mean proof beyond a shadow of doubt. The law would fail to protect the community if it admitted fanciful possibilities to deflect the course of justice. If the evidence is so strong against a man as to leave only a remote possibility in his favour, which can be dismissed with the sentence 'Of course it is possible but not

in the least probable', the case is proved beyond reasonable doubt, but nothing short of that will suffice.

These explanations come from cases of some antiquity, but they remain relevant, emphasising how deep-rooted and much respected the principle is.

As an example of how the principle of 'beyond reasonable doubt' might work in practice, suppose a young man is accused of driving with excess alcohol. The police caught up with him after he had parked his car and gone into his house. The bonnet of the car was still warm and the young man did not deny that he had driven it. The car belongs to him and he is the usual driver. He was arrested and, while on the way to the police station, tried to jump out of the police car and run away. At the police station he again did not deny he was the driver, but later, a friend of the defendant says that he and the defendant had been out with a number of other friends, and one of the others had been driving. Because the defendant had tried to run away, and because he had not said straightaway that someone else had been driving, the magistrates may give this story no credibility, taking the view that it is too late and too unconvincing to cast a reasonable doubt on the police evidence, and so decide to convict the accused.

As noted above, sometimes the defendant has to carry the burden of proof to establish a particular defence. A common example is a person who is said to have been driving without insurance, who must produce a certificate of insurance in order to disprove the case. Another example is in connection with the offence of carrying an offensive weapon in a public place 'without lawful authority or reasonable excuse, the proof whereof shall lie on' the accused. Here the defendant must prove the defence, but the test is the lower one, 'on the balance of probabilities', the meaning of which is discussed below. So if a person is found with a machete in his car, and says he was on his way to his mother's house to tidy up her overgrown garden, but neither he nor his mother in fact has a garden, the court may be disinclined to accept the defence. But he may fare better if his mother comes to court and confirms that she did indeed have a very neglected garden, was unable to do anything about it herself, and had arranged for her son to come and tame it. Another example is where a driver says that he drank alcohol after driving but before providing a specimen of breath or blood for analysis, and that he would not otherwise have been over the limit, it is for the driver to show that he drank between driving and providing the specimen, and that it was that drink which took the driver over the limit.

On the balance of probabilities

This second test, *on the balance of probabilities* applies in civil cases and, as we have seen, to defendants seeking to establish certain defences. It is easier to prove something 'on the balance of probabilities' than 'beyond reasonable doubt'. 'On the balance of probabilities' is often paraphrased as 'more likely than not', which comes from the 1947 case mentioned above, when Lord Denning went on say that proof on the balance of probabilities:

> must carry a reasonable degree of probability, but not so high as is required of a criminal case. If the evidence is such that the tribunal can say 'We think it more probable than not', the burden is discharged; but if the probabilities are equal, it is not.

Statutory presumptions

The law has also developed certain presumptions of law which modify the normal standards of proof. For instance, the Criminal Justice and Public Order Act 1994 contains provisions to prevent the intimidation of witnesses and jurors. It makes it an offence to do something:

(a) which intimidates, and is intended to intimidate another person,
(b) knowing or believing that the other person is assisting in the investigation of an offence or is a witness or potential witness or a juror or potential juror in proceedings for an offence, and
(c) intending thereby to cause the investigation or the course of justice to be obstructed, perverted or interfered with.

The Act goes on to say that if (a) and (b) are proved by the prosecution, then it is presumed that (c) is also proved unless the defendant can establish otherwise.

Another such presumption, which magistrates are likely to come across more often, is the presumption in the Road Traffic Offenders Act 1988 that the proportion of alcohol in a driver's body at the time of driving was not less than in the specimen provided later.

PERVERSE DECISIONS

Clearly, decisions must accord with the weight of the evidence. Magistrates must not reach conclusions which are 'perverse' or allow themselves to be swayed by doubts which are unreasonable. Thus a decision in which 'the justices allowed their hearts to rule their heads' was overturned on appeal. So too in a case where justices found that evidence given by a forensic scientist was 'unsupported' and chose to disregard it, for no apparent reason other than a misplaced sympathy for the defendant.

A case in 2004 concerned the legislation which requires motor cyclists to wear safety helmets. The motor cycle in question was unusual, in that it had a rigid cell in which the rider sat, and other advanced safety features. The driver admitted he had not been wearing a helmet. The magistrates found that the cycle fell within the statutory definition of a motor cycle. They also decided that a person who was 'on' a motor cycle had to wear a helmet, but that a person who was 'in' a motor cycle, as in this case, did not. They acquitted the motor cyclist. On the prosecutor's appeal, the High Court ruled that the legislation clearly applied to anyone driving or riding on a motor cycle. The magistrates had reached a perverse decision. The High Court overturned that decision and directed the magistrates to convict.

JUDICIAL NOTICE AND LOCAL KNOWLEDGE

While the decisions of magistrates must be based on the evidence they have heard, they may take judicial note of matters which are common knowledge, or so obvious that proof would be superfluous, for example, the fact that 19 December 2011 fell on a Monday, or that the breath analysis device has been approved by the Secretary of State. Such matters can be taken into account by magistrates without being proved.

In the same way, magistrates may make use of their local knowledge, as for example, of the location of a police station or the fact that a car park is left open at night and used by members of the public. If they intend to use such local knowledge, they should make it known to the parties so that they have the opportunity to comment.

More specialised knowledge on the part of the justices is in a rather different category. In a case where a defendant said he had had a fit and so had a reasonable excuse for failing to supply a specimen for a laboratory test, the prosecutor argued that the fit was false. In the retiring room, one of the magistrates, who was a doctor, suggested to the other magistrates that the fit may have been genuine. The magistrates found the defendant not guilty. The prosecutor appealed successfully, the Divisional Court finding that a magistrate should not, in effect, give evidence in private.

STRUCTURED DECISION-MAKING

All magistrates are now trained in 'structured decision-making'. This is a way of sifting evidence, identifying the relevant and eliminating the irrelevant; defining the issues to be decided and discarding the red herrings; evaluating and weighing what has been said in court; and seeking agreement based on the material issues. It has many advantages, not least that it increases certainty that the decision reached is correct. It can also reduce the potential for disagreement between magistrates in the retiring room. It gives magistrates greater confidence in the decisions they reach, and insights which make future cases easier to deal with. Last, but not least, in complicated cases it makes decision-making easier and faster.

How a decision is structured for these purposes may vary a little from case to case, but the essential elements are the same: a step-by-step analysis of the case leading up to the decision.

Guilty or not guilty?

The way to decide whether a defendant is guilty or not guilty, according to the structured method, is illustrated below, by reference to a sample case. Suppose X has been summoned for driving without due care and attention or without reasonable consideration for others using the road. It is said that he drove his red Vauxhall Astra into the back of a blue Ford Fiesta that had stopped at a pedestrian crossing to let someone cross. The incident occurred at 5.30 p.m. on a clear, dry, summer day. The driver of the blue Ford says that for a quarter of a mile or so before stopping at the crossing, she had been aware that the red Vauxhall behind her was gaining on her and she thought it was going too fast for the road, which is subject to a 30 m.p.h. speed limit. She saw a pedestrian about to step onto the crossing and stopped to let him cross. The pedestrian had just passed in front of her car when an impact from behind made her car catapult across the crossing and come to a halt the other side, causing extensive damage and distressing the driver. The pedestrian for whom she stopped gives evidence that he too saw the Vauxhall advancing on the blue Ford and thought it was going too fast. He confirms what the driver of the Ford has said about the collision. The defendant enters the witness box. He agrees he was driving the Vauxhall in question and that he did indeed collide with the Ford. He says he lives in the area and knows the road well. He says he was not speeding, but that shortly before the collision, a bee had flown in through the car window; it was buzzing around his head and distracting him; he was trying to flick it away with his hand with the result that he did not see the car waiting at the pedestrian crossing. The court's legal adviser tells the court about a case in which a swarm of bees had entered a driver's car causing such a distraction that the driver could not be found guilty of driving without due care and attention.

The magistrates, taking a structured approach to their decision, would adopt a five-stage procedure something like this:

(i) *What standard of proof is required?* Standards of proof have already been discussed above, and in this case the accusation of careless driving must be proved beyond reasonable doubt. If the magistrates are unsure which standard applies, the legal adviser will clarify.

(ii) *What constitutes the offence?* What elements must be proved by the prosecution? In our example, it would have to be shown that the accused 'drove a mechanically propelled vehicle on a road or other public place without due care and attention or without reasonable consideration for other persons using the road or place'. A Vauxhall Astra is clearly a mechanically propelled vehicle and no one has suggested otherwise, so this question can be disposed of immediately. But if it had been a motor cycle, and no one had confirmed during the case that this was indeed a 'mechanically propelled vehicle', it might have been necessary to check with the legal adviser. The incident took place in the High Street, and so the 'road or other public place' requirement is met.

More important is the question, did the defendant drive 'without due care and attention'? In other words, did the driver fall below what would be expected of a competent and careful driver? This is a question of fact for the magistrates alone, and to answer it, we move on to the next stage in the structure.

(iii) *Reviewing the evidence.* If the evidence has been long and complicated, perhaps given by witnesses who are not very articulate, or who do not speak clearly, magistrates may wish to re-read their notes, comparing them with the notes made by their colleagues and by the legal adviser. The magistrates should identify those parts of the evidence which are unclear, contradictory or confused and about which, therefore, decisions need to be made. The process will also highlight those parts of the evidence which are not in dispute; these may well be taken into account when reaching a decision, but the magistrates do not need to decide which, of two or more versions, they are going to accept. At the end of this stage all members of the bench should be clear about what matters are agreed and what matters are not.

Thus, in the example, the magistrates might come up with two lists:

Agreed facts

- At 5.30 pm on Thursday 9 June 2011 the defendant, driving a red Vauxhall Astra, drove into the back of a stationary blue Ford Fiesta which was waiting to let someone cross the pedestrian crossing outside Marks and Spencer, High Road, Middlemarch.
- The amount of traffic on the road was average for the time, date and place.
- The weather conditions were good.
- The defendant has lived in the area for a number of years, drives the particular journey every weekday and is thoroughly familiar with the road and the pedestrian crossing.

Disputed facts

- The speed at which the defendant was driving immediately before the impact.
- The reason he ran into the Ford.

The questions to be answered can then be formulated as follows:

- Did a bee enter the defendant's car?
- If not, is there any other explanation for the collision? Was the driver simply going too fast? If not, must the facts speak for themselves, i.e. must the magistrates assume the driver was simply not paying sufficient attention?
- If a bee did enter the car, is this the same thing as a whole swarm of bees?
- If a bee did enter the car, is the way the defendant dealt with it within the standard of the reasonably prudent and competent driver or would that person have slowed down and pulled over?

(iv) The next stage after clarifying the questions to be answered and the evidence by reference to which they will be answered, is *assessing the evidence* – deciding whom to believe and whom not to believe, and how important each piece of evidence is. More ideas on how to do this are given later in this chapter.

In our sample case, when deciding whether or not to believe that a bee flew into the car, the magistrates will note that other witnesses did not see it (although of course, they may well not have done); and that no one said they saw the defendant trying to flick the bee away with his hand as he claimed he had done, although again, this is not conclusive – he could perfectly well have done this without anyone seeing. More significantly, the defendant did not mention the intrusion of the bee to the witnesses after the collision, or when questioned by the police. So the magistrates decide not to believe the bee story. But if they had, they would have had to go on and decide whether a single bee should be considered in the same way as a swarm of bees. They would also have to decide how a prudent and competent driver would react to such a visitor. Should he have tried to get it out of the car while driving along, or slowed down and pulled over? If it was not possible to slow down and pull over, should he have simply put up with the bee buzzing around in the interests of the safety of others? Would a reasonably prudent and competent driver be alarmed by the bee? These may be more difficult to answer, and different people will have different views.

(v) *Finally, the magistrates reach their decision.* Having eliminated the bee defence, they have to decide whether or not the defendant measured up to the required standard of driving. The magistrates give some weight to the evidence of the pedestrian who said the defendant was going too fast, but not too much, since he did not have a speed gun in his hand and most people have trouble estimating accurately the speed of a passing car. But what he said was corroborated by the driver of the Ford who said the defendant was advancing on her, and this lends it a little more weight. But that is still not sufficient to establish careless driving beyond reasonable doubt. The magistrates decide instead to let the facts speak for themselves. The defendant drove into the back of a stationary car causing an impact which pushed the car forward a certain distance; in the absence of any acceptable explanation, the magistrates have to conclude that he simply could not have been looking where he was going and/or was going too fast. This is below the required standard. They find him guilty of driving without due care and attention.

Of course, many cases are very much simpler than the example above, and there is often only a single issue to decide which is instantly recognisable, and it is not always necessary to follow all the steps in the structure. But it is hoped that the above fairly detailed example illustrates how the system works to clarify just what decisions need to be reached, and how a careful review and assessment of the evidence before reaching a final conclusion is likely to lead to more reliable decisions in which the magistrates can have confidence.

Sentencing

The structured approach is also used when deciding on sentence. It was seen in Chapter 9 that the Criminal Justice Act 2003 contains provisions on assessing the seriousness of an offence, taking into account the harm it caused and the culpability of the offender. A preliminary view on the appropriate sentence can then be reached, before considering whether there is anything about the particular offender which argues for reducing that sentence. A reduction for a guilty plea may be allowed, and the court considers whether it is appropriate to make a compensation order or other ancillary order. In more detail, the structure may be expected to follow the stages described below.

First, the appropriate sentencing guideline is identified, with the assistance of the legal adviser if necessary. For example, the guidelines on driving with excess alcohol are different from those on being in charge of a vehicle with excess alcohol.

The next step is, looking at the offence in isolation from the offender, to begin the process of assessing seriousness by establishing the starting point given in the sentencing guideline. This may be a question of deciding which of the examples given in the guideline most closely aligns with the case in point. A simple instance is the drink-drive offences, where the lower the reading, the lower the starting point for the penalty. More detailed guidelines apply to certain other offences, such as common assault, where various factors may indicate greater or lesser harm, and higher or lower culpability. Sustained or repeated assault, or the fact that the victim was vulnerable, are among the matters which would indicate greater harm. If the injury seems relatively slight in the overall context, that may suggest lesser harm. Culpability is greater if the offence features hostility based on the victim's sexual orientation or disability, but may be lower if, for instance, there was exceptional provocation. An evaluation of these factors enables the magistrates to decide if the assault in question falls into one of three categories – high seriousness, medium seriousness or low seriousness.

Once the category of seriousness has been decided, the magistrates can identify from the guideline the penalty starting point, and the range of penalties available.

The next stage in determining seriousness is to examine individual factors concerning the offence in question. Such factors may make the offence more or less serious. It has already been noted in Chapter 9 that statute provides that the court must view an offence as more serious if the offender has recent and relevant previous convictions, and/or if the offender was on bail at the time of committing the offence under consideration. Other aggravating features may relate to the time and place of the offence, the amount of planning that went into it, the degree of fear to which the victim was subjected and whether or not the offender abused a position of power or of trust.

This exercise in assessing seriousness should result in a conclusion that the offence is average for its type, towards the lower end of the range or close to the top of the range. The magistrates can now make a preliminary assessment of where, on the range given, the offence seems to fall. But that is not the end of the matter.

The next step is to think about the individual offender to see if anything about him or her makes the bench want to change its mind about what kind of punishment fits the crime. This is a question of reviewing any points of mitigation personal to the offender. They may include genuine remorse, or that the offender was subjected to an exceptional degree of provocation. If the offender pleaded guilty, that is also taken into account. The appropriate reduction in sentence is one third if the guilty plea was entered at the earliest possible opportunity, reducing to ten per cent if it was not entered until the day of trial.

At this point it should be possible for the magistrates to pinpoint the most appropriate point in the range of guideline penalties for the offence and the offender in question. This may include deciding whether or not the custody and/or community sentence thresholds are met:

- is this offence so serious that only custody is appropriate?
- is the offence serious enough for a community penalty?
- is compensation, a fine or a discharge (conditional or absolute) suitable?

If the bench has in mind to send the offender to prison or to impose a community penalty, it may wish for more information and ask for a pre-sentence report from the Probation Service. If a report has already been prepared, the magistrates should take careful note of the information provided. Thus, difficult personal circumstances such as illness, bereavement or family breakdown may argue for a lower penalty. So too the fact that an offender admitted the offence at an early stage, although if he or she was caught 'red-handed' this does not necessarily carry quite the same weight. The court also considers the effect a particular sentence is likely to have, although the fact that an offender has sole care of small children should not necessarily deter a court from passing a sentence of imprisonment if that is otherwise appropriate.

The next stage is to consider the purpose of the sentence. Sentencing objectives are reviewed in detail in Chapter 9, from which readers will gather that rehabilitation as an objective of sentencing is giving way to ideas of restriction of liberty and compensating the victim.

Finally a decision on the actual sentence to be imposed must be made. The bench may be unmoved by what has emerged since they assessed the seriousness of the case, or they may take a different view altogether. Suppose a young man pleads guilty to drink driving, having registered 115 on the breath analysis device. Looking at the offence alone, this is an extremely serious matter for which, according to the sentencing guideline, a community order seems appropriate. But when the circumstances of the offender are revealed, it transpires that a year ago he was a victim of a tragic road accident which left him mentally impaired; he is undergoing intensive psychiatric treatment and has become wholly dependent on his mother; he has already voluntarily surrendered his driving licence to the Driver and Vehicle Licensing Agency, sold his car and taken steps to ensure he does not have access to any other car. A long civil case for compensation for his injuries is in process. On the occasion when he drove, he was suffering a particularly bad episode of instability. The magistrates may decide that, in all these highly exceptional circumstances, the offence has fallen below the community order threshold and that a long period of disqualification alone is the most appropriate way to deal with the case. Since, strictly, disqualification is an order ancillary to a penalty, this would be done by imposing a fine or an absolute or conditional discharge for the offence itself, but making an ancillary order of disqualification. The magistrates should also explain, when announcing their sentence, the reason for departing from the guideline.

Fixing the level of the penalty brings in many other considerations. If the offence is so serious that only imprisonment is suitable, how short can the sentence be and could it be suspended? In setting a fine, the offender's financial circumstances are relevant, as explained in Chapter 9. If more than one offence is being dealt with, should there be separate penalties? Should they be concurrent or consecutive? Where several offences are being sentenced together, the magistrates may well decide to draw up a careful list and double check that every offence has been dealt with, and that, for instance, the total sum to be paid takes account of the payer's means.

The court must give reasons if it passes a sentence which is harsher or lighter than usual for the type of offence, and at this final stage the magistrates would also come to an agreement on that. It may be a simple matter of announcing a reduction for a timely guilty plea, or may relate to the particularly difficult social situation of the offender.

The court must also consider whether there are any subsidiary matters to deal with such as a costs order, penalty points, disqualification or an order to destroy illegal drugs. It may be appropriate to make an order for compensation, discussed in Chapter 9, or, in the case of an offender convicted of certain football-related offences, an order banning the offender from attending specified football matches.

The value of considering the offence and the offender separately can perhaps be illustrated by another example. Suppose a driver admits a drink-driving offence and a reading in breath of 120; he was convicted for drink-driving eighteen months earlier. His counsel, who is articulate and eloquent, explains that his client is a person of some standing in the area where he lives; he has a demanding and lucrative job; he is ashamed and embarrassed about what he has done; yes, he is probably addicted to alcohol, but is about to embark on an intensive rehabilitation course at a private clinic. Not addressing the fact that the offence could lead to a sentence of imprisonment, the advocate goes on to say that his client could not perform community service because his time would be completely taken up by his work and the rehabilitation course; that a community order is unnecessary since it would only duplicate the therapy to be given as part of the rehabilitation programme; and argues for a fine.

Distinguishing the offence from the offender, the magistrates recognise the offence as one of the most grave of its kind – certainly one for which a community penalty, and perhaps even imprisonment, would be appropriate. They decline to accept the suggestion that providing one's own therapy is an acceptable substitute for a sentence of the court, and adjourn the case for a pre-sentence report, preferring to wait for the more objective assessment of the Probation Service before deciding whether there is anything about the defendant's personal circumstances which should modify the sentence that is normally appropriate to the offence.

The sentencing process sounds complicated, and it is certainly true that many factors may have to be reviewed and evaluated. The sentencing guidelines themselves are extremely helpful in setting out the order in which the issues should be tackled, and giving examples of the many matters which may need to be taken into account. An illustration may help. Suppose there has been a disturbance outside a nightclub. A group of clubbers – maybe ten or twelve of them – were out on the street at 1 a.m., making quite a lot of noise. They had all been drinking, and suddenly there is further commotion and one of the group hits another on the face with his fist, bringing him to the ground, and then kicks him several times in the ribs. The police are called and the victim is taken to hospital. He is bruised and scratched, but fortunately no bones were broken and the victim fully recovers within a week or so.

The offender pleads guilty to common assault and the magistrates have to decide sentence. First, how serious was the incident? There was certainly injury, and the fact that the offender kicked the victim once he had brought him to the ground makes matters considerably worse and constitutes, the court decides, an element of greater harm. On the other hand, there is nothing to suggest higher culpability: there is no suggestion that race, sexual orientation or disability came into the matter or that there was any premeditation; no weapon was used; although both the offender and the victim were in a group of people at the time, the offence was not a group action; the victim was not particularly vulnerable. The offender says he lashed out because the victim was particularly abusive about the offender's girlfriend, but the bench decides that this does not amount to any exceptional degree of provocation.

So there is an element of greater harm, but no element of higher culpability. The magistrates therefore categorise the offence in the middle level of seriousness. The starting point is a medium level community order, but the range of penalties is very wide, from a band A fine to a high level community order.

The court then looks at features of the offence itself which might make it more or less serious. The defendant admitted he had been drinking quite heavily. The offence took place in the midst of a group of people, who may well have been put in fear. These aggravating features suggest that a sentence towards the higher end of the range would be right.

Turning next to the offender's personal mitigation, he admitted the offence immediately and pleaded guilty at the first opportunity, has apologised to the victim, and is extremely regretful for having had too much to drink and assaulting someone who had, until the night in question, been his friend. He is aged twenty-five and is in full-time work as a retail assistant. He has no previous convictions. The defendant's sudden outburst constituted an offence of some gravity, and the court decides to ask for a pre-sentence report to help them decide on an appropriate sentence. Given the range of sentences available, the court keeps all its sentencing options open, but asks that the report should deal with the defendant's use of alcohol.

The report reveals that the defendant has been under stress. His brother was injured in a serious car crash a few days before the incident, and he is worried that he may be about to lose his job in a cost-cutting exercise by his employer. There is nothing to suggest that he abuses alcohol. The offender has now restored his friendship with the victim. The court takes the view that while all those matters may help explain the defendant's conduct, they do not excuse him from losing control of himself. It decides to accept the probation officer's recommendation that a community order be imposed. The principal purpose of the sentence is, the court agrees, to punish the offender and deter him from committing another offence, and the protection of others. It imposes a community order with a supervision requirement and a requirement to perform 140 hours of unpaid work (because of the guilty plea, the number of hours has been reduced by one third from 210). This is near the top of the scale (the maximum is 300 hours), but reflects the factors which went to the seriousness of the offence. The court also makes a compensation order of £500, a sum reached by taking into account the nature of the injuries and the offender's income.

The adjournment decision

Since the Criminal Procedure Rules came into force and as case management by the courts becomes more robust, applications to adjourn (or postpone) a case to be dealt with at a later date are becoming less common. We have seen in Chapter 4 that the overriding principle of dealing with cases justly includes dealing with them efficiently and expeditiously. The case management functions of the magistrates' courts were examined in Chapter 5, where it was seen how the court uses its powers to avoid delay. Magistrates' courts are courts of summary justice, 'summary' meaning that justice should be dispensed quickly. The proceedings should be brief and without needless formality, while at the same time fairness must not be compromised.

Matters under the Children Act are subject to the general principle that any delay is likely to prejudice the welfare of the child. In other cases before magistrates it is fair to make the same assumption, and the magistrates have a responsibility for avoiding delay by not granting adjournments unless it is absolutely necessary to do so. A defendant awaiting trial is presumed innocent until proved otherwise and it is an injustice to subject a defendant to the stress and anxiety of unnecessary delay, regardless of whether he or she is finally acquitted or convicted. Anxious witnesses and victims should be heard as soon as possible. Evidence is more reliable the sooner after the event it is given.

In a number of appeals in the last few years, the High Court has criticised magistrates' courts for granting too many adjournments, stressing that they must rigorously scrutinise applications, and must take into account the need for expedition.

We have seen that the usual practice is for a defendant to plead guilty or not guilty when first appearing in court. If the plea is one of guilty, the court proceeds to sentence. The circumstances in which such a case may be adjourned are restricted to those where a pre-sentence report is required and cannot be prepared that day, or where the case is being sent to the Crown Court for sentence. The procedures for these are explained in Chapter 9.

If the accused person pleads not guilty, a date for trial is set and the court goes through the case management exercise described in Chapter 5. The expectation is that in a contested case, there should be only two court appearances – the first to enter the plea, the second for the trial.

As we have seen in Chapter 5, adjournments are not normally granted on the day of trial. If the defence has prepared the case and is ready for the trial, but the prosecution has not, it is rarely in the interests of justice for the prosecution to be allowed an adjournment, and the prosecution may therefore fail. On the other hand, if the defence is not ready because it has not completed its preparations, then the defence is not allowed to benefit from that, and likewise is not normally allowed an adjournment.

There remain, however, circumstances in which the court may have to consider an application for an adjournment. While there is no particular structure for a decision to adjourn, applications must be examined with great care and the court must be satisfied that an adjournment is the only just way forward. The fact that both sides may agree to an adjournment is immaterial; it is for the court to examine the application and make a decision. All the circumstances must be taken into account, and the following questions may be relevant:

- What is the history of the case? How long ago did the alleged offence take place and how many times has the matter already been before the court? The longer the history, the less likely it is that further adjournment is appropriate.
- What should have been done in preparation for today and why was

it not done?
- Can the concerns of the party requesting the adjournment be dealt with today? For example, by standing down the case for half an hour?
- What will happen if the case is not adjourned? Will it have to be dismissed? Is there any reason not to allow that to happen? Examples of exceptional cases where a court may decide it *is* appropriate to adjourn a trial may be where the victim is a particularly vulnerable person, or there is a strong community interest in the trial taking place.
- Can a trial proceed fairly even though one of the witnesses, whether for the prosecution or the defence, is absent? Why has the witness not attended? Did the defence, if it is a defence witness, or the prosecution if it is a prosecution witness, do everything possible to ensure the witness attended?
- If the defence is asking for an adjournment to obtain documents or other items from the prosecution, is the defence entitled to have those things? How important are they? Can the case go ahead without them? Can they be handed over now? Why have they not been handed over already?
- Would an adjournment compromise the right to a fair trial? Would refusing an adjournment compromise the right to a fair trial?
- What is the true justice of the matter? Would anyone be seriously prejudiced by postponing the case?
- If an adjournment seems the only fair way forward, how short can it be and what is its purpose?

The bail decision

Chapter 8 is devoted to bail and sets out the statutory right to bail and the circumstances in which it may be withheld. Again, decisions on bail can be expressed in a structured way, beginning with the defendant's right, in almost all cases, to unconditional bail. The court may then need to consider whether or not bail should be denied. The grounds for doing so depend on whether the offence is either-way or summary-only, and on whether an offender may be imprisoned for it. The prosecutor may have drawn to the court's attention a particular ground or grounds for refusing bail, or the court itself may need to work through all the possibilities. The court may decide that, although there are no grounds for refusing bail, unconditional bail is not appropriate, and go on to consider possible conditions to be attached to bail. All these matters are dealt with in an orderly way in Chapter 8, and a properly structured decision process should take into account all the relevant matters listed there.

Other structures

Structures to guide magistrates in their thinking have also been devised to deal with mode of trial decisions, 'no case to answer' decisions, enforcement proceedings and others. These are not dealt with in detail here, other than to note that they all adopt broadly the same approach of clarifying the questions to be answered and applying the relevant law. Mode of trial and 'no case to answer' are dealt with in Chapter 5, and enforcement in Chapter 9.

DECIDING WHO AND WHAT TO BELIEVE

All that has been said above about structured decisions helps magistrates identify the decisions they need to make. But it tells us little or nothing about which side to come down on when the evidence conflicts, is inconsistent or plain muddled. How do magistrates go about sorting the truth from the untruth, fact from fiction, reliable evidence from invention? Given that witnesses can misinterpret events, forget, elaborate and invent, intentionally or unintentionally, innocently or maliciously, how does the bench recognise misperceptions, errors and exaggerations? And how do magistrates decide how important each piece of evidence is relative to others? The remainder of this chapter sets out some ideas on how to distinguish lies from truth, spot mistakes, identify unreliable evidence and how to attach varying degrees of weight to different elements of the evidence.

First, though, it is worth bearing in mind that many of the rules and regulations which bear on how trials and other proceedings are conducted are themselves designed to promote fairness and balance. A lawyer need not necessarily believe the case he or she is presenting, but is bound by professional rules which prohibit misleading the court. The general rule that hearsay is not admissible in evidence is intended to eliminate the possibility of putting before a court matters which cannot be tested. Leading questions are not allowed because they put words into the witness's mouth – words which might not otherwise have occurred to the witness. The purpose of cross-examination is to highlight inconsistencies and inaccuracies. All these are designed to ensure that the process itself is as conducive as possible to truth and accuracy, but there are clearly severe limits on what can be achieved by rules of this kind.

It is worth remembering, too, that apparent conflicts in evidence can sometimes be resolved by a question from the bench, although the magistrates should of course confine questions to clarifying the evidence which has been given; they should not introduce new matters or perspectives. Thus, for example, where the prosecution, in opening its case, referred to a blue car, but the prosecution witnesses referred to a green car, a question from the chairman of the magistrates produced the elucidation that, during the course of preparing the case, the word 'sapphire' had erroneously come to be used to describe the colour of the car; it was in fact the name of the model.

Motive

First, does the witness have a motive to lie? For a defendant, avoidance of conviction is an obvious motive. A friend of the defendant likewise may wish to cover up. A co-defendant may seek to place more blame on the other defendant(s). The victim of a crime may lie to encourage the conviction of the accused out of a misconceived sense of revenge. It has transpired, in a small number of high profile cases, that police officers have lied to secure convictions.

On the other hand, professional witnesses such as doctors are subject to professional rules and are less likely to be motivated to lie, and independent witnesses who have no direct interest in the case, again, are unlikely to have any reason to lie. But it is conceivable that a professional witness might exaggerate out of vanity or a desire to impress. And the evidence of an otherwise independent witness may be tainted by personal bias or prejudice, or the witness may, out of sympathy for a victim, unwittingly elaborate the evidence against the accused.

But motive alone is rarely definitive. A relative of the defendant may have acquittal as a motive for lying, but could equally well adopt the opposite standpoint – a responsible parent may wish justice to prevail, regardless of the consequences for his or her son or daughter. The reasons for lying or putting a slant on evidence are many and varied.

Attitude

The attitude of a witness – the way in which he or she gives evidence, also known as the witness's demeanour – makes a nebulous but sometimes important contribution to assessing the evidence. It comprises many aspects: how the witness is dressed; how he or she speaks, for example, accent, tone, volume and clarity; whether any bias or hostility is displayed, for example, in favour of the defendant, against the police in general, for or against members of a certain cultural group, and so on; body language, for example, whether or not the witness meets the questioner's eye or looks away; whether the witness remains cool when challenged or becomes flustered. Where a witness gives evidence through an interpreter, the magistrates can see gesticulations, signs of distress and other visible manifestations of the witness's state of mind, but if they do not understand the language, they do not necessarily catch certain nuances of meaning or changes of intonation.

But what does all this mean? Unfortunately, there are few hard and fast rules. Many witnesses appear nervous or uncomfortable. This may be because they are lying and/or exaggerating – all the time or some of the time – or they may simply be overawed by the experience of being in court or embarrassed by the questions being put. Witnesses who appear calm, confident, consistent and articulate are not necessarily telling the truth: members of Her Majesty's Government and a former President of the United States have been found to have lied. A person who is slovenly in appearance or contemptuous in answering questions may not endear himself to the magistrates but is not necessarily telling less than the truth. If a defendant says he lives on income support yet comes to court in the latest designer labels, carrying the most fashionable mobile phone, he may look 'all wrong', but may still be truthful – it is certainly possible that he acquired these accoutrements of style before becoming unemployed, or that they were given to him by an indulgent and well-heeled girlfriend. A person may be hesitant because he is trying to remember what he said before so that his lies are consistent with each other; on the other hand, he may simply be searching his memory for the right answer, or may not quite have understood the question. A person may say he does not remember because he genuinely does not, or because it is to his advantage 'not to remember'. A young man, when asked 'Was Martin driving the car?' counter-questioned 'Do I have to answer the question?'. He was told yes, and confirmed that Martin had been driving. But the eyebrow-raising interjection could have meant 'Yes, Martin truly was driving the car and I really wish I didn't have to confirm it because Martin is my friend and he is in trouble'; or it could have meant 'I am reluctant to answer this question because in doing so I intend to tell a lie'.

And so again, attitude or demeanour alone does not add up to much, and can only go into the melting pot with everything else.

Realism and credibility

To turn to a more helpful way of gauging the accuracy of evidence, we can look at how realistic it is. First, is it consistent? If a witness says that at 10 p.m. he was drinking in the Dog and Duck, and later says that at that time he was in the Flounder and Firkin, both cannot be true. Is he lying or has he just confused the names of his two favourite pubs? Magistrates may be inclined to discount both versions.

Apart from inconsistency within what an individual witness says, there may be inconsistency between what two different witnesses say. One may have seen a man of over six feet tall coming out of the pub; another may have seen a short, fat man. Can they possibly both be referring to the same person? Is there any explanation for their having such differing perceptions? Is one right and one wrong, or are they both wrong? On the other hand, if a number of witnesses give evidence of a series of details, all in uncannily identical terms, consistency may militate against accepting the evidence. For example, if three witnesses, all of whom saw the person in question only fairly fleetingly, all say words to the effect that 'he was six feet tall, had a limp, wore spectacles, was bald, was wearing a black bomber jacket, blue jeans and trainers', the evidence may be almost too good to be true. Is it realistic, bearing in mind the period of time for which the witnesses saw the person, that they all remembered exactly the same details, and so many of them?

If different witnesses give evidence about a sequence of events, they are more likely to be believed if the evidence as a whole hangs together, and even more so if the witnesses are independent of each other. A shopkeeper says a woman became abusive and threatened violence while in the shop; another witness says she was waiting at the bus stop outside the shop and saw a woman in the shop waving her arms around and heard her shouting; a third witness says she was almost knocked over in the shop doorway by a woman storming out in a rage. But, without further explanation, it would not have fitted together quite so neatly had the second witness said she had been looking in the shop window at the time and saw the defendant looking at the merchandise in a perfectly calm and ordinary way.

Weight to be given

The circumstances from which the witness's testimony arose may add to or reduce the weight which the court attaches to it. Thus the longer the period over which a witness observed a state of affairs, closeness to an incident, favourable light and weather at the time, all go to increase the likelihood that it is reliable. A fleeting glance in twilight will carry less weight than a half-minute observation in daylight. A qualified motor mechanic's version of the condition of a car may well carry more weight than that of the driver of the vehicle with which it collided.

The ability of the individual to observe and remember has a bearing; it is said that the old and weak are often favoured as victims, precisely because they are less capable than others of perceiving and remembering details about their assailants. By way of corollary, because the police are trained in observation and note-making, in this respect their evidence is likely to be relatively reliable.

Features of the event in question may also affect recollection. Thus the victim of a street robbery will probably remember vividly the tug as her shoulder bag was pulled away from her, but out of shock, and the speed with which the event happened, may have a far hazier recollection of how many boys were in the group of attackers, how old they might have been, what they looked like and what they were wearing.

A witness may have been under the influence of drink or drugs at the relevant time and that impairment casts doubt on the witness's ability to remember correctly.

A lecturer on criminal law used to test his students by arranging to be called out of a lecture to take a telephone call. While out of the room he would change his tie (this was a long time ago, when university lecturers still wore ties). Very few students, when later asked to describe what their lecturer had been wearing, noticed the change.

Sometimes, sheer volume of numbers counts. Thus if three witnesses give evidence pointing in one direction, and one gives evidence to the opposite effect, the version given by the first witness and corroborated by the second and third is more likely to be accepted as long as it is realistic and credible.

Inferences from circumstantial evidence

Sometimes, circumstantial evidence – evidence of secondary but material matters which may lead to certain inferences – may have to be assessed to work out what conclusions can properly be drawn from it. Circumstantial evidence often has to be relied on if no one witnessed the offence itself, as where it was committed in darkness or away from any other person. The prosecutor may, for instance, be able to show that the accused was in the right place at the right time, and had the opportunity to commit the crime. But more will be needed to prove the offence, and so, if it can also be shown that the proceeds of the theft in question were found under the defendant's bed the next morning, the magistrates may well decide that he did indeed commit the theft, unless he comes up with some other plausible explanation for the booty under the bed.

Making up your mind

Looking at the various elements of deciding who and what to believe, and the relative importance of those parts of the evidence which are accepted, leads to no hard and fast rules about how to come to conclusions. It is only when the totality of the evidence is assessed, bearing in mind all the factors which go to render it credible and reliable, and all the factors which militate against its credibility and reliability, that an overall judgment can be reached. In assessing the complete picture, the undisputed facts often help interpret the disputed matters. And the magistrates will keep in mind that for a criminal case to succeed, the facts must be proved beyond reasonable doubt. If the magistrates are left with a reasonable doubt, they must resolve that doubt in favour of the defendant and acquit.

The more factors weighing in favour of trusting prosecution witnesses, and the greater the credibility of their evidence, the more likely it is that the defendant will be convicted. Suppose the prosecution has brought two independent witnesses and they both confirm what the police have said in the case, both give broadly consistent versions of the facts, and neither seems to have any axe to grind. The defendant and his witness, a friend from work, both say the defendant was somewhere else at the time, but are vague about quite where that 'somewhere else' was, and the defendant had not mentioned being somewhere else when he was being questioned by the police. It is likely that the magistrates will find this case proved beyond reasonable doubt. On the other hand, if there is a single police witness whose version of events differs in some significant respect from that of the defendant – the defendant perhaps has some circumstantial evidence to back up his story, and the indications are that the defendant is trustworthy and that the police could be mistaken – the magistrates would probably be left with a doubt, and so find the defendant not guilty.

Another insight into how decision-making is based on the totality of the evidence, using all the many and varied ways of interpreting it, can perhaps be gained from considering newspaper reports of cases. A newspaper report may give the impression that the sentence was too light or too severe. Of course, the sentence may not have been the most appropriate, but on the other hand the apparent anomaly may be explained by the fact that the reporter has missed out, whether deliberately or unwittingly, some essential element which weighed heavily with the magistrates or judge. Under the headline 'Holiday Maker Walks Free After Road Rage Attack', we may read a description of a vicious and inexplicable attack, but that the offender was only put on probation. We may or may not also read that there was also evidence of provocation, or that pre-sentence reports revealed significant mitigating features. Reporters do not necessarily absorb what they hear in the same way as do the magistrates; they may omit parts out of error or to sensationalise; the contents of a pre-sentence report are confidential and so not available to journalists. These possibilities not only make for caution in accepting at face value reports of cases which do not on the face of them 'stack up', but also illustrate the way in which courts take into account all the material factors in coming to a decision.

Chapter 11

Legal Aid

INTRODUCTION

Article 6 of the European Convention on Human Rights confirms what has long been the law in England and Wales: those charged with criminal offences have the right to defend themselves in person or through legal assistance of their own choosing, but if they do not have sufficient means to pay for legal assistance, they are to be given it free when the interests of justice so require.

Legal aid is a system of state funding for persons involved in legal proceedings who cannot afford to pay for a lawyer themselves. To be eligible for legal aid, a person has to qualify under two sets of criteria: one relating to the person's means, the other relating to the nature of the case. Legal aid is governed by the Access to Justice Act 1999, which established the Legal Services Commission. The Commission runs the Criminal Defence Service (CDS). The object of the service is to ensure that those suspected or accused of a crime have appropriate advice, assistance and representation. This includes advice for those being questioned at police stations, and presenting defendants' cases in court. The Commission is also responsible for the Community Legal Service, which provides assistance in civil and family cases. It performs these functions by commissioning services from solicitors, barristers and other advice agencies.

In the year 2009/2010 the Commission spent over £1 billion on the CDS, assisting in 1.5 million cases. Despite that, deep cuts to the legal aid budget in recent years have been highly controversial and have led to a large increase in the numbers of defendants who no longer qualify for legal aid. The Legal Services Commission reports that about half of all defendants at magistrates' courts receive legal aid, as do three quarters of those appearing before the Crown Courts. This leaves substantial minorities who must either find the money to pay for lawyers themselves, or do without. Further changes to the system are expected when the Legal Aid, Sentencing and Punishment of Offenders Act 2012 comes into force.

THE DUTY SOLICITOR SCHEME

The duty solicitor scheme is part of the CDS and provides advice at police stations and at the preliminary stages of cases in the magistrates' courts. To act as a duty solicitor, an individual has to meet certain requirements, relating mainly to experience and training, and must belong to a firm contracted to the CDS to provide duty solicitor services.

When a person at a police station requires legal advice, the police contact the Defence Solicitor Call Centre which arranges for a solicitor to attend or, in less serious cases, to give advice by telephone. The Legal Services Commission is required to make sure that people are aware that a duty solicitor is available.

People being questioned

People who are being questioned by the police about an offence, whether at a police station or elsewhere, whether or not they are suspects, and whether or not they have been charged, have a right to free legal advice. They may ask to consult a solicitor of their own choosing, a solicitor from the list kept by the police or the duty solicitor. Whoever they choose, at this stage, legal aid is free and does not depend on the person's means.

A duty solicitor is available to suspects twenty-four hours a day. The solicitor on duty must accept a case referred by telephone, unless already engaged on another case. If the suspect is drunk or violent, the solicitor can postpone giving advice, but must advise as soon as the suspect is capable. After giving initial advice, the solicitor must, in certain circumstances, for example where the suspect says he or she has been seriously maltreated by the police, go and see the suspect at the police station. Otherwise it is for the solicitor to decide whether it is in the interests of the suspect to go and see him or her at the police station.

At court

The CDS, in consultation with local law societies and magistrates' courts, decides which courts should have duty solicitors in attendance and when, and makes arrangements for duty solicitors to be available to defendants in courts where a duty solicitor is not routinely present at court. Some courts have a duty solicitor in attendance all the time, or mornings only or on certain days only. Others may have more than one duty solicitor – one dealing with defendants in custody, the other dealing with defendants on bail.

The services of the duty solicitor are available without charge to those accused of offences for which, if convicted, they may be imprisoned. All defendants must be told that a duty solicitor is available. This is often done by means of notices in court reception areas, and/or leaflets given to defendants when they arrive at court. Often, magistrates themselves remind defendants that they may speak to the duty solicitor. This may be appropriate if the magistrates think a defendant is in need of advice, perhaps if a defendant is pleading guilty but it seems he or she may in fact have a defence, or is pleading guilty simply to 'get it over with'. Although the court may try and persuade a defendant to take advice, it may not of course require him or her to do so.

A defendant is not obliged to consult the duty solicitor of the day; indeed duty solicitors must tell defendants that they are entitled to instruct anyone they choose.

A duty solicitor at court is required to advise defendants in custody and to make a bail application if so requested by a defendant. The duty solicitor must also represent a defendant who is in custody on a plea of guilty. The duty solicitor must advise and represent a defendant who is before the court for failing to pay a fine or other sum ordered on conviction, or for failing to obey an order of the court, if the defendant is at risk of imprisonment. The duty solicitor must represent any other defendant if the solicitor believes it is necessary. Finally, duty solicitors must help defendants apply for legal aid for subsequent appearances.

Duty solicitors may not, under the duty solicitor scheme, represent defendants in committal proceedings or on not-guilty pleas; nor, normally, should they represent defendants accused of non-imprisonable offences.

CRIMINAL LEGAL AID

Criminal legal aid is available for criminal proceedings before a magistrates' court (including the youth court), the Crown Court, the Criminal Division of the Court of Appeal and certain other higher courts. It extends to preliminary appearances and bail applications as well as to trial and sentencing.

The application

An application for legal aid is made in writing by completing the appropriate forms which are then submitted to the CDS. The application form requires the applicant to give personal details, to say what he or she is accused of doing, give the date of the next court appearance, and say whether any other criminal matters are pending. The applicant is also asked whether certain state benefits are paid to the applicant or the applicant's partner. (These are the benefits which entitle a person to free legal aid provided the interests of justice test is passed – see below.) Finally, the applicant must give reasons for wanting legal aid. The form sets out a number of possible reasons, based on the interests of justice criteria.

A completed financial statement must accompany the application. Here the applicant gives details of income from employment, and from state benefits, pensions, maintenance payments received and any other income of the applicant or the applicant's partner. There are questions about housing costs, child care costs and maintenance paid. Property and capital must also be declared. The statement must be supported by documentary evidence, such as pay slips, bank statements, and rent or mortgage statements. This is the basis of the second test of eligibility – financial means, which depends on both income and capital.

The interests of justice test

The first test for deciding eligibility for legal aid is that it must be in the interests of justice to grant it. The Access to Justice Act 1999 provides that in making this decision, the following factors must be taken into account:

- whether, if anything in the proceedings is decided against the defendant, that would lead to loss of liberty or livelihood, or damage to reputation;
- whether any matter arising might involve consideration of a substantial question of law;
- whether the individual may be unable to understand the proceedings or to state his or her own case. This might be because the defendant's knowledge of English is inadequate, or because of mental illness or other mental or physical disability, or the nature of the defence may be such that witnesses need to be traced and interviewed, or a witness for the prosecution expertly cross-examined;
- whether it is in the interests of another person that the individual be represented.

Means

If the case passes the interests of justice test, legal aid for proceedings in the magistrates' courts is free to those who are under eighteen, or receive one of the following state benefits:

- income support,
- income-based job seeker's allowance,

- guaranteed state pension credit, or
- income-related employment and support allowance.

A person who does not qualify automatically under the above criteria may still be eligible for free legal aid, depending on income. Annual income of below £12,475 qualifies, as does annual income of between £12,475 and £22,325 if the person's disposable income is less than £283 per month. Otherwise, the person must pay privately for a lawyer or represent himself or herself. For proceedings in the magistrates' courts, a person either qualifies for free legal aid or does not. There is no system of contributions.

By contrast, where the proceedings are in the Crown Court, all applicants who submit fully completed application form(s) are taken to pass the interests of justice test, but may, depending on means, have to make a contribution. Any such contribution is returned with interest if the person is acquitted at the Crown Court. A person who is acquitted at the magistrates' court is normally awarded costs against the Crown.

PAYMENTS TO SOLICITORS AND BARRISTERS

Solicitors and barristers are paid for the legal aid work they do according to scales which set out fixed fees for various types of work. Cuts to the legal aid budget in recent years have meant that the rates paid to lawyers have fallen. Indeed, some solicitors and barristers have seen their incomes drop to such an extent that they have withdrawn from legal aid work altogether.

UNREPRESENTED DEFENDANTS

Perhaps even more importantly, reductions in the legal aid budget mean that many defendants are without legal representation in court. Some, of course, may choose to speak for themselves and are perfectly free to do so. We have already seen that the legal adviser has a duty to assist an unrepresented party to present his or her case, but without going so far as to appear to be an advocate for the person. Alternatively, a person may appear in court with a 'McKenzie friend'. The name originates from a 1970 divorce case in the Court of Appeal, where the friend first featured. Such a person is usually not a lawyer, and has no right to address the court on behalf of the defendant. But the McKenzie friend may accompany the defendant, sit beside the defendant, suggest questions the defendant may want to ask, take notes and generally offer support.

CIVIL LEGAL AID

The Legal Services Commission is responsible not only for the CDS, but for the Community Legal Service, which deals with legal aid for civil matters. Whether or not legal aid is granted for a particular case depends on the means of the person seeking legal aid, and the merits of the case. There must be a reasonable chance of winning the case and it must be worth the money it will cost to fund it. In the magistrates' courts, civil legal aid is most relevant in cases under the Children Act 1989. The Legal Services Commission has produced a funding code setting out in detail how it assesses applications for various levels of funding in family cases. As in the criminal courts, so in the family proceedings courts – legal aid is less freely available than it used to be, and many parties are having to appear without a lawyer to speak for them.

Chapter 12

Life as a Magistrate

INTRODUCTION

Life as a magistrate has certain individual and personal aspects, and makes considerable demands. Some of these, strangely, seem not to be widely aired elsewhere, although others are the stuff of training courses. In this chapter, an attempt is made to review some of these matters.

OPEN-MINDEDNESS

Much is said elsewhere about recognising prejudice and eliminating it from reactions to what is said and done in court and from decision-making. It need not be further elaborated here other than to reiterate that prejudice, personal predilection, and partiality are in direct opposition to the principles of simple fairness and open-mindedness with which magistrates approach their tasks. They militate against the overriding objective under the Criminal Procedure Rules (discussed in Chapter 4) that criminal cases be dealt with justly. Everyone is equal before the law, and in taking the judicial oath or affirmation, magistrates espouse this principle. New magistrates rapidly realise that they can listen to a prosecution case and find it entirely convincing, only to discover that, having then listened to the defence, the case has taken on an entirely different complexion. It is a simple truth that no one is in a position to make up his or her mind until they have heard both (or all, for there may be more than two) sides of the story.

PERSONAL INTEREST

Since justice must be as transparent as possible, there are times when, because of some personal circumstance, an individual magistrate should not participate in a case, since others may perceive that, whether or not it is in fact so, he or she may not therefore be able to approach the case impartially. We have already seen (Chapter 4) that a magistrate who is a member of a local authority may not take part in a case in which the local authority is concerned. There are other situations, not provided for by statute, where a magistrate may have a conflict of interests. Thus a magistrate should not sit on a case involving a friend or relative, the magistrate's employer, or anyone with whom the magistrate, or members of the magistrate's family, has dealings. Nor should a magistrate sit on a case which might affect the magistrate's financial interests, or those of a relative or close friend. Examples of these situations might be:

- the defendant turns out to be someone you worked with some years ago, your son's girlfriend or your next-door neighbour;
- the defendant is accused of stealing from his employer, X Co., a major national company. You too work for X Co., but at a different location from the defendant, even though you have never seen or heard of the defendant;
- the defendant is accused of illegally abstracting electricity and you own shares in the electricity company concerned;
- the defendant is accused of making illegal video recordings; you work in the media and participate in industry discussions about stamping out this practice.

In cases like this, sometimes only the magistrate concerned knows there is potential for conflict. The defendant may recognise the magistrate, but not necessarily realise its implications. It is up to the magistrate to volunteer that he or she has an interest, in the first place to colleagues and to the legal adviser. The test is whether a fair-minded and informed observer, knowing all the relevant circumstances, would conclude that there is a real possibility that the court would be biased if the magistrate continues to sit. If, on that test, it is agreed that a magistrate should not sit on the case, an open announcement that the magistrate has disqualified himself or herself from the case is made. The case may then be moved to another court which is in session, or the magistrate in question may simply leave the courtroom while the matter is dealt with by the colleagues remaining.

IGNORING SOMETHING

On the other hand, there are rare occasions when magistrates have to close their minds to something. Suppose a witness has made a remark in breach of the rule against hearsay and the bench has been asked by the legal adviser to ignore it. For example, 'I know he was there because my mum told me she saw him', and the witness's mum is not being called to give evidence. This may be a very revealing piece of information in the context of the evidence as a whole, but if the bench is told it is not admissible, they must accept that it is not and proceed as if it had not been said. This is in fact simpler than it might sound. The remark is omitted entirely from the steps in structured decision-making and so is afforded no weight or relevance. Put another way, it is simply a matter of imagining how the case would be viewed had that remark not been made at all, and proceeding on the basis of the information which remains. Experience confirms that is not nearly such a feat of mental gymnastics as might first appear.

Another problem may be a lawyer or witness whose manner or tone is irritating, pompous, arrogant, condescending, long-winded, repetitive, boring or plain silly. If a person is positively rude, the chairman may have to find some dignified and non-emotive words to request a modification of behaviour. When it comes to deliberations in the retiring room, the attitude of a witness may, as we have seen, be relevant when weighing that person's evidence, but that of the lawyers is another matter. It is important to distinguish reactions to the lawyer's behaviour from the evidence itself. It is not the defendant's fault if his lawyer has not performed as well as might be hoped, and the defendant certainly should not suffer because the lawyer has an unfortunate manner. The same is true in reverse: articulateness, intelligence, elegance of argument, charm, good humour, and even good looks, do not of themselves enhance the quality of evidence.

STRESSFUL CASES

In the same way that prejudice is to be eliminated, so too emotional reactions must be identified and taken out. Often, what magistrates are told about defendants arouse sympathy, as where the defendant was in dire poverty, or recently bereaved or his partner had just left him. While circumstances of this kind often temper the sentence, they rarely have a place in decisions about guilt or innocence. Most of the abjectly poor and those who endure tragic personal circumstances are nevertheless scrupulously honest. They too deserve justice.

Emotional reactions come in at another level and call for a measure of detachment. Cases may sometimes, although fortunately rarely, be distressing. Defendants suffering mental illness are probably the commonest example. At the extreme can be a case in the family proceedings court where, having carefully weighed all the evidence, the magistrates conclude there is insufficient evidence to make an emergency protection order. Forty-eight hours later the child in question is found injured and the parents have been arrested, suspected of having caused the injury. This is indeed distressing, but magistrates need to be dispassionate. If they did their job properly, examining each piece of evidence, assigning weight, credibility and relevance to each, they will have confidence that the decision they made was the right one on the basis of the information they had. The family court is a court of law and must not speculate or try to look beyond the evidence before it. There may have been other evidence which could have been gathered and put to the court, but was not; that is a matter for the authority which brought the proceedings, not the magistrates. At the end of a court session, a magistrate should be able to come away with a degree of certainty that he or she has done the best that could have been done.

APPEALS

Against that, however careful they are, magistrates can never be one hundred per cent sure that they have got it right, which leads to the subject of appeals. Many decisions of magistrates are of course confirmed on appeal, but sometimes not. In most magistrates' courts there is a system for announcing the outcome of appeals. It may be disconcerting to learn that a decision has been overturned or the sentence adjusted. An appeal to the Crown Court against a conviction in the magistrates' court is, as we have seen, by way of rehearing; the case is heard all over again without reference to what happened in the magistrates' court, except that the Crown Court may take into account inconsistencies between the evidence given in the magistrates' court and that given in the Crown Court. So it is possible that by the time a case is reheard, a crucial new piece of evidence has been found which leads to acquittal, or perhaps the defendant's lawyer has found a way of countering a piece of damning prosecution evidence.

Reports of appeal decisions usually come with a short note of the reason, which may or may not be enlightening, for example, a sentence may have been reduced at the Crown Court because the defendant gave many more details about his financial circumstances, leaving the magistrates wondering why this did not come out sooner.

The purpose of the right to appeal is of course to give redress to those who have been wrongly convicted or too harshly sentenced. Sometimes the only way to reconcile what the Crown Court decides with the conclusion the magistrates reached is to accept that the magistrates simply went wrong, perhaps misconstruing the evidence, not taking proper account of the guidance given by the legal adviser, or failing to take proper heed of mitigating circumstances.

Magistrates are wise always to bear in mind the potential for errors, but should not be unduly undermined by having their decisions reversed. It is a strength of the system that convictions and sentences are susceptible to re-examination by others, and leads to the enhancement rather than the diminution of justice.

WORK

Employers have long been required to allow magistrates time off work to perform their judicial duties. The most recent embodiment of this is in the Employment Rights Act 1996, which says that 'An employer shall permit an employee of his who is a justice of the peace to take time off during the employee's working hours for the purpose of performing any of the duties of his office'. It goes on to provide that 'An employee may present a complaint to an industrial tribunal that his employer has failed to permit him to take time off as required ...'. But an employer is not required to pay an employee magistrate while at court, although some do, perhaps accepting in return extra unpaid work from the employee.

Employers vary considerably in their approaches to employee magistrates, some being very much more accommodating than others, perhaps taking the view that they should contribute to the justice system by freeing the employee, or wishing to 'reward' the employee, or even believing that a magistrate employee enhances the image of the company. As mentioned in Chapter 1, anyone who is in employment and thinking of applying to be a magistrate is well advised to talk to his or her employer about it at an early stage, and certainly before submitting an application. No matter how helpful an employer wishes to be, the nature of some types of business, the structure of certain organisations, market conditions and many other factors inevitably restrict the scope for flexibility.

ALLOWANCES

Magistrates are entitled to claim travelling expenses. If a magistrate uses his or her own car or motor cycle, there is a 'per mile' allowance varying according to the engine size of the car. There are also subsistence allowances to cover the costs of meals for magistrates who are away from home for more than four hours. The amounts are amended from time to time, but at the time of writing (October 2012), the subsistence allowance is from £7.45 to £19.60 depending on the number of hours away. And there are certain allowances for loss of earnings; higher rates are paid to the self-employed who are subject to income tax on these payments.

Details of the current rates, and how to claim them, appear in most retiring rooms.

DRESS AND APPEARANCES

Not much need be said about how magistrates should dress, except that their clothes should accord with the neutrality of the office and should not include any items which could, even remotely, suggest bias or indicate individual views, such as club ties or political campaign badges. Like legal advisers and other lawyers appearing in court, magistrates should simply appear neat and dignified.

Some magistrates seem to object to defendants having their hands in their pockets, but most agree that the magistrates themselves should not slouch, yawn, clean their spectacles, flick through books or otherwise appear inattentive while in court.

In an appeal to the Divisional Court in 1996, it was said that the defendant had not been afforded a fair trial because one of the magistrates had, while the defendant was being cross-examined, 'conspicuously ceased to demonstrate any overt interest in the testimony … [she] averted her gaze entirely … ceased any form of note-taking … and … started to occupy herself by reading through the Magistrates' Association Guidelines on Sentencing…'. The Divisional Court allowed the appeal, saying that 'It is important … that justices, and indeed judges at any level, give, and are seen to give, their full and undivided attention to the case before them'.

In giving judgment in that case, the court referred to two earlier cases, one in which the chairman of the bench seemed to have fallen asleep. The defendant's solicitor had asked the court clerk if the case could proceed with only two justices, but the chairman had declined to withdraw. An appeal succeeded, the court saying that justice must be seen to be done. Although it was accepted that the chairman had not in fact been sleeping, the court emphasised that it was the appearance that mattered.

In yet another case, a magistrate spent ten or fifteen minutes while the defendant was speaking, signing warrants. Again, an appeal succeeded, the court saying that it is 'a judicial duty to give the case … undivided attention. The devotion of that attention must be both actual and apparent, the latter because it was necessary for the maintenance of public confidence in the fairness of the administration of justice'.

ENTRANCES AND EXITS

Magistrates make their entrances and exits in a calm and quiet way. At the beginning of a session, the legal adviser will already have made his or her way into the courtroom before the magistrates. The chairman of the court usually agrees with colleagues in advance who will sit on the left and right, so they can enter in the appropriate order. If the chairs are awkwardly positioned and magistrates are unable immediately to get to their places (more likely in some cramped courtrooms), it is wise for them simply to stop and move the chair. Taking time over this is far safer than risking the indignity of tripping. The same applies, obviously, when leaving.

NAMES AND LETTERS

It has already been noted that the terms 'magistrate' and 'justice of the peace' are generally interchangeable. In court, legal advisers and lawyers generally address them as 'Sir' or 'Madam'. Police officers seem to prefer the quainter 'Your Worship(s)', although most magistrates probably agree that the simpler 'Sir' or 'Madam' is a sufficient token of deference to the office they hold.

The use of the letters 'JP' seems to cause certain difficulties. Some magistrates avoid these difficulties altogether by never adding 'JP' after their names, but for those who wish to do so, the Lord Chancellor has given some guidance. The general principle is that the suffix may be used, but magistrates must not appear to be deriving any financial or other benefit from the office of magistrate. The letters should not be used to further a trade, profession or business, or for any political purpose. The letters 'JP' may be added to private and business letter-headings and other similar materials in the same way as suffixes denoting orders and decorations, and academic or professional qualifications. Even so, magistrates should bear in mind how others may interpret this usage, and the letters 'JP' should not, for example, be given greater prominence than other qualifications or honours. Any attempt to use the status to gain benefit could amount to misconduct (dealt with below).

Particular issues arise in the context of political activities. While magistrates are permitted to refer to themselves as magistrates as a matter of fact and as evidence of commitment to the community, they must not do so in a way which might reasonably appear to cast doubt on their political impartiality while sitting on the bench. It is of paramount importance to maintain the neutrality of the magistracy. The local advisory committee (see Chapter 1) can advise in case of doubt.

There is also a convention about the order in which qualifications and awards are listed after a person's name. 'JP' is among the most important, since appointments to the office are made in the name of the Queen, and it therefore comes before, for example, university degrees.

THE MEDIA

Since the work of the magistrates is of considerable local and national importance, it is unsurprising that members of the press or representatives of radio or TV stations may approach a magistrate for an interview of some kind. Again for reasons of preserving independence and neutrality, some care is needed when reacting to such an invitation. Since the fact of being a magistrate does not in itself restrict how a person may behave out of court, there is no reason in principle why a magistrate cannot participate in such an interview, particularly if it is in no way connected with the fact that the person is a magistrate, as, for example, where it concerns a local arts festival in which the magistrate happens to be taking part, or what it is like to be one of the slowest runners in the London marathon. Nor is there any prohibition on magistrates giving talks to local groups about the work of the magistrate in general.

If a magistrate is contacted directly by a representative of the media in connection with any judicial matter, the magistrate need not agree or disagree straightaway, but should first contact the bench chair and the justices' clerk, either of whom may be a better person to deal with the inquiry. Alternatively, the Magistrates' Association or the Judicial Communications Office (part of the Judicial Office for England and Wales) can advise.

Guidance given jointly by the Lord Chancellor and Lord Chief Justice is as follows:

- the advice of the justices' clerk should always be taken;
- before giving an interview, it is wise to find out what questions are likely to be asked, how the material will be used (broadcast, printed, or electronically published, for example), how the interview will be conducted and who else, if anyone, is to appear in the same programme;
- if speaking to the press in any capacity, public statements which might cast doubt on the magistrate's impartiality are to be avoided;
- involvement, whether direct or indirect, in politically controversial issues is to be avoided;
- decisions in particular cases must not be commented on;
- a magistrate should think carefully about how that role fits into any

media interview, even if giving it in another capacity;
- if a magistrate gives an interview in a private capacity and the interviewer knows the interviewee is a magistrate, the magistrate should insist that the interviewer does not refer to that fact, and understands that the magistrate does not represent the views of the magistracy as a whole.

The other side of the media coin is that the magistracy in general is often publicly criticised, perhaps for being out of touch, too stuffy, too severe, too lenient, comprised of unsuitable people, not representative, too old, too secretive, and so on. Because magistrates occupy public positions and their proceedings are public, and not least because what they do and say are matters of public concern, it is inevitable that they sometimes attract criticism, and this should rarely cause any particular concern. Like many other groups of people in the public eye, it is the oddball and one-off events – the 'man bites dog' element – that attract attention, while most of the work that goes on invites no particular comment. Often criticism may be misconceived, perhaps being based on an incomplete picture of a case. Or there may be an answer to it – in Chapter 1 some of the reasons why the magistracy is still not, despite efforts, fully representative of the populations it serves have been examined. All in all, magistrates are probably wise to borrow from the media industry the view that bad publicity is better than no publicity.

POLITICS

What has been said above about communications with the media is of special relevance to those active in politics. Since magistrates must take scrupulous care that they cannot be seen as partial in any way, any public remark to the effect that, for example, the magistrate thinks a particular Criminal Justice Act is misconceived and should be repealed immediately jeopardises public perception of his or her neutrality in applying the laws in force.

This principle goes further, in that personal perceptions of the acceptability of particular pieces of legislation should not affect decisions made in court. Magistrates must enforce the law as enacted; refusal to do so may well amount to conduct incompatible with the office of magistrate. An example was the introduction of the victims' surcharge, discussed in Chapter 9. Many magistrates disapproved in principle of the way the surcharge was devised and introduced. Some resigned in protest, while others simply went about levying it in a perfectly neutral way. A magistrate who so strongly disapproves of a particular piece of legislation which impinges on work in court that he or she really cannot be neutral about it should probably consider leaving the bench. Indeed he or she may well feel that that is an effective way of expressing the depth of their disapprobation.

CONFIDENTIALITY

Magistrates are of course free to discuss the work of the courts in general terms, so promoting understanding of the system. They may, for example, take part in the annual national mock trial competition between schools, or in the Magistrates in the Community project (mentioned in Chapter 1). But most of the details of their work are confidential. The deliberations of magistrates in the retiring room are private and should not be discussed with persons outside the court. They can be, and often are, discussed at length within the court, between magistrates who participated in the case and with other colleagues and with legal advisers, and perhaps in a bench meeting when considering the results of appeals.

Anything which has been said in open court should not give rise to problems if repeated or commented on elsewhere, although this does not of course apply to family and youth courts which are conducted in private.

Many documents read by magistrates are confidential and should not be discussed, or their contents disclosed, elsewhere. These include pre-sentence reports and statements and reports in family cases, which are now usually endorsed with an express statement of their confidential nature.

LEGAL CASES

It has already been mentioned that the fact of being appointed a magistrate does not deprive a person of any civic right. Thus, sitting on the local bench does not prevent you taking action against the local store for having supplied faulty goods, or issuing a claim to recover an unpaid debt. But the magistrate should tell the chairman of the bench and the clerk to the justices if something like this happens, in accordance with the undertakings signed before or upon appointment as a magistrate (see Chapter 1). The same applies if a magistrate is a party to civil proceedings as a defendant. It may be appropriate for the magistrate to discontinue sittings until the case is resolved. The principle is that the magistrate must be seen as impartial when sitting as a magistrate.

Of far greater gravity would be where a magistrate is summonsed for, or charged with, a criminal offence. The magistrate should talk to the chairman of the bench and/or the justices' clerk without delay. It may mean refraining from taking part in any of the court's activities until the case has been determined, and it goes without saying that anyone convicted of a serious offence would be expected to resign from the bench.

A separate regime applies to road traffic offences. These need to be reported only if the magistrate, as a result, is disqualified from driving, or has six or more penalty points on his or her driving licence.

Attending a speed awareness course following a fixed penalty notice for speeding, penalty charge notices for matters such as illegal parking, and fixed penalty notices for matters such as littering need not be reported.

On the other hand, penalty notices for disorder, cannabis warnings, anti-social behaviour warnings and formal cautions must be reported.

JURY SERVICE

Magistrates are expected to serve on juries if summoned to do so. They should not, though, sit on a jury at the Crown Court to which they normally commit cases, for the obvious reason that there would be a risk of being allocated to a case which might already be familiar to them if they have dealt with it at an earlier stage. If summoned to sit at the 'home' Crown Court, the magistrate should ask to be transferred to another court.

A magistrate sits on a jury as an ordinary private citizen and has no special status. It is for the individual to decide whether or not to tell other jurors he or she is a magistrate.

PERSONAL DIFFICULTIES

Occasional, short-term illness is unavoidable and can be dealt with simply by rearranging sittings or, in the worst case, cancelling a sitting at the last moment.

More long-term difficulties, such as impairment of hearing which cannot satisfactorily be corrected, pose a greater problem and may lead a magistrate to have to consider whether or not he or she should continue on the bench.

Sudden illness during a session in court simply has to be dealt with in the best practical way possible. A magistrate who suddenly feels ill while sitting should simply ask for an immediate retirement in the hope of an equally rapid recovery, or, failing that, withdrawing from the day's proceedings.

Anecdotes about magistrates falling asleep abound, and an example of the consequences of merely *appearing* to be asleep was given above. Magistrates can take obvious precautions – light meals without alcohol, for instance, but most are familiar with the occasional apparently interminable, repetitive and soporific speech from an advocate. A magistrate who feels in danger of giving way to sleep might ask for a short retirement – coffee may help. A magistrate who thinks a colleague is becoming drowsy may also suggest a retirement or perhaps speak or pass a note to the 'victim'.

A magistrate who is suffering from some particularly stressful personal circumstances, such as the long and grave illness of a spouse, may arrange to be relieved of sittings for a prolonged period. The local advisory committee deals with requests for leave of absence of three months or more.

COMMUNICATIONS ON THE BENCH

Talking to colleagues while in court during a case can be difficult. Magistrates huddled together whispering is not conducive to the dignity of the court or, depending on the size and acoustics of the courtroom, to the confidentiality of deliberations. On the other hand, frequent retirements are costly in terms of time. Practice varies as to whether magistrates should communicate with each other orally or by notes.

In many cases it is obvious whether or not it is appropriate to retire. A retirement may be necessary, for example, to read a pre-sentence report or decide a sentence, or, at the end of a trial, to decide guilt or innocence. In other cases it may be obvious that it is probably not necessary to retire – the decision to grant or refuse an adjournment, for example. The chairman consults colleagues about whether or not they wish to retire, and it sometimes happens that, having first thought they did not need to retire, the magistrates soon realise that things are not as simple as first appeared, and change their minds. A magistrate, even if not the chairman, should not hesitate to ask for a retirement if it seems appropriate, as where he or she takes a different view from the others and wishes to talk it through.

IN THE RETIRING ROOM

Tradition is that, although the chairman of the bench opens discussions in the retiring room, shaping the structure of a decision, he or she usually saves his or her opinion until last, allowing colleagues to put their views first. In Chapter 10, the process by which decisions are made was discussed at length. But what happens if the magistrates disagree? First, the use of an analytical, structured method, as we have seen, reduces the potential for conflict by eliminating extraneous matters which could give rise to disagreement, and by introducing a step-by-step approach which, at certain points, leads to inevitable, logical conclusions which are difficult to challenge. But what if colleagues take fundamentally different views of the significance of a particular piece of evidence, or of the credibility of a witness?

Magistrates have a joint responsibility to find consensus, and they are 'on the same side' – the side of seeking the just outcome. 'We' is often a more neutral pronoun than 'I'. For example, 'yes, but if we come to that conclusion, does it take sufficient account of what witness X said?' rather than, 'you can't say that because you're ignoring what X said'. This is also an example of the benefit of putting a point by way of a question rather than a categoric statement. A question invites the hearer to consider the question; a statement may be more likely to invite a contradiction.

Humour may have a place too in keeping the heat out of a discussion, and can often be introduced without in any way compromising the gravity of the decision being made.

If the magistrates begin a discussion with different views, and end it with a consensus, then clearly someone must accept that they are wrong. Anything which makes this easier – allowing someone to 'save face' – facilitates the discussion. In the example above, the person apparently not taking account of the evidence of witness X may simply have forgotten about it, and can probably gracefully admit to having done so in response to the question. The other side of this coin is that in retiring room discussions, magistrates should never be afraid to give way when they realise they have misunderstood something or just got it wrong.

Of course, a bench of three magistrates, whether they have known each other for years or have only met that day, can often thrash out a difficult question on which they at first disagree without any risk of offending each other, and this is as it should be. All magistrates have different approaches and personalities and that is one of the strengths of the system. Discussing a difficult case is often absorbing and challenging, and finding agreement after a vigorous but courteous debate is one of the most satisfying aspects of the work.

More difficult may be the situation in which a magistrate strongly disapproves of some element of a colleague's behaviour. What if a magistrate makes a remark which a colleague believes displays prejudice, lack of neutrality or partisanship? Worse still, if the chairman makes such a remark in court?

A magistrate may need to muster some courage to deal with a situation like this and, since it goes to the heart of the system, should not let it go by. It may mean asking for an immediate retirement. A strong magistrate may be able to take a direct approach – 'Could what you said be taken to indicate bias? I am worried that it might be interpreted that way?' Or it may be wise to break off a retiring room discussion to speak to the most senior magistrate at court that day, or the justices' clerk, to express concern and seek guidance. In extreme cases, the bench disciplinary procedure may need to be invoked.

THE ADVISORY COMMITTEES

The role of the advisory committees in the selection of magistrates was discussed in Chapter 1. The committees are also responsible for ensuring that magistrates fulfil their undertakings to sit in court, and complete required training. If a magistrate sits too often or not often enough, the advisory committee draws this to the attention of the bench chair and justices' clerk. The minimum number of sittings is thirteen full days or twenty-six half-days, and the maximum is thirty-five days (or fifty for magistrates who sit in the youth or family court as well as in the adult court). There may be good reasons for falling outside these limits, although if a magistrate is repeatedly unable to achieve the minimum number of sittings without good reason, the person might well be expected to resign.

The committees have the task of reviewing decisions by the Bench Training and Development Committee that a magistrate has not reached the required standard of competence and, in an extreme case, makes any formal recommendation for removal to the Lord Chief Justice and Lord Chancellor.

DISCIPLINARY MATTERS

While complaints about judicial decisions may be dealt with by way of appeal, discussed in Chapter 9, concerns about the personal conduct of individual magistrates, whether it be something said in court or in the retiring room, or about some aspect of their behaviour out of court, are subject to a separate procedure. The complaint may be made by a fellow magistrate, a member of the staff, or indeed any member of the public. While it may be the chairman of the bench who first receives a complaint, only the Lord Chancellor, with the agreement of the Lord Chief Justice, has power to take disciplinary action against a magistrate, and complaints are investigated on his behalf by the local advisory committee. Complaints are expected to be handled expeditiously, sensitively, impartially and with full regard to the magistrate's judicial independence. The Office for Judicial Complaints has drawn up a set of rules which advisory committees follow when dealing with complaints. Fortunately, this procedure is needed extremely rarely and is not a matter for concern for most magistrates. In the year to March 2011, there were only 64 cases in which advisory committees recommended disciplinary sanctions.

On that rather serious note, this short review of some of the private concerns of magistrates comes to a close. In all cases of individual difficulty, a magistrate can turn to the chairman of the bench, the clerk to the justices or the Magistrates' Association. There is a wealth of experience to draw on, and it will be rare that a particular problem has not cropped up before and an answer found. Serious difficulties are truly rare. For the most part, life as a magistrate is challenging, interesting and rewarding.

Glossary

Adjournment: postponing a case to a later date.

Administrative Court: part of the Queen's Bench Division of the High Court; hears certain appeals from the magistrates' courts.

Adult Court Bench Book: issued by the Judicial College, essential guidance for all magistrates. Downloadable at www.estudo.co.uk/jsb/course.

Affirmation: a promise to tell the truth, which carries as much weight as an oath taken on a holy book.

Appraisal: process to assess magistrates' competences.

Arrest: the detention of a person who is committing, is about to commit, or has committed an offence, or is suspected of so doing.

Attachment of earnings order: an order requiring an offender's employer to deduct specified sums of money from the offender's earnings and send them to the court, usually to pay off a fine.

Attorney General: chief legal adviser to the Crown; has overall responsibility for the various prosecuting bodies. See www.attorneygeneral.gov.uk.

Bail: the freedom afforded to most defendants before their first court appearance and between court appearances.

Balance of probabilities: the standard of proof in civil cases, and (in criminal cases) to establish certain defences; lower than the usual criminal standard of 'beyond reasonable doubt'.

Bench: all the magistrates appointed to a particular local justice area, or the magistrates sitting in a particular court on a particular day.

Bench Training and Development Committee (BTDC): each local justice area has a BTDC, which is responsible for training and appraising magistrates, and keeping a list of approved chairmen.

Beyond reasonable doubt: the standard of proof in a criminal prosecution.

Binding over: a power of magistrates to require a person to keep the peace for a specified period, or forfeit a set sum of money.

Burden of proof: see *Balance of probabilities; Beyond reasonable doubt.*

CAFCASS (Children and Family Court Advisory and Support Service): a non-departmental public body which works with families and children and advises the family proceedings court. See www.cafcass.gov.uk/.

Care proceedings: court action taken by a local authority concerning a child who is believed to have suffered harm or to be at risk of harm.

Case management: the process by which the court takes control of a case, to meet the overriding objective to deal with cases justly. See Chapter 5.

Case stated: a method of appeal where the issue is a point of law.

Chairman: the spokesperson for the magistrates sitting in court; also the elected leader of the magistrates in a particular local justice area.

Charge: a formal process by which a criminal case against a suspect is begun; see also *Summons* and *Requisition.*

Civil law: the body of law, distinct from the criminal law, concerning relationships between individuals and companies – contracts, negligence, divorce, probate, landlord and tenant, for example.

CJSSS (Criminal justice – simple, speedy and summary): an initiative to improve the speed and effectiveness of the magistrates' courts.

Clerk to the justices: each local justice area has a clerk to the justices who has overall responsibility for giving the magistrates independent advice on the law; see also *Legal adviser.*

Committal for sentence: sending a case from the magistrates' court to the Crown Court for sentence because (usually) the magistrates consider their maximum sentence is inadequate.

Committal proceedings: a procedure (gradually being phased out) by which more serious cases are 'committed' by the magistrates' court to the Crown Court to be dealt with there.

Common law: law deriving from legal tradition, which has not been codified into statute.

Community order: a sentence carried out in the community. One or more requirements (such as unpaid work, a curfew, drug rehabilitation) are attached.

Competences: expression used to refer to the skills expected of magistrates.

County courts: courts dealing with less serious civil law cases.

Court of Appeal: comprising the criminal and civil divisions, hears appeals from lower courts.

Court of Justice of the European Union: sitting in Luxembourg, dealing with matters of European Union law.

Criminal Justice Board: a local board with responsibility for criminal justice, co-ordinating the activities of all the bodies concerned.

Criminal law: the body of law concerning behaviour for which an individual can be proceeded against by the state (usually the Crown Prosecution Service).

Criminal Procedure Rules: rules made under the Courts Act 2003, setting out the overriding objective of the criminal justice system, and governing the procedure for conducting criminal cases. See www.justice.gov.uk/courts/procedure-rules/criminal.

Cross-examination: questions put to a witness about the evidence the witness has given.

Crown Court: courts dealing with the more serious criminal offences, where trial is by judge and jury; also hears most appeals from magistrates' courts.

Crown Prosecution Service: the body responsible for prosecuting almost all criminal offences. See www.cps.gov.uk/.

Curfew: a court order that a person remain at a given address between specified hours, often monitored by electronic tagging.

Custody officer: senior officer at a police station who is independent of the investigation process and has duties relating to the welfare of suspects and detainees.

Deduction from benefits order: an order requiring the deduction of specified sums of money from an offender's state benefits, usually to pay off a fine.

Director of Public Prosecutions: The head of the Crown Prosecution Service.

Distress warrant: a warrant authorising bailiffs to seize and sell goods, usually to pay off a fine.

District judge (magistrates' court): a legally qualified, salaried judge sitting in the magistrates' courts; formerly known as a stipendiary magistrate.

Divisional Court: part of the Queen's Bench Division of the High Court; hears certain appeals from the magistrates' courts.

Double jeopardy, the rule against: the principle that a person should not be tried twice for the same offence.

Duty solicitor: gives free legal advice to anyone at a police station, and to defendants at certain preliminary stages of a case in the magistrates' court.

Either-way offence: an offence of medium range seriousness which may be tried either in the magistrates' court or the Crown Court.

Emergency protection order: a short-term order to remove a child where it is believed the child has suffered harm or is at risk of harm.

European Convention on Human Rights: incorporated into the law of England and Wales by the Human Rights Act 1988, setting out fundamental rights, including important rights concerning criminal procedure. Downloadable at www.echr.coe.int/nr/rdonlyres/d5cc24a7-dc13-4318-b457-5c901491 6d7a/0/ englishanglais.pdf.

European Court of Human Rights: established under the European Convention on Human Rights, sitting at Strasbourg.

Evidence: matters put before the court, orally or in writing, or physical objects, which go to prove or disprove a fact.

Examination-in-chief: the evidence given orally by a witness in response to questions put by or on behalf of the party (prosecution or defence) which called the witness.

Family panel: the panel of magistrates specially trained to sit in the family proceedings court.

Family Procedure Rules: rules made under the Courts Act 2003, setting out the overriding objective of the family justice system, and governing the procedure for conducting family cases. Downloadable at www.justice.gov. uk/courts/procedure-rules/family.

Family Training and Development Committee: the committee responsible for training and appraising magistrates, and keeping a list of approved chairmen, to sit in the family proceedings court.

Fast delivery report: a type of pre-sentence report, appropriate in respect of offences of low to medium seriousness.

Fixed penalty notice: a notice alleging an offence (often a motoring offence) and allowing the recipient to pay a penalty or dispute liability.

Full argument certificate: a document produced by a court which has withheld bail, setting out the grounds for withholding bail, and the reasons for applying those grounds.

Guardian: an officer of the court appointed in family proceedings cases to report to the court on a child's welfare.

Her Majesty's Courts and Tribunals Service (HMCTS): part of the Ministry of Justice, responsible for organising and managing all the courts in England and Wales, including the magistrates' courts. See www.justice. gov.uk/about/hmcts.

High Court: comprising the Queen's Bench Division, the Family Division and the Chancery Division, deals with the more serious civil cases, and certain appeals from the magistrates' courts. See www.judiciary.gov.uk/you-and-the-judiciary/going-to-court/ high-court.

Home Office: the government department responsible for drugs policy, crime, counter-terrorism and the police. See www.homeoffice.gov.uk/.

Hospital order: an order made in respect of a defendant suffering a mental illness.

Indictable-only offence: a serious offence which can be tried only at the Crown Court.

Information: material (written or oral) put before a court setting out the facts in support of an application for a summons or warrant. It should identify the informant and the defendant, and give particulars of the alleged offence and the relevant statute.

Initial details: documents provided to a defendant outlining the case, enabling the defendant to enter a plea or deal with mode of trial.

Judicial College: oversees and guides the training of magistrates throughout England and Wales, providing training materials and training the trainers. See www.estudo.co.uk/jsb/.

Judicial notice: the process by which the court accepts matters of common knowledge without evidence.

Judicial oath: a formal promise to deal with cases justly and without bias, made by every new magistrate upon appointment.

Judicial review: a method of appealing appropriate where the appeal is based on the manner in which the proceedings were conducted.

Judiciary of England and Wales: www.judiciary.gov.uk, an excellent website packed with information about all the judiciary (including magistrates) and what they do.

Jurisdiction: the extent of the powers of the court, in terms of the cases it may deal with, and the sentences it may impose.

Justice of the peace: another term for a magistrate.

Justices' clerk: see *Clerk to the justices.*

Legal adviser: qualified in law, sits in court with the magistrates and advises them on the law.

Legal aid: the system of state funding for people involved in legal proceedings who cannot afford to pay for a lawyer.

List caller: see *Usher*.

Local advisory committees: appointed by the Lord Chancellor to advise on the appointment of new magistrates, and to deal with matters relating to the training and conduct of magistrates.

Local justice area: the geographic areas by reference to which the magistrates' courts are organised.

Local knowledge: the magistrates' knowledge of their own area, which they may usually take into account without evidence.

Lord Chancellor (Secretary of State for Justice and Lord Chancellor): appoints magistrates on behalf of the Queen.

Lord Chief Justice: head of the judiciary (including the magistrates); has overall responsibility for their training; represents the views of the judiciary to government.

Magistrates in the Community: a project run by the Magistrates' Association to increase public awareness of the role of magistrates.

Magistrates' area training committee: draws up annual plans for training in its courts board area.

Magistrates' Association: a charity dedicated to educating magistrates and others in the law, the administration of justice, the treatment of offenders and the best methods of preventing crime; publishes the journal *Magistrate*. See www.magistrates-association.org.uk.

Magistrates' Court Sentencing Guidelines, issued by the Sentencing Guidelines Council (now the Sentencing Council): an essential collection of guideline sentences and explanatory material. Downloadable at http://sentencingcouncil.judiciary.gov.uk/docs/ MCSG_complete_version.pdf.

McKenzie friend: someone who is not a lawyer but who assists a defendant in court.

Mentor: an experienced magistrate who helps, supports and advises a newly appointed magistrate.

Ministry of Justice: the government department responsible for criminal law, the courts, sentencing, offenders, prisons and probation. See www. justice.gov.uk.

Mitigation: facts and arguments put before the court by or on behalf of an offender to persuade the court to be lenient in its sentence.

Mode of trial: the procedure leading to a decision whether an either-way offence is to be dealt with in the magistrates' court or the Crown Court.

No case to answer: the situation where the prosecution case is not strong enough for the court to continue further with a trial.

Oath of allegiance: a formal promise of allegiance to the monarch, taken by every new magistrate upon appointment.

Overriding objective under the Criminal Procedure Rules: that criminal cases are dealt with justly.

Plea: the defendant's statement that he is either guilty or not guilty.

Plea and directions hearing: the hearing at which a defendant first appears before a Crown Court; the plea is taken and directions given.

Pre-sentence report: a report requested by a court and prepared by a probation officer, to assist the court in deciding the most appropriate sentence for an offence.

Precedent: a system to promote certainty, under which lower courts follow principles laid down in decisions made by higher courts.

Presumption of innocence: the long-standing principle of law that a person is innocent until proved guilty by the prosecution.

Prisoner Escort and Custody Service (PECS): responsible for escorting prisoners between prison and court.

Private law: proceedings brought by private individuals in the family proceedings court, usually disputes about where a child is to live, or about contact with a child.

Probation Service: responsible for preparing pre-sentence reports, and for supervising people subject to community orders and offenders released on licence from prison.

Public law: proceedings brought by the state in the family proceedings court, usually a local authority in child protection cases.

Re-examination: final questioning of a witness by or on behalf of the party which called the witness, following examination-in-chief and cross-examination.

Reasonable doubt, see *Beyond reasonable doubt.*

Register of judgments, orders and fines: a statutory public register, open to all. See www.trustonline.org.uk/understand-judgments-fines/the-registers-for-judgments-and-fines.

Requisition: a new streamlined system of commencing criminal proceedings as an alternative to a charge or summons.

Retiring room: the room or other place to which magistrates withdraw to consider their decisions.

Section 9 statement: written evidence about matters to which no objection has been raised.

Section 10 admission: written acceptance of a fact or facts, so that evidence need not be called.

Sentencing Council for England and Wales: publishes sentencing guidelines for all criminal courts, designed to promote consistency. Most of its members are senior judges. See http://sentencingcouncil.judiciary.gov.uk/index.htm. See also *Magistrates' Court Sentencing Guidelines.*

Special measures: steps taken to safeguard vulnerable witnesses.

Standard delivery report: a type of pre-sentence report, appropriate in more serious cases.

Statutory declaration: a statement of facts formally made before a magistrate and countersigned by the magistrate.

Statutory instrument: rules or regulations promulgated by a government department, under authority conferred by an Act of Parliament, and laid before Parliament before coming into force.

Structured decision-making: a process for making decisions aimed at consistency and reliability, focusing on the relevant issues and giving each appropriate weight. See Chapter 10.

Subordinate legislation: see *Statutory instrument.*

Summary-only offence: an offence of lower seriousness which may be tried in the magistrates' court only.

Summons: a document notifying the person to whom it is addressed that proceedings are being commenced; an alternative to a charge and used for less serious cases.

Supplemental list: the list of magistrates who have retired or resigned.

Supreme Court: the highest court in England and Wales, hearing appeals in the most important cases.

TICs (taken into consideration): offences for which an offender agrees to be sentenced along with the principal offence before the court, saving the need for separate charges in relation to the other offences.

'Totting up': the accumulation of twelve penalty points on the driving licence, leading to automatic disqualification from driving.

Usher (or list caller): the person who calls on cases before the court (and much else).

Victim personal statement: a statement by the victim of a crime, which a court may take into account when sentencing.

Victim Support: an independent charity providing support for victims before, after and in, court.

Warrant: a process by which a court (or a single magistrate) authorises a defined action, such as, to enter and search premises.

Witness support: part of the Victim Support scheme in relation to witnesses who are not themselves victims.

Youth Justice Board for England and Wales: the body which monitors the youth justice system as a whole.

Youth offender panel: a panel made up of members of the local community, to whom young offenders may be referred with a view to agreeing measures to make reparation and prevent further offending.

INDEX